3

D1593064

## ESCAPE FROM THE
## NINETEENTH CENTURY

### AND OTHER ESSAYS

PETER LAMBORN WILSON

This book is dedicated to
Douglas Emory Wilson,
eminent Emersonian

ISBN: 1-57027-073-2

AUTONOMEDIA
Box 568
Williamsburgh Station
Brooklyn, New York 11211

autonobook@aol.com
www.autonomedia.org

Frontispiece, half-title page: View of Monona Mound Complex
from *Journal of the Ancient Earthworks Society*,
Madison, Wisconsin

Book design: Ben Meyers and Jim Fleming

Printed in the United States of America

# ESCAPE FROM THE NINETEENTH CENTURY

## AND OTHER ESSAYS

PETER LAMBORN WILSON

AUTONOMEDIA
1998

ACKNOWLEDGEMENTS

An earlier version of the essay on Fourier was performed, with music by Steven Taylor, at the Jack Kerouac School of Disembodied Poetics at Naropa Institute in Boulder, Colorado, in July 1992. Subsequently that version appeared in *Disembodied Poetics: Annals of the Jack Kerouac School*, edited by Anne Waldman and Andrew Schelling (Albequerque: University of New Mexico Press, 1994). My thanks to the editors and publishers for permission to re-use this material for the new and expanded version published here.

The idea of the eternal return of the nineteenth century originated long ago in a schtick by Jake Rabinowitz that he and I worked up into a sketch and published in our zine, *The Moorish Science Monitor*. The present essay, "Marx and Proudhon Escape from the Nineteenth Century" is dedicated to my comrade Mark Sullivan because he loaned me all the books. (I've still got them!)

The "Emblematick Mounds" section of "The Shamanic Trace" emerged from several happy "seasons" with the ad-hoc "Avocational Archaeology Group" at Dreamtime Village in West Lima, Wisconsin; group members are thanked individually in the notes to that section. But I should emphasize that the Group would not have existed without the advice and help of two major "informants": Professor J. Scherz of the University of Wisconsin at Madison, and Merlin Redcloud, a Ho-Chunk (Winnebago) lore-master. Thanks to them, the attempt to interpret Effigy Mound Culture was transformed from idle sightseeing into an intellectual adventure. My interpretations (and mistakes), however, are mine and no one else's—although I do not believe that my interpretations clash with Scherz's Pre-Columbian Contact theories, nor with the wisdom of the Winnebago Elders. So little interpretive work has been done on the Mounds that there exists, I believe, room for any number of competing and complementary "readings" and cross-fertilizations. In any case all agree that *the Mounds must be preserved*, and/or restored, lest nothing remain to be interpreted.

After finishing the section of "The Shamanic Trace" dealing with "left-wing Hermeticism" I came across two works that would have vastly improved my treatment of the subject. James H. Billington's *Fire in the Minds of Men: Origins of the Revolutionary Faith* (New York: Basic Books, 1980); chapter 1 especially provides a wealth of information and bibliography on Hermetic rebels, filtered through the author's strange CIA-informed conspiracy theory of the occult roots of the Left. The second work is *Access to Western Esotericism* by Antoine Faivre (Albany: State University of New York Press, 1994), especially Book One, chapters 3-5. Faivre is the leading French scholar of Hermeticism, and has an interesting take on left- and right-wing brands of esotericism; his bibliography is also useful. I hope to pursue this subject in my forthcoming book *Hieroglyphica: Hermeticism, Iconoclasm, and Money*.

I must thank Jordan Zinovich for introducing me to carto(grapho)mancer Adele Haft, who introduced me to her student K. Cheppaikode, who drew the excellent maps in "A Nietzschaen Coup d'État". Thanks to Alex Trotter for the splendid index, to Valery Oisteanu, dada co-conspirator, and once again to James Koehnline for the cover. And as usual, to Jim Fleming and the Autonomedia Collective, and especially Ben Meyers.

# CONTENTS

# FOURIER!—OR,
# THE UTOPIAN POETICS

(FOR ANNE WALDMAN)

feeling lonely like you, aging bachelor in Paris rented rooms overgrown with flowers—ever since you were a boy and the flowers took over your room—burst their pots, dirt spread over the floor under the bed, black manurey soil with flowers metamorphosing your room into small cubical Douanier Rousseau-like jungle—the loneliness of modern life, let's not dignify it with such grand terms as "alienation," began as long ago as 1799, obviously, since you, Fourier, felt it even then, aching cold of static streets where no one knows anyone else's name—and the frigid disgust of Sunday family suppers before the TV hearth in Civilization, late in Civilization.

*Accordingly, men who are well acquainted with Civilization give, as a rule for success, the precept, cringing mediocrity.* *(PHS II 186)*

## THE SEXUAL ANGELICATE

which in Harmony means the man and woman who preside over the Court of Love, that game/machine at the center of the dream of the Phalanx—the two *perfecti* of the entire Polygynal Series of Passional Attraction, who can make even pity an erotic act—Fourier himself combines these two angels in one hermaphroditic mind.[1]  Fourier himself was "ambiguous"—as witness his special mania for sapphists which he discovered only in his late thirties—in fact Fourier considers love itself an "inversion", since in

*We are going to speculate about…an order of things in which marriage and our other customs will have been forgotten, their very absence having inspired a host of amorous innovations which we cannot yet imagine.* *(UVCF 327)*

*…the family is a group that needs to escape from itself… (HM 236)*

*Thus we see beings unite in marriage and other affairs who have no personal passional affinity, and whereof the approximation, the bringing together, is nothing but a subdued disgust. (PHS II 44)*

1 One of the American Phalansteries of the 1850s chronicled by J. H. Noyes in his *American Socialisms* (see bibliography) was called "The One Mentian Community".

true love a "superior" (in strength, age, sophistication, etc.) bends to the will of an "inferior." This romantic voluntarily erotic slavery, which Fourier considers natural, is generally impossible in Civilization. Fourier was the alchemical androgyne. Yes, the Masonic Fourier! The occult messiah!

*If love is to be a source of generosity, we must base our speculations on the collective exercise of love. (UVCF 374)*

*In Harmony…amorous celebrity can entitle a person to a world-wide monarchy and to other lucrative & magnificent offices. (UVCF 368)*

## HYMN TO THE DAWN
[SEE APPENDIX A]

To read Fourier with feeling gives the same thrill as discovering a new lost cult of ancient times with strange and gnostic truths. If you really love someone, buy rare old yellowing Fourier pamphlets and let your beloved discover them as if by accident in musty library of deceased uncle, or leftist used book store in Montmartre, dusty pages of cheap acidic nineteenth-century paper flaking away like ivory scurf, quaint elongated fancy typefaces, elaborate pseudomathematical diagrams. At first your beloved believes that *no one else* knows about this unique forgotten genius…then your beloved discovers that there are others…that *you* are one of them! What a pure and ennobling pleasure!

## FOURIER'S HEAD IN MARBLE

resting on his grave as on some Salomean platter—an obvious invitation to necromancy. Candles and incense, invocatory rhodomontade, pallid young men in neat raincoats, shabby-genteel old ladies, disciples gathered in Montmartre Cemetery…Sunday afternoon seances in the April mist, perhaps. Doctrines as beautiful as these were destined to be enshrined in a cult, a poor small religion of lodginghouses and badly lit meetinghalls, illuminated certificates of entitlement and orders of chivalry, faded velvet banners, memorabilia enshrined in glass like reliquaries. Fourier's monument—a stone structure standing where the rue Caulincourt hits the Place Clichy in the IXth arrondissement, just down from Montmartre—it was worn and truncated, the writing on the stone illegible. In October 1960 the journal *Combat* reported the wish of a municipal councillor that the monument be removed. André Breton protested. The monument still stood in 1970 (what have 24 more years done to it?). In his *Ode to Fourier* Breton relates this experience:

> Et voilà one little morning in 1937
> that would be about 100 years by the way after
> your death
> in passing I noticed a very fresh bouquet of violets at your
> feet
> it is rare that anyone beflowers statues in Paris…

I observed casually in days that followed the bouquet
was renewed
the dew and it made one
and you, nothing would have turned your eyes from
the be-diamonded muck of Place Clichy

## THE ANALOGIES

Stars and planets are sexual beings. Gravity on the physical plane serves as a metaphor for the erotic attraction which really moves the universes:— the Aromal Emanation. Each cosmic body shoots out multi-colored rays of aroma by which they copulate with each other and propagate their kind in a continual orgy of creation. These rays crisscross Space in a veritable multidimensional web of color just as Space on another level is a webwork of light. Each of the Passions corresponds to a numeral, a musical note, color, mathematical process, geometric form, alchemic metal—thus the Cabalist Passion is symbolized by an indigo silver spiral. Different kinds of love can be represented by iris, tuberose, carnation, hyacinth. Did Fourier spontaneously re-create the occult theory of analogy out of his own imagination, or had he read Paracelsus? No wonder the Martinists, Illuminists and Swedenborgians thought Fourier was one of them, an adept. Aromal influences in the coming era of Harmony will cause the seas to turn to lemonade. *Everything* is erotic, every-

*...rustic altars are placed at the summit of a knoll. They are bedecked with flowers or shrubs & the statues & busts of patrons of the sect (the "Thousand Flower Series") or of the individuals who have excelled in work & have enriched it by inventing useful methods. These individuals are the mythological demi-gods of the sect or industrial Series. A corybant opens the session by burning incense before the demigod... (UVCF 293. For the 1000 Flower Series, see Appendix B)*

*A star can copulate: 1. with itself like a vegetable, the north pole copulating with the south; 2. with another star by means of outpourings emanating from contrasting poles; 3. with the help of an intermediary; the tuberose was engendered by three aromas emanating from the south pole of the Earth, the north pole of the planet Herschel, and the south pole of the Sun. (UCVS 401)*

| *Subversion* | *Transition* | *Harmony* |
|---|---|---|
| *Night* | *Twilight* | *Day* |
| *Caterpillar* | *Chrysalis* | *Butterfly* |
| *Comet* | *Concentrated body* | *Planet* |
| *Winter* | *Half season* | *Summer* |
| | | *(PHS II 412)* |

thing yields to the influence of Passional Attraction—the only possible society is one composed entirely of lovers, therefore the only possible politics is a politics of the impossible, and even a science of the impossible, erotico-pataphysics, dada epistemology, the Passional Calculus.

## NORTH AMERICAN PHALANX

The longest-lived Fourierist experiment was the North American Phalanx in Monmouth County, New Jersey, 40 miles south of New York City. Between 1843 and 1858 there may have been a hundred or so phalanxes in America. In an alternate universe none of them failed ignominiously or vanished into the dustbin of lost crackpot history—they succeeded wildly, and America-prime became the cradle of universal Harmony. Our alternate selves are all living in big phalansteries and the very weather has changed, balmy and crackling with erotic energy, orgone skies and lemonade oceans, so that everything we do, even harvesting pears, gives us hard-ons or wet vaginas. We need only three and a half hours of sleep a night, eat five meals and two snacks a day, flit from task to task and pleasure to pleasure like butterflies.2 We're seven feet tall, live to 120, and the most advanced have tails with a hand on the end, and an eye in the palm of the hand: the *archibras*.

## MONEY

Since Fourier took the opposite point of view to all philosophy (*l'éclat absolu*, absolute doubt and difference), and since "philosophers" invariably disdain and disparage wealth, he was for it. He recognized the erotic and "childish" purity of money as money rather than as frozen abstraction and oppression. Even if he were to consider money as "filth" he would still approve it, as he was far from ignorant of the erotic power of filth, at least for certain Series. Every pleasure condemned by the moralists of Civilization he applauds as a force for Harmony—a revaluation of all values leading not to Nietzsche's chilly loneliness but to the elegant perversity of the horde, the band, the tangle of bodies in "touch rut."3

## THE LITTLE HORDES

at dawn, under their Little Khans, they march, barbaric banners flying, out into the still-misty fields, to rid the furrows of vermin and serpents, to spread manure—boys attracted to danger and filth. A few girls, and adults, the Bonze/Druids, who still share these tastes, accompany them. The whole Phalanx honors them for the

*...the mutiny of love is only the more effective for being hidden and concealed behind all sorts of masks. (UVCF 340)*

*I have now said enough to make it clear that this corps of children (the Little Horde), who indulge all the inclinations that morality forbids, is a device which will realize...Sweet Fraternity. [Harmony] encourages the dirty inclinations which are repressed with heavy-handed whippings by a tender morality that*

2 Fourier's "butterfly Passion," strangely pre-echoed in Chuang Tzu's Butterfly and echoed in Lorenz's "Butterfly", Strange Attractor of weather. According to Allen Ginsberg, Walt Whitman adopted his butterfly symbol from Fourier. [Personal communication.]

3 Touch and taste are the highest, hearing and sight the minor senses, with smell as the "ambiguous pivot."

distasteful work and thinks of them as little knights. Who knows what mischief they're up to later out behind the barn, in the dump, the junkyard, the privy overgrown with honeysuckle—what rituals of filth?

*makes no effort to utilize the passions as God gave them to us. (UVCF 321-2)*

*Children are nature's echoes against morality; they are all in league to escape its rules. (UVCF 165)*

## THE FOURIERIST BANQUET

Gastrosophy—the art and science of good taste—Fourier's most beautiful and perfectly typical invention. I used to apply the term gastrosophy not only to Fourier but also to Brillat-Savarin, author of *The Physiognomy of Taste*; imagine my surprise to discover that they were related and knew each other well! True, Fourier disdained Brillat-Savarin's gourmandism as "simple" in comparison with the compound or composite complexity of cuisine in Harmony—nevertheless (as Barthes points out) it was probably Brillat-Savarin who introduced Fourier to *mirlitons*, the little spiced cakes of Paris which he loved and praised as harmonian food. Therefore a Fourierist banquet might well feature Brillat-Savarin's famous recipe for turkey, almost the only recipe contained in the *Physiognomy* (which is a meditation on food, not a cookery book). Fourier also loved fruit, especially pears, melons, and apples, and fruit compotes (because they were "composite") made with sugar, which the Harmonians will eat instead of bread. Bread, except for very fine dinner rolls, seemed boring to Fourier, and the labor of raising wheat too dull; moreover, the sugar of the future will (due to aromal emanations) lose its "wormy" unhealthiness. Bread is too *Civilized*—and Harmony is the Big Rock Candy Mountain of childhood dreams. If the Fourierist banquet is to contain dishes much discussed by the

*...the science named Gastrosophy...will place good cheer in strict alliance with honor and the love of glory. (PHS 133)*

*...the most clever gastrosophers will be in their lifetime promoted to saintship, of which they will have the rank and the title.
(HM 94)*

*...when a well-assorted company can, in a short evening party, place itself in full composite by mixtures of material and spiritual pleasure—gallantry, the ball, the dainty supper, and, above all, cordiality—then everyone is enraptured with this state of delight, so rare in assemblies. Everyone says, why does not this state of festivity and intoxication always last? why does it not revive every day? If you return after this to your dismal home, and to the routine of business and morality, you think yourself fallen, like Apollo, from the heavenly abode into a place of exile.*

*These moments, when parties rise to the delight of the composite, are infinitely feeble pictures of the delight that the Harmonians will constantly enjoy.... (PHS II 7)*

Founder, then serve a stew made from a "tough old hen" (or two hens and a rooster), "marinated and served in a braising pan, or in gelatine," in honor of one of *Moderation is good as a channel of refinement of the pleasures, but not as a deliberate privation. (PHS II 101)*

Fourier's famous illustrative fables, about a series of chicken-loving gourmets with extreme tastes; and served with cous-cous and slightly rancid butter, in honor of Barthes and his friend (see *Sade/Fourier/Loyola*). Omit Provençal-type dishes made with "hot oil," garlic, saffron "and other villainies," of which the Founder disapproved (v. PHS I 316). Also note: "How many 'hidings' have I endured (as a child) because I refused to swallow turnips, cabbage, barley, vermicelli, and (other) moral drugs, which occasioned my vomiting, not to mention disgust" (ibid., 344). Even if we happen to like some of these things, we'll omit them in honor of the hero we celebrate. April 7 is his birthday. Plenty of wine and cognac, and "ices, orangeade, sparkling wines." Table set with flowers. Twelve toasts, one to each Passion—and one more for the Founder. (See Appendix D.)

## FOURIER STIRNER NIETZSCHE

We need warm Fourier to counterbalance cool Stirner and Nietzsche, and we need Stirner and Nietzsche to even out Fourier. Stirner exterminates a few spooks still rattling around in Fourier's head; for "altruism" sometimes appears in Fourier detached from the interest of individuals, floating free as an abstraction; at other times however Fourier makes it clear that *... in order not to have the trouble of forgetting the books of philosophy, I have never taken the trouble to read them. (PHS I 117)*

*The Series needs discords as much as it needs harmonies. (UVCF 231)*

self-interest alone is sufficient motivation to bring about Harmony, since the individual can only realize full individuality in a social setting where need ("work") and pleasure are nearly synonymous, and where one's own passions are complemented and fulfilled by *others* of the appropriate Series. The Phalanx can thus be seen as one possible form for the Stirnerite "Union of Egoists" (or more accurately, "unique-ones"). It has been argued (by Gustav Landauer for example) that "Ego" for Stirner still retains—despite all Stirner's determination—a taint of the Absolute, in the same way that "Society" (or Association) does for Fourier. In this case, Nietzsche appears as a positive/ambiguous third term or pivot of reconciliation between the two extreme cases, first in his image of the "free spirit", which could stand for Stirner's and Fourier's ideals as well; and second, in his "perspectivalism," which precisely puts the two extreme perspectives *in perspective*. Moreover, Nietzsche and Fourier agree on the question of the Necessary Illusion, the social myth; in this light one might interpret the Phalanx as the "will to power" of the combined Passional Series and Groups. All three thinkers are "radical aristocrats," disbelievers in equality and democracy. Believing in the possibility of a synthesis of these three cranky geniuses may involve the aesthetic of the well-known mating, on operating table, of sewing machine and umbrella; but that's old hat. Indeed, we can add a few more "impossibles" to the mix, and hope for six before breakfast. For example: a number of nineteenth-century American utopianists managed to reconcile Fourier's theory of Attraction with Josiah Warren's "Society of Individual Sovereigns"—particularly Stephen Pearl Andrews, founder of the UNIVERSAL PANTARCHY and of "Modern Times," the anarchist community in Brentwood, Long Island. In fact Fourierism dovetails nicely with what might be called the "left" wing of Individualist anarchism, its labor movement-oriented side, represented by Tucker and Mackay. A similar synthesis was made in the "pleasure politics" of Situationism, which probably absorbed Fourier through Surrealism. Fourier's *Nouveau monde amoureux*, his most overtly erotic work—which never appeared in his lifetime and was lost—finally made it into print for the first time in 1967; if it was not a precipitating factor of the following year's "Events," it was surely a symbolic premonition.

The biggest area of difference between Fourier and Stirner/Nietzsche, and the biggest area of difference between Fourier and the whole later development of socialist anarchism, is the area of religion. Stirner/Nietzsche did not believe in "God," and neither did Proudhon or Kropotkin (who both read Fourier with "fascination" when young). But Fourier did believe in something. He attacked "Religion" as an aspect of Civilization, but he spoke without hesitation of a "God" and of "UNIVERSAL DIVINE PROVIDENCE" (as a necessary axiom to the proof that all humans should enjoy an economic and erotic "minimum," without which it would become necessary to accuse "God" of injustice). Fourier's theory of correspondences is also metaphysical or "occult." Fourier's deity, however, cannot be identified with that of Abrahamic Monotheism, since His most essential feature is His approval of all passions and forms of sexuality, indeed His virtual *identity with* the Passions. Fourier's monist pantheism invites comparison with the non-Religious spirituality of certain radical mystics and heretics (such as William Blake), and also with certain contemporary movements such as anarcho-Taoism or anarcho-paganism. (These in turn are of course updated versions of earlier heresies such as the Brook Farmers' Transcendentalism, a sort of mix of Fourier and Unitarianism. Spiritualism and Swendenborgianism were also rife amongst nineteenth-century radicals.)

THE PHALANSTERY

—big victorian palace, pseudo-chateau—"the caravanserai...the temple, the tower, the telegraph, the coops for carrier pigeons, the ceremonial chimes, the observatory, and a winter courtyard adorned with resinous plants," wide verandas, oriel windows, bay windows, stained glass, all wood and shingle, an american Versailles in the midst of Jersey truckfarm fields humid and cheerfully vulgar, flat and green. Corn tomatoes chickens cherries apples pears plums herbs hemp turkeys pigs cows dogs cats[4] sunflowers hollyhocks 1620 people under one roof (with outlying gazebos and cot-

---

4 A strange thing about Fourier and cats: in one passage he condemns them for being antisocial, yet the biographers mention that he habitually shared his rented rooms with a number of cats.

tages for allies and hermits)—like the castles of Sade's libertines the Phalanstery is a closed space, *hortus conclusus* or artificial paradise rising originally in all its elaborate and obsessive architecture and detail *A Session in the Court of Love: the band of adventurers moves forward through a cloud of perfume and a rain of flowers. (UVCF 387)* out of masturbation fantasies. The one big important difference between Sade and Fourier is that in the Phalanstery everyone's rich and happy—not just the libertines. In our modern Phalanx the "Bourse" or Exchange, the complex daily process of scheduling and book keeping, is aided by computers—otherwise, however, reproductive and mediating technologies are not very popular. We prefer to make art rather than passively consume "leisure" and "entertainment." Our chief modes of creativity are the banquet, the "OPERA" (which Fourier already understood as the synthesis of all art forms), and the orgy. Of course in our alternate universe we expend as much energy and eros on mere work as you (in your sad reality) on the finest art and most exquisite pleasures. Our food, our art, our eroticism, receive the influx of sheer genius, and exist on a higher plane of intensity than you can imagine except in fleeting moments of ecstatic realization. Our quotidian routine has the same texture as your highest adventure.

## HIEROGLYPH

The foul emanations of Civilization have caused the Moon to die. By the unalterable law of Passional and Aromal rays, our present Moon will be destroyed and replaced under Harmony by five different-colored satellites. So enjoy the pallid and sterile glow while you can, dupes of Civilization, for it is inexorably doomed.

*The material world being in all its details hieroglyphic of the passional, God must have created emblems of the passions in all the degrees. (PHS 16)*

*This is to say that the properties of an animal, a vegetable, a mineral, and even a cluster of stars, represent some effect of the human passions in the social order, and that EVERYTHING, from the atoms to the stars, constitutes a tableau of the properties of the human passions. (UVCF 397)*

## PARANOID CRITICISM

—a term invented by S. Dali—everything is alive, and even consciousness is more universal than poor Reason could ever allow—For Fourier, life and history are shaped by occult forces, specifically by the unconscious, by desire—but also by actual conspiracy, "breathing together." Analogy—everything means something else—no "coincidences." An aesthetic derived from this theory would of course approximate Surrealism. Fourier remained silent about the art of his time and limited himself to foretelling a future when the borders which Civilization enforces in aesthetics would

*Let us begin by pointing out that in the eyes of morality all the most distinguished personality types, the truly sophisticated ones, are dangerous. (UVCF 222)*

fall and be replaced by (for instance) the Harmonian OPERA. Thus Surrealism is justified in considering him an ancestor; moreover Fourier himself exhibited a definite "paranoid" streak, convinced of a vast conspiracy against him and his mission, orchestrated by the philosophical establishment and its lackeys in the press and government. The art he predicted indeed came into being—but not the social form which ought to support it, uplift it, surround it, and carry it on to universality. In this sense the historical avant garde became the unacknowledged legislators of a nonexistent and still totally *imaginal* world, a counterworld or utopia in the literal sense of "no place." In the alternate universe where Harmony reigns, Art has been "suppressed and realized" because every Harmonian is an "artist." In our world, however, the avant garde has actually fallen into the gulf that separates vision from actuality—the avant garde has "disappeared" into the abyss created by a *tragic* contradiction (between, for example, Surrealism and Stalinism). In the twentieth century art had to make a revolution or else die. Its revolution failed and indeed all that remains of it is an exquisite corpse. So—hey presto—Art has already been "suppressed". What remains now is its "realization"—in the free play of creative imagination *outside* the total area of reproduction and mediation, outside the entire dialectic in which a term like "avant garde" makes semantic sense. What form might this endeavor take? I don't know—I'm still engaged in producing books, despite Fourier's prediction that the libraries would fall. Still, reading and writing are also *passions*.

FIAT LUX(E)

In Harmony everyone will be an artist, since each will perform "useful labor" with the same creative intensity now bestowed only on art. But no one will be only an artist, since the Butterfly Passion (the lust for variety) will give each of us at least thirty vocations. In effect the Phalanstery IS a work of art, in all its movements, rituals, processions, pavilions, banquets, set-pieces, cabals, assignations, and operas. Its aesthetic is rooted in *luxury* and *light*, or "brilliance," one of Fourier's favorite words. The "mathematical poem" or science of Attraction is also an art, or rather, it takes the form of a language whose grammar is musical and whose content is erotic. This atmosphere evokes a resonance with psychedelic aesthetics, and indeed the phalansteries of the 1840s lie buried beneath the

*…the birth of social happiness is dependent on the discovery of two means: 1. luxury, without which harmony cannot be organized; 2. the theory of harmony, without which you cannot make use of luxury. (UVCF 213)*

*We have heard the sensitive Anacreon, who prefers men to women, extol the orgies of young pederasts and intrepid drunkards among the sooth-sayers. If the champions of antiquity admire excess, so condemned today, it is because they quite agree that orgy is one of man's natural needs. (HM 278)*

*The courts of love are based on the principle that every fantasy is good; they look for the most unknown, the most disdained, in order to give it prominence*

floors of the communes of the 1960s— like lost archaeologies—or ancestors whose names are forgotten but whose genes are immortal. Consider the "Museum Orgy," a Harmonian artform "offering no more than visual gratification and designed to encourage the development of the aesthetic faculties of the Harmonians" (as Beecher describes it, *UVCF* 392). Just as the border between producer and consumer is erased by attractive labor, so the line between audience and work of art vanishes in the Museum Orgy, as each Harmonian becomes simultaneously the object and subject of desire, both sign and signified in the language of Passion. Fourier predicts that Harmonians will eat and enjoy certain foods which to us are poisons, and he specifically mentions mushrooms; surely he would have approved of magic mushrooms, enhancers of luxury and erotic sensation,

*and to create its partisans the world over. (HM 114)*

*Amorous love fantasies, whether infinitely rare as is foot fetishism, or common as are the sects of flagellation, cannot be subject to debate regarding honor or proper comportment, nor can they require the intervention of a council. Everyone is right in matters of amorous mania, since love is essentially the passion of unreason. (HM 112)*

*In Harmony great efforts will be made to bring together the devotees of...extremely rare manias. For each of them the meeting will be a pilgrimage as sacred as the journey to Mecca is for Moslems. (UVCF 348)*

most "brilliant" of the hallucinogens. The aim of Fourierist aesthetics resembles that of Taoist or of psychedelic aesthetics: identity of subject and object, overcoming the dichotomy of self and other.

## THE HARMONIAN BODY
(A READING OF *PASSIONS OF THE HUMAN SOUL*, VOL. I)

None of the commentators seem to have given a full description of the amazing differences between our Civilized bodies and those of the Harmonians in their full "evolution" (which will depend not on genetics but on the brilliant influence of *social mutation*—not proto-Darwinian but proto-Lamarckian). Some commentators have noted with amusement the *archibras*, that fingered tail so useful no doubt in fruitpicking and orgies, and most have recalled that Harmonians will have longer childhoods (puberty at fifteen or sixteen), longer lives (nearly one-eighth will live to 144), more perfect health, greater statures (average seven feet), and more ravishing beauty than we can

*What dupes men are that they have compelled themselves to wear a dreadful chain; what punishment they endure for having reduced women to bondage.... Freedom in love, joy and good will, insouciance, and more, are not dreamed of because philosophy habituates us to regard the desire for true good as vice. (HM 204-5)*

imagine. But what an alien beauty! Few modern sci-fi writers have dared to envision a future humanity so radically altered, or rather self-altered. No puny bulbbrains dependent on robots and prosthesis! Fourier's future body-image is based not on body hatred but on the glorious apotheosis of the individual/collective will, expressed on a somatic level so deep as to resonate with the very plasm or life-forces of Nature, and on a psychic level so high as to make the boasts of shamans and magicians look picayunc by comparison.

*The shades of white differ according to the planetary degrees; the white of our epidermis is false—it is a rosy grey. The Jupiterians have already the rosy alabaster white; the Solarians, higher in rank, have the white epidermis of rosy musk color.*
*(PHS I 228)*

Science fiction abounds in masking-images of body-fear and hatred—immortality, decorporealization, Cyberspace, the airlessness and anti-organicity of "Space" itself—which reveal an underlying neo-Gnostic or neo-puritanical body-image in which material is bad, spiritual (or rather mental) is good. Fourier too has tinges of Dualism, which lead him to despise *our present body*, but he overcomes his own extreme idealism by advocating a *spiritual materialism* (*i.e.*, making *life* the high value) so radical as to amount to a potential deification of the body. "There is...nothing more unsuited to us, who are a *cardinal star*, a star of high nobility, than the moral pleasures,—the turnips of Cincinnatus and the black broth of the philosophers. We need an immense luxury, and a bi-compound harmony, which ought to apply to all the faculties of our soul and of our senses, far removed in their actual [present] state from this brilliant [future] destiny" (PHS I 54).

This destiny includes, for example, the albino, a pre-echo of the Harmonian body in "his properties of equinoctial whiteness and conocturnal vision, with which the race born in Harmony will be endowed" (63). Fourier is particularly informative on the future becoming of *vision*—not only will we see at night, we will also come to enjoy the "amphi-vertical or diverging polar eye of the chameleon" who possesses the "beautiful faculty of simultaneously casting the eyes to opposite poles." *Convergence* for Fourier is always a restriction, a limitation. Our present civilized eyes converge and are thus severely limited: the Harmonian eye *diverges* and thus expands its scope, increasing the pleasure or "*luxe*" of the Passion of vision. That which diverges gives variety, like the divergent sexualities of the "manias" and so-called perversions. That which converges is monotonous, like morality or simple binoptic vision. The Harmonian will acquire "Co-aromal vision," allowing the perception of some 800 colors, each belonging to a different aroma (light is only one aroma, and we see only 7 of its 12 rays); we shall even watch in the sky the rays of aroma darting between stars as they copulate, noting their myriad shades in our "sidereal gazettes" (87). The vision of the *somnambulist*, who walks everywhere safely with eyes closed, "proves to us that we can experience sensations without the aid of the senses" (*i.e.*, ESP), since we can psychically tune in to the "sensual faculties of the planetary body," Earth herself, who "sees and hears like ourselves, but through very different means" (105). We seem to be approaching Taoism here, and are not surprised to learn that Harmonians (like Taoist sages who plunge beneath the sea to meet with dragon kings) are amphibious, or that they fly through the air without wings (169), that they possess invulnerability (174-75), ambidexterity, and prehensile toes. Fourier's theory, however, is *physical*, not magical: he proposes the existence of twelve atoms or basic particles making up all material things and organs. Our civilized eyes lack the co-solar vision of the eagle (the ability to see through fire, such as the Solarians or inhabitants of the Sun enjoy) and the co-nocturnal vision of the cat, because "one of the five sharp or five flat atoms is combined in a contradictory way in our eyes.... These disorders are only temporary, and humanity will remedy them by backing itself with the *societary system*, which alone can raise our bodies to extreme vigor, and favor the new combinations of atoms of which we are corporeally susceptible" (91). Moreover, social change will influence planetary destiny, so that climate will change. Earth will lose its single "mummy" Moon and acquire a plethora of satellites and Saturn-like rings, and once again be bathed in the aromal influences of other planets and stars (as it was before Civilization literally knocked our world from its course); new aromas will circulate in our atmosphere, giving "new faculties to the beings, animals and plants. This spring [*i.e.*, this source] alone would suffice to occasion all the specified changes [in the body and Nature]" (92).

Fourier refrains from outlining the development of other senses and organs, allowing us to make use of the Passional Calculus to deduce for ourselves the future of the sense of *touch-rut*, and indeed the future of the *genitals*, which must be even more extraordinary than that of sight and optic tissue. For our sight, he predicts, will ultimately render all "animate bodies" (and reality itself) *transparent* as "very limpid crystal," like "the silk-worm on the eve of its transformation, and the glow-worm in the dusk." Thus "the human eye will be in the condition of a man from whom a cataract has been removed, and who distinguishes forms and shades where before there was nothing but opaqueness and obscurity" (123). Clearly Fourier preaches a mysticism of the senses, or a sensual mystique, in which everything is embodied, but in *bodies of light*.

## MANDALA

Fourier's *future* would impose an injustice on *our present*, since we Civilizees cannot hope to witness more than a foretaste of Harmony, if it were not for his highly original and somewhat mad eschatology. He conceives of reincarnation not as a means of getting off the Wheel, but rather as a promise of an infinity of merry-go-round rides, in which we will trace as individual souls our trajectories through the future of Harmony and even to the emergence of entire new universes more stupendous than our present immensity. His critique of the *dullness* of all reli-

*(bi-compound or aromized or transcendent fire)…might be surnamed the material God of nature…since fire is the body of God, and ought in this wise to hold the rank of focus among the elements. (PHS I 188)*

gious nonmaterial conceptions of paradise leads to a *Diffraction: instantaneous* materialist eschatology—to the virtual eternity of self *light of harmony piercing* and body—since otherwise Fourier's God would have *the centre of subversion,* to be accused of injustice both to the living and the *(as when) a plumage of* "dead." One of the things we can do with Fourier's *black feathers, or a hat of* system is to hold it within our consciousness and *black felt, being placed* attention in the form of a mandala, not questioning *between the eye and the* whether it be literally factually true, but whether we *Sun, reflect like a prism of* can achieve some sort of "liberation" through this *crystal the seven rays on* strange meditation. The future becoming of the solar *their edge. (PHS II 414)* system, with its re-arrangement of planets to form dances of colored lights, can be visualized as a tantric adept uses a yantra of cosmogenic significance, like a Sufi meditation on "photisms" or series of visionary lights, to focus and integralize our own individual realization of the potential of harmony within us, to overcome our "prejudices against matter, which is represented to us as a vile principle" by philosophers and priests (*PHS* I 227). Like Nietzsche's Eternal Return, the Fourierist eschatology need not lose all value for us if we consider it metaphorically; or better, mandalically rather than as literal dogma. Both Systems are meant to *symbolize* (*i.e.*, to be, and to represent that which it is, simultaneously), to make present a similar Yes to material existence, to becoming, to life; a Yes which—despite all their differences—sounds like the same Yes in both Nietzsche and Fourier.

## THE TAO OF HARMONY

By sheer coincidence while reading Fouri- *Civilized education…intervenes sys-* er I happened to visit several charming *tematically to fight against our desire* Taoist temples in San Francisco (thanks *to be carefree, a desire that will be* to my friends at City Lights, who also *unfettered in Harmony. (UVCF 143)* supplied me with a copy of Breton's *Ode*). The temple of the Phalanstery, centuries from now, will have become encrusted with just such a luxury of red and gold, incense and banners; moreover, the Taoist empha- sis on spontaneity, work-as-play, wealth, health, longevity, sexual "alchemy", com- plex cuisine, and even sensual pleasure[5] also accords well with a Fourierist religion. K. White points out in his intro to the *Ode* that when Fourier excoriates 3000 years of Civilization for "struggling insanely against Nature," and boasts that he is "the first to have yielded to her," he is speaking only for Europe, while in the *Tao Te Ching* one may read "Let Nature take its course / By letting each thing act in accor- dance with its own nature, everything that needs to be done gets done / The best way to manage anything is to make use of its own nature / For a thing cannot func- tion well when its own nature has been disrupted." In the Yang Chu Tractate of *The*

---

5 Taoism is not a monolithic tradition; not every Taoist maintains all these values. I'm thinking particularly of such poets/bon-vivants/"madmen" as the famous Seven Sages of the Bamboo Grove.

*Book of Lieh Tzu* (which I bought the same day I visited the temples) I found:

> Give yourself up to whatever your ears wish to listen to, your eyes to look on, your nostrils to turn to, your mouth to say, your body to find ease in, your will to achieve. What the ears wish to hear is music and song, and if these are denied them, I say that the sense of hearing is restricted. What the eyes wish to see is the beauty of women, and if this is denied them, I say that the sense of sight is restricted. What the nostrils wish to turn to is orchids and spices, and if these are denied them, I say that the sense of smell is restricted. What the mouth wishes to discuss is truth and falsehood, and if this is denied it, I say that the intelligence is restricted. What the body wishes to find ease in is fine clothes and good food, and if these are denied it, I say that its comfort is restricted. What the will wishes to achieve is freedom and leisure, and if it is denied these, I say that man's nature is restricted.
>
> All these restrictions are oppressive masters. If you can rid yourself of these oppressive masters, and wait serenely for death, whether you last a day, a month, a year, ten years, it will be what I call "tending life". If you are bound to these oppressive masters, and cannot escape their ban, though you were to survive miserably for a hundred years, a thousand, ten thousand, I would not call it "tending life".

## Addendum to the Fourierist Banquet
## (A Note On Music)

Given that for Fourier all measured series can be expressed in musical terms, so that music acts for him as a principle of social becoming, it seems only natural that *reading* Fourier enhances the ear for certain music, as I've discovered just now listening to Telemann, whom I already credited with being a Yea-sayer, a proponent of human happiness, and who I would now argue deserves to survive into the era of Harmony. Fourier himself mentions the operas of Gluck with praise—the only specific reference to a composer I've found so far in his work. Amongst the moderns one suspects he might have liked Satie. Fourier speaks rather mysteriously of a "masonic and musical eye," which sounds Mozartian as well as synaesthesic. And we know he enjoyed marching bands. (See Appendix C.)

## Revisionism

It's amusing that every one of Fourier's admirers has wanted to argue with him, to accept part of his system and reject part, from Victor Considerant, his chief disciple, all the way down to his modern commentators and biographers. I could have done the same, if such a course had not seemed to lack dignity and tact. Instead I've managed something better, and have ascertained by means of a series of Swedenborgian/Spiritualist seances that Fourier (who presently inhabits the "planetary soul" while awaiting re-incarnation as a Solarian) has changed his mind about certain aspects of his thought, for as he said, "Did I myself not write that 'a penchant for exclusive systems is one of the radical vices of Civilization, and it will be avoided in Harmony.'?" He's given up all his former racial prejudices, for example, but insists his cosmology was more-or-less correct. At first he rather liked Marx and Engels, who praised him when they were young—but later when Marx condemned him for silliness and the taint of the brothel, Fourier came to dislike him intensely, and points out that he was unkind and patriarchal toward women, "always a bad sign." The ghost of Paul Goodman introduced Fourier to Wilhelm Reich and the modern erotic liberationists and convinced him to rethink his position on infant and childhood sexuality.

"I now realize that both Hypermajors and Hyperminors are present in all four Groups, thus:

| In the 1st phase, or Childhood: | In the 2nd phase, or Adolescence: |
|---|---|
| 1 Friendship | 1 Love |
| 2 Ambition | 2 Friendship |
| 3 Love | 3 Ambition |
| 4 Familism | 4 Familism |

(Note: Three and four of the first phase are missing in the former system.)

| In the 3rd phase, or Virility: | In the 4th phase, or Old Age: |
|---|---|
| 1 Ambition | 1 Familism |
| 2 Love | 2 Ambition |
| 3 Familism | 3 Friendship |
| 4 Friendship | 4 Love |

"This," he said, "makes a great improvement in the chart on page 84, Vol, II, of your copy of *The Passions of the Human Soul*."

"When I said that children are a third sex," Fourier went on (via *planchette*), "I meant they were asexual. When Henry de Montherlandt lifted my saying (without attribution) he meant to indicate that children are another sex with its own and proper sexuality. Needless to say, I was quite prepared to grant full sexual freedom to pubescents, but failed to grasp that children and even infants possess their own erotic natures as well. Of course, I still have the honor of being the first social inventor to propose the liberation of all the passions, including pederasty and sapphism— including even the passion for chastity! To admit now that the Passional Series contains all humans, regardless of age or sex, does not impair the strength of my system, but rather strengthens and *completes* it."

## MANDALA (II)

The microcosmic architecture of the Phalanstery mirrors the macrocosmic architecture of the universe, and in this way can be seen *in toto* as a temple; for all temples are miniature universes. The key that links phalanstery and cosmos as mutual hieroglyphs is to be found in Fourier's radical play with scale, perspective, and closeness. The future of the solar system, for instance, involves Earth's acquisition of five new satellites, Juno, Ceres, Pallas, Vesta, and Mercury, which will leave their present orbits out of sheer *attraction* to the new Harmonian Earth and move much closer to us and to the Sun. The rest of the solar system will also squeeze closer together, so that Venus, Mars, and Jupiter will appear to us nearly as large as our own satellites, and we will behold even Herschel (Uranus) with its eight moons (La Faquiresse, La Bacchante, La Bayadère, La Galante, La Coquette, La Romanesque, La Prude, and La Fidèle). Our night sky will blaze with huge glowing multi-hued globes ("the effect of a garden illuminated with colored lamps")—we'll see Saturn's rings bare-eyed, Venus like a lilac moon, Jupiter a jonquil moon—Vesta will be of a "subversive tint," possibly "burnt sienna, like the back of a cock, or rather like the lees of wine." The planets will crowd together like warm bodies at an orgy, and we'll be so close we'll be able to see and converse with the inhabitants of the other spheres via the Extramundane Planetary Telegraph ("Thus we shall be able, in the Sun as in Jupiter, to see and count the passengers and the windows"—PHS I 213). Moreover the sky will be criss-crossed with aromal rays, like aurora borealis focused into lasers, shooting around the universe like jets of galvanic jism. On the *scale* of the individual phalanstery the same grand *perspectives* will be paradoxically combined with a similar *closeness* and crowding together. The neoclassical, ornate and HUGE palace of the Phalanx, the single roof under which its Harmonians dwell, opens its two wings like arms to the Sun, that visible emblem of the "material god," the "transcendent fire" or life-principle. The phalanstery provides an even more exact emblem of the universe—and vice versa—since each of the thirty-two Choirs or main Series corresponds to one of the thirty-two celestial bodies, with the Sun representing the Synod—"for there is no detail of planetary harmony that is not reproduced in passional harmony." Thus the rose represents hieroglyphically the Vestalate under the influence of Mercury, while the Troubadours are represented by the carnation, flower of puberty and first love, beneath the sign of Jupiter's fifth moon. Each individual is a star, linked and drawn close together by Attraction to all others, connected by "rays" (the radiants or complex movements of work/play, the Passional Series, etc.) and by "orbits". The chief orbit will be described by the Street Gallery, an indoor passageway connecting all the wings and running continually along the second story of the Phalanstery. Fourier never ceased praising this invention, which summed up for him the very style of Harmony. Europe's nineteenth-century covered galleries, pale imitations of Fourier's ideal, fascinated Walter Benjamin, and the unitary concept of the built community exemplified by Fourier's Street Gallery finds echoes in certain playful twentieth-century theories such as Arcology, Situationist Urbanism, or *bolo'bolo*. Because Fourier's cosmology has been largely ignored, commentators have failed to recognize the hieroglyphic nature of phalansterian architecture; moreover, unlike the "druids" who built Stonehenge, Fourier was not basing his scheme on an *existing* universe, but rather on an imaginal one, an *improved* one, which will only come into being when human society virtually brings it into being by the power of Attraction and unleashed Passion—a force great enough to literally pull planets from orbit.

COMPARING FOURIER WITH WILLIAM BLAKE
(for Anselm Hollo)

you might well begin to think that the *moment of desire* had come to European Civilization with the inescapability of a comet or a steam engine, and of course that the complex which gave birth to it was the French Revolution—one of those

*(In Harmony, men will) work quickly at replanting the mountains, and painting certain rocks, so that the luxury of landscapes...may be preserved. (PHS I 59)*

historical events which is *still going on* in our time, like the Roman Empire or the Neolithic—which makes Fourier as much a proto-Romantic as Blake, but which also makes both of them our exact contemporaries. Two marginal cranks in rented lodgings, both mistaken for occultists but both prophets of the body, far more radical than most of the nature-mystics, reformers, and ideologues who came after them: they made the big breakthrough almost simultaneously, they overcame Western philosophy both Aristotelian *and* Platonic, they overthrew Religion—each of them had one foot in the eighteenth century and one in the twentieth (or twenty-first!)—they skipped the nineteenth century—and maybe the other shoe hasn't yet dropped, even now! They were both "mad". If Fourier was a "logothete" then so was Blake—he even defined it: make your own system or be enslaved by someone else's. Meanwhile, what did Blake think about *fruit?* The moment of recovery from sickness induces a powerful mystique of material objects, smells, tastes, colors. Such moments lie behind many of Nietzsche's best insights. Fruit symbolizes this kind of moment. In winter: pears and apples of course, cellared since October, persimmons, oranges and grapefruit sent from the tropics on trains, and compotes of last summer's peaches, apricots, and cherries. Arboriculture! Somehow it seems to evade the curse of the "Agricultural Revolution", somehow it seems easy, not like real work at all, or in any case "attractive labor". New York was once an orchard state—literally hundreds of species of apples have disappeared since the turn of the century due to evil american capitalist conspiracy against variety and taste in favor of shelf-life and uniformity of product. And now (as it begins to snow—January 8, 1991) a complete hallucination: it's summer and Blake and Fourier are playing miniature golf in a run-down beach resort somewhere on the Atlantic coast, maybe South Jersey or Rhode Island, a warm night but not stifling, clear with plenty of stars, they've been drinking sangria in big iced pitchers stuffed with fruit, melons, lemons, strawberries, blackberries, plums, black cherries, Spanish brandy, and sugar—they're pretty high and missing most of their shots. Behind them comes a party of kids, 13/14 year olds in short shorts and hi-top sneakers, giggling, flirting, making fun of the two looped old geezers in a friendly cosmic way, and everyone laughing at the sheer stupid pleasure of it.

## POETICS OF TOUCH

Fourier wanted to expand the alphabet to thirty-two letters to harmonize with the number of bodies in the solar system, number of teeth, number of choirs in the Phalanx, etc. The Phalanx is also called a *tourbillon* or Vortex, which gives a sense of its turbulence and its attractiveness, calling up the mathematical image of a "catastrophic basin" toward which all points will collapse by attraction. It may even be that we can think of the Phalanx as a "Strange Attractor", borrowing a term from modern chaos mathematicians. Fourier speaks of an "Alphabet of Attraction" or of the Passions, and a "musical grammar." The thirty-two letters—including those which exist though we can't hear them, just as five colors (rose, fawn, maroon, dragon green, and lilac) exist in the spectrum of light even though we can't see them (on the analogy of the five unplayed notes in an octave)—these letters are flying around and around in a vortex, like a swirl of autumn leaves, ring-of-roses, all fall toward the middle, making a magnetic rose, rose of the winds. The letters flame up in transcendent fire, each revealing a number, flower, aroma, color, note, banner, animal, PASSION. This is a Cabala of Desire, a gematria of erotic analogies. Fourier has little to say of aesthetic theory (other than a nod to the Aristotelian unities which he himself ignored) but his real contribution to *poetics* can only be assessed by weighing the entirety of his writing. Barthes was right to class him as a logothete, like Sade and Loyola, one for whom words have a life of their own and can be used to create new realities. With his neologisms, number mystique, theory of correspondences, etc., he used language very much as does a Ceremonial Magician, to call up images from the will into being. The difference between Fourier and other hermetalinguists, however, lies in the source/origins or "springs" of his words, and it is here that he parts company with all Illuminists and Platonists. The passions are not inferior shadows of higher, more supernal realities—they ARE supernal realities. The letters spring from the passions as if from angels' mouths, each one a ray of the spectrum of desire. Here's the key to the Surrealists' fascination with Fourier: language defined as a system of marvels, mantras, and magic spells, but not emanating from any bloodless castrated spiritomental flesh-despising religious mysticism—no, language emanating from passion, from the body, and returning to passion, and to the body, in a vortex of incalculable power. I want to consider this *poetics* Fourier's most precious invention, but perhaps I'm wrong to do so. When I've experienced Harmony and lived in a Vortex I'll know that this poetics is no end in itself, but a weapon, a tool, a strategy by which to make Civilization tremble and crack—but only a foretaste of real pleasure, real luxury, real *poetry*: life lived in the incandescence of passion.

APPENDIX A: THE HYMN TO DAWN (PHS II 109FF.)

At a quarter before five, some chimes sound the summons to the lesser parade and the hymn of dawn; the company prepare in the rooms of the refectory to descend in the course of five minutes; on descending you find under the porch the instruments of the musicians, the decorations of the priests and officials of the parade, &c. Five o'clock strikes; the athlete Conradin, aged 14, and the major of the service, commands the groups to form. I have stated on a previous occasion that the officers of the lesser parade are drawn from the choir of athletes, thus the *aides-de-camp* of Conradin are, like himself, aged 13 and 14; they are the athletes Antenor and Amphion for the groups of men; the athletes Clorinda and Galatea for the groups of women.

Amphion and Galatea go on the one hand to form the orchestras, Antenor and Clorinda go to prepare the order of march. They fall in, in the following order:—

I suppose that the muster consists of four hundred persons, men, women and children, and that the sum total composes twenty groups ready to start for different points of the adjoining country. The twenty standard-bearers place themselves in line and at a distance, facing the front of the palace and behind the flags. The troop is formed into an orchestra by vocal and instrumental divisions, having a priest or a priestess at the head of each group. Before the priest a lighted censer and an infant of the same sex that holds the perfumes, with a hierophant or high-priest between the columns of the two sexes; the drums or trumpets are on both sides of the porch, the animals and the cars are ranged along the sides of the court.

In the centre is the major Conradin, having at his side the *aides-de-camp* and before him four children of the choir of neophytes. They carry signal flags, and manoeuvre to transmit the orders to the signal tower, that repeat them to the domes of the neighboring castles, to the groups already spread in the country, and to the palaces of the neighboring cantons.

When all is ready the roll of drums imposes silence, and the major commands the hail to God. Then the drums, the trumpets, and all the military music make themselves heard; the chimes of the surrounding domes play together, the incense rises, the flags wave in the air, and the streamers float upon the pinnacles of the palace and of the castles; the groups, already in the fields, unite in this ceremony, the travellers place foot to ground, and the caravans assist in the holy salute before quitting the station.

At the end of one minute the salute ceases, and the hierophant gives the signal of the hymn by striking three measures upon the diapason of universal unity; the priests and priestesses placed over the vocal and instrumental parts thunder forth the chant, and then the hymn is sung by all the groups in chorus.

The hymn being finished, the little khan causes the muster to be beaten to the flags, the orchestra breaks up its ranks, deposits its instruments, and everyone goes to range himself beneath the banner of his industrial group; it is in this order that the troop files off in various masses and in all directions, for being formed of different ages, from the child to the old man, they would look awkward if they filed off in line and step as the quadrilles of the grand parade do. They range themselves in artificial disorder, and direct themselves first towards the animals; each group takes its cars at the passage, and making them advance abreast with itself, they file off successively before the grand peristyle, beneath which certain dignitaries are stationed, such as a paladin of the sovereign wearing his escutcheon, if it is a minor parade, and if it is a grand parade, a paladin of the emperor of Unity bearing the cycloidal crescent.

Each group, on passing, receives a salute proportioned to its rank; the groups of agriculture and masonry, which are the first, are saluted by a high flourish, equivalent to the drum that beats to field; thence they proceed each one to its destination.

The salute of praise to God regularly traverses the globe in different directions; if it is a day of equinox, there is a grand parade at sunrise, and the spherical hierarchy presents at dawn a line of congregations or phalanges two or three thousand leagues in length, whose hymns succeed each other during the space of twenty-four hours all round the globe, as each longitude receives the dawn. At the two solstices, the hymns are chanted at once upon the whole globe and by the entire human race, at the instant corresponding to the noon-day of Constantinople.

The morning salute is performed like a running fire of artillery, that during the summer travels from the north pole to the south pole, and in the opposite direction during winter. The public *fêtes* follow the same order: the day of the summer solstice, the whole northern hemisphere dines together *en famille*, or in descending groups, and the whole southern hemisphere in quadrilles or ascending groups;* the two hemispheres dine in an opposite order on the day of the winter solstice.

This morning assembly is interesting also as a session of afterchange, where negotiators go to modify arrangements and agreements entered into the preceding day at the return session of nightfall. These numerous stimulants form a mixed transit of different ingredients, and these stimulants of the dawn suffice to set on foot the whole canton from the early morning. It will be seen that there exist plenty of other motives of matutinal diligence, amongst others the vestal court. Accordingly in harmony you must be either infirm or ill to make up your mind to stay in bed after four o'clock in the morning. A man whom they purposely neglected to wake would be disconcerted on going two hours later to the sessions of the different groups; he would have lost the thread of the intrigues, and his spite would be extreme.

## APPENDIX B: THE 1000 FLOWER SERIES
(This version quoted from Breton's *Ode*; see also *UVCF* 292-3)
"If the cherrytree series is united in large numbers in its great orchard, a mile from the phalanstery, it should, in the four o'clock to six o'clock evening session, see coming to meet it and its neighbours:
1. A cohort from the neighbouring phalanx of both sexes come to help the cherry gardeners;

* "Ascending and descending groups," here signify groups of the ascending phases of life, friendship and love, or youth and adolescence; groups of the descending phases of life, ambition and familism, or middle and declining age.—H.D.

2. A group of lady florists of the district, coming to cultivate a hundred-foot line of Mallows and Dahlias forming a perspective for the neighbouring road, and a square border for a vegetable field adjoining the orchard;
3. A group of the vegetable gardener series, come to cultivate the vegetables of this field;
4. A group of the thousand-flower series, coming for the cultivation of a sect altar, set between the vegetable field and the cherry orchard;
5. A group of strawberry maidens, coming at the end of the session, after cultivating a clearing planted with strawberries in the adjoining forest:

At a quarter to six, swing-carts out from the phalanstery will bring the afternoon snack to all these groups: it will be served in the castle of the cherry-gardeners, from quarter to until quarter past six; then the groups will disperse after forming bonds of friendship and arranging industrial or other reunions for the days to follow."

APPENDIX C: "HARMONICON", BY STEVEN TAYLOR

APPENDIX D:

Fourierism was a very *New York* phenomenon. Brisbane and Greeley lived and published in New York, and most of the founders of the North American Phalanx were New Yorkers. Steven Pearl Andrews, founder of the UNIVERSAL PANTARCHY, also lived in New York. Compare the following passage from Pearl Andrews with the quote from Fourier about parties (page 9, with the section on gastrosophy, "The Fourierist Banquet"). The influence of Fourier on Andrews will become apparent:

> The highest type of human society in the existing social order is found in the parlor. In the elegant and refined reunions of the aristocratic classes there is none of the impertinent interference of legislation. The Individuality of each is fully admitted. Intercourse, therefore, is perfectly free. Conversation is continuous, brilliant, and varied. Groups are formed according to attraction. They are continuously broken up, and re-formed through the operation of the same subtle and all-pervading influence. Mutual deference pervades all classes, and the most perfect harmony, ever yet attained, in complex human relations, prevails under precisely those circumstances which Legislators and Statesmen dread as the conditions of inevitable anarchy and confusion. If there are laws of etiquette at all, they are mere suggestions of principles admitted into and judged of for himself or herself, by each individual mind.
>
> Is it conceivable that in all the future progress of humanity, with all the innumerable elements of development which the present age is unfolding, society generally, and in all its relations, will not attain as high a grade of perfection as certain portions of society, in certain special relations, have already attained?
>
> Suppose the intercourse of the parlor to be regulated by specific legislation. Let the time which each gentleman shall be allowed to speak to each lady be fixed by law, the position in which they should sit or stand be precisely regulated; the subjects which they shall be allowed to speak of, and the tone of voice and accompanying gestures with which each may be treated, carefully defined, all under pretext of preventing disorder and encroachment upon each other's privileges and rights, then can anything be conceived better calculated or more certain to convert social intercourse into intolerable slavery and hopeless confusion? [Andrews, 1848: 2]

Andrews is usually considered a Warrenite Individualist Anarchist. He was instrumental in founding Modern Times, and also the "Brownstone Utopia" in New York [see Stern, 1968]. But his later thinking, the global structure of the Pantarchy, and his universalist religion all seem to owe something to Fourier.

APPENDIX E, 1997: NOTES ON FOURIER'S *THEORY OF THE FOUR MOVEMENTS*

*Theory of the Four Movements*—the title seems to suggest the possibility of an experience which combines and surpasses the power of thought and the power of music. A symphony has four movements; and *theoreia* originally means "vision", in the sense of direct experience or "taste", an unveiling which outshines mere discursive reason, and even burns up words themselves. Thus theory reveals a "musical" or "metasemantic" aspect of thought. A language of words which is forced to bear the weight of this double musicality may seem to strain and even crack under the burden.

And the *Theory of Four Movements* is indeed cracked, coming apart at the seams, bursting, not so much a book as a bulging bag, splitting open, spilling fragmented prismatic shards of musical light. If Fourier is a "logothete" [originally a title in the Byzantine Court]—someone who (like Sade, Loyola, Swedenborg, Blake) makes a world of language and then inhabits it—nevertheless that language is always straining against the limitations of a *logos* which excludes music— language seeks to overcome itself, and the book itself becomes the field wherein this struggle occurs. To the conventional reader the book may seem littered with the shrapnel and chaos of such a battle, but the reader who is attuned to Fourier's essential musicality will grasp the HARMONY that wants to emerge from this apparent cacophony (which extends even to the bizarre pagination of the original *Quatre Mouvements*). If this is a symphony (1808) it is already "Romantic"; and in some strange ways it even foretells the Modern (Fourier appears to have intuited the possibility of twelve-tone composition, based on analogy with his theory of the Twelve Passions). But it might be more helpful to imagine Fourier's texts as *operas* rather than as "pure" musical works. Fourier's words "sound" strange on the printed page because they lack an apparent musical dimension; the reader must supply it through imagination. Fourier loved opera and gave it a central role in the world he called *Harmony* precisely because it united every art and could be expressed collectively. In later works, such as the *Nouveau monde amoureux* where he indulged his narrative talents, Fourier created conceptual operas, scenes of daily phalansterian life played out to the endless (and seamless) accompaniment of music, charades, ballet, grand processions, carnival, masked balls, rival orchestras, utopian architecture, and the complete aestheticization of social reality. The *Theory of Four Movements*, which makes less use of narrative, might still be seen as the libretto for a sort of one-man opera, a series of recitatives and arias, performed by the character Fourier:—visionary crackpot, eccentric Balzacian bachelor, poverty-stricken gourmet, traveling salesman, self-proclaimed savior ("demi-messiah"), living in a series of rented rooms with his cats and pots of flowers, churning out endless revisions, versions, improvements, revelations, repetitions, scribbling, scribbling. It would be wrong however to imagine that Fourier created himself as this "character"; never was there a less divided self. Fourier can be quite funny, quite sarcastic, witty, but he is *never ironic*. Neither were Sade, Loyola, Swedenborg, or Blake. The *Theory of Four Movements* is not a representation of Fourier, therefore, but a *presentation*. That is, it is *present* (and therefore still very "readable") and it is a present, a gift, Fourier's gift—a New Song—an entire universe we never imagined—the "truth".

Not the *naked* truth, however. Fourier is sincere, but far from naive. His metanoia involves more than a touch of paranoia. What else are his principles of *Absolute Doubt* and *Absolute Deviation* but a kind of "paranoia critique"? Slyly, Fourier hides various parts of his revelation even as he seems to explode with it in every direction. Perhaps someone might *steal his ideas*? Or perhaps his ideas, especially his sexual ideas, might overstrain the capabilities of his readers? No, even in the exuberance of his utter present-ness, Fourier already *withholds* something. The *Theory of Four Movements* is a book defined by absences as well as presence—by silence as well as "music".

Clapp and Brisbane, the Americans who translated and published *Theory of Four Movements* (1857) worried about the "shocking" aspect of the work. A half century of "victorianism" had intervened, and a transplantation from "Latin" to "Anglo-Saxon" culture. Fourier inherited something of the libertinism of the 18th century, and the romantic freedom of expression of a Rousseau, and both modes were alien to American culture. Brisbane predicts that consensus morality will brand Fourier's sexual ideas "as false and immoral" or "harsh, severe, coarse, vulgar"; in fact, even Emerson and Hawthorne rejected the full implications of the "Passional Series". Fourier's full treatment of sexuality in Harmony, the *Nouveau monde*, remained unpublished even in France till 1967—but the erotic message cannot be edited out of Fourier except by the kind of anthologizing practiced by, say, Charles Gide—and criticized so justly by André Breton—which amounts to sheer bowdlerization and misrepresentation. Gide attempted to depict Fourier as a "precursor" of the cooperative movement, and thus selected only passages discussing the idea of Attractive Labor; Breton argued that Fourier must be read complete, implying that Attractive Labor, for example, cannot be understood in isolation from the complete theory (or rather, from the complete text, since the theory itself is never *complete*)—that Attractive Labor must be seen as a Passion, or a sexualization of social production, and as an aspect of that *cosmic desire* which (like divinity) actually creates the material multiverse.

But even the 1960s anthologies of Fourier in English, which attempt to do justice to every aspect of his thought, fail to do him the justice Breton demanded—aesthetic or critical justice—recognition of Fourier as an *artist*. Brisbane translates a preface to *Theory of Four Movements* for an edition "published in Paris by the disciples of Fourier, after his death":

> "The book is a first explosion of genius; it is a startling and marvelous eruption, throwing out on every side floods of poetry, of beauty, and of science, the sudden flashes of which open to the mind myriads of horizons, new and immense, but shut out instantly from the view, and which produce upon the intellect the effect of a dazzling fairy scene, of a gigantic Phantasmagoria..."

...that is, in a word—a word not yet invented—*surrealism*. By reading the whole text, Breton discovered that Fourier was a surrealist. And yet even this fails to do justice to Fourier, whose politics were far more advanced than Breton's in many ways (he was neither misogynist nor "homophobe", for example—two besetting sins of the Surrealists); and whose style is at all times (unlike some surrealist writing) transparent and translucent, even and especially when it is most severely "cracked".

Recognizing the excitement which only the *whole text* can induce in the reader of Fourier—the "enthusiasm", as it was called (by analogy with Protestant extremism)—Clapp and Brisbane wisely decided to drop the whole bomb of the *Four Movements* rather than anthologize it into a chrestomathy of damp squibs. Boldly they quote the French Preface again: "if... it is contrary to Morality, so much the worse for Morality." One other work by Fourier to appear in English, *The Passions of the Human Soul* (edited by the "English" Fourierist Hugh Doherty—surely an Irish name?—who stormed Versailles with the Revolutionary mob of 1848) also includes innumerable passages dealing with Fourier's dottiest notions (interplanetary telegraphy, sexual life of the planets, etc.) and his most erotic fantasies as well. It's commonplace to assert that Fourier's American followers were shielded from his weirdest ideas, but in fact they were not—although for some reason Clapp and Brisbane decided to eliminate the chapters on "Gastrosophy" from *Theory of Four Movements*, as if Fourier's extraordinary obsession with food were even more shocking than his notions about "The Relations of the Sexes." (And Fourier certainly would have despised the tee-totaling Grahamite-vegetarianism of his American followers at Brook Farm and the North American Phalanx.) Fourier's full theory was certainly diluted in America (and in France as well, for that matter), but it was not stripped of all its true radicalism—it was not distorted. Fourier had a profound effect on the mid-19th century "Reform" Movement called "Free Love", even after the phalansterian experiments had failed. The Individualist Anarchists at "Modern Times", (the utopian community on Long Island, 1851-ca. 1865) like Stephen Pearl Andrews and the Christian Perfectionists at Oneida (1848-1880) under J. H. Noyes, owed their Free Love doctrines in large part to Fourier, if not to Fourierism.

In Beecher's biography of Fourier (pp. 116ff) we learn that the author himself considered *Theory of Four Movements* a "riddle". For one thing, it was given a false place of publication (Leipzig), and signed only by "CHARLES à Lyon". After giving a summary of the book's contents, Beecher remarks:

> An outline such as the above can convey some sense of what the *Théorie des quatre mouvements* is "about," but it cannot convey the impression produced on the reader by Fourier's text or even by a glance at his index. For between each of his major sections is inserted a bewildering variety of preambles and epilogues on such subjects as "the destitution of moral philosophy," "the proximity of the social metamorphosis," and "methodical mindlessness." The book as a whole has no discernible logical continuity; references are repeatedly made to future volumes and to aspects of the doctrine that Fourier does not choose to discuss; and within each section one

encounters long and apparently gratuitous notes and digressions on everything from the breakup of the Milky Way and the melting of the polar icecaps to the decadence of the French provincial theater and the *maîtrise proportionnelle*. Finally, the whole is preceded by an "Introduction," a "Preliminary Discourse," an "Argument" and an "Outline," followed by "Omitted Chapters," a "Note," a "Nota," a "Notice to the Civilized," several epilogues, and a huge fold-out "Tableau of the Course of Social Movement" beginning with the first infection of the seas by stellar fluid and culminating with the cessation of the earth's rotation on its axis. [Beecher 119—120]

At one point, *Theory of Four Movements* describes itself as "absurd, gigantic, [and] impossible."

In 1816 Fourier wrote an apologia or "Explanatory Preamble to the First Announcement" to explain the riddle of *Theory of Four Movements*; he called the text *Sphinx Without Oedipus*, however, suggesting that the explanation would prove less than exhaustive. He describes the book as a work of "studied bizarreness," "a parody before the play," a "trial balloon." He had donned the garb of Harlequin—the "masks of inspiration, salaciousness, and pedantry," as Beecher says—on purpose to lure out his opponents, to trick them with "a snare for snarling critics." He boasted that when some of his friends read in proofs the book's "Preliminary Discourse" and praised it as "soberly written," he at once added another introduction composed in his most "visionary" tone. "My mind," he remarked proudly, "is naturally bizarre and impatient with methods. Thus it suited me to speculate on the use of my natural propensities." Beecher rightly proposes that this description could apply equally well to any of Fourier's later works, and not merely to *Theory of Four Movements*. We could call it a piece of "experimental writing", but only because it came first; Fourier's "voice" however is already fully developed and will *never change*. Till the last he will continue to withhold, he will continue to organize his texts almost as free-associational monologues, and he will continue to be "bizarre". His self-masking is never a self-doubling; he is always FOURIER, the same prophet of unity without uniformity, the same crank, the same *writer*.

We however can read Fourier not only as post-Surrealists but also as post-Deconstructionists and post-Post-Modernists. We are obliged neither to posit an absolute authorial category (with its reduction toward mere psychologism) nor a radical decentering of the author in favor of the text (with its reduction toward disengagement from "meaning"). Fourier is perhaps our contemporary; not that we have solved the riddle, but that we have entered into the enigma and become as "bizarre" as Fourier himself. Fourier's text has the same power of the "explosive" and "marvelous" for us as it did for his disciples, but for us the shock owes more to recognition than to strangeness. We come to Fourier through the Situationists (who perhaps read *Nouveau monde amoureux* in 1967), through Foucault, Deleuze and Guattari, the Autonomists, through "driftwork", critical theory and theories of "desire"—and through the "death of Communism". We no longer ask of an author that the work transcend the "personal" or that it mask itself as ideology. We need not therefore read Fourier as a failed "Utopian Socialist" nor even as a proto-Surrealist. The "science-fiction" aspects of his work simply reflect our childhood fantasies, familiar in their very strangeness; and his sexuality belongs to us in the same way. It is as if Fourier's whole revolutionary project had not only not failed but rather succeeded— but only in the world of reading, the "logothetic" world of book-universes, revealed by Borges and Calvino (who wrote a very sympathetic essay on Fourier, by the way). Owen, Comte, St.-Simon, even much of Marx and the Anarchists, all have become more or less unreadable, while Fourier's readability only seems to increase. In some strange way (and not at all the way he hoped), Fourier's time has come.

We find ourselves in a "post-ideological" situation in which we must *create values* in order to have values at all, and in which the only creative powers accessible to us arise from desire, and from the imagination. If Civilization cannot accommodate desire (as Freud maintained), then Fourier offers us the possibility of overcoming Civilization itself in the realization that desire is not only centrifugal and "chaotic" but also centripetal, a source of "spontaneous ordering". Realized desire, according to Fourier, leads not to the "transgressive" or Sadean moment, but to the moment of Harmony. This is not an entirely original idea. Hesiod's cosmogeny depicts Chaos, Desire, and Matter as the spontaneous ordering forces of existence; and Avicenna's cosmology imagines *archangelic desire* as the organizing principle of becoming. But Fourier was the first to expose the revolutionary implications of this "reading" of desire as the only possible principle of the Social as well as the cosmic. Over and over again Fourier dismisses the French Revolution as a failure, not because it "went too far", but because it did not go far enough:—it should have liberated desire. Not until Surrealism, or even till 1968 was such a critique heard again. "Power to the Imagination" implies that we may have the values we desire (if not the "goods") because we are capable of *imagining* those values. In this task we may derive from Fourier a *Utopian Poetics*, a dialectic of uncovering our "true desires"—which are also our greatest "virtues". The Nietzschean liberation of the "self" mirrors and complements the Fourierist liberation of the "other"—a whole society of *uber*-beings could have no better realization of will to power than the phalanstery—the real "goods" at last—"jam today," as Alice put it.

[Note: Nietzsche can be used to counter some of Fourier's defects, such as his "anti-Semitism". Fourier liked to characterize himself as a semi-literate provincial clerk, and he failed to overcome prejudices lingering in that part of his personality. But his racial attitudes fail to amount to *racism*. In Harmony, it goes without saying, the "Cabalistic Passion" of the "Jews" will be transformed into a positive force for social movement and individual pleasure. As for Fourier's absurd dislike of China, gleaned from a few ill-digested newspaper articles, one likes to imagine that in Harmony Fourier would have discovered not only the gastrosophic delights of Chinese cuisine but also the appeal of Taoism (the hedonics of Yang Chu, for example, or the communal orgies of the Yellow Turbans). (For an excellent comparison of

Fourierism and Taoism, see the introduction to the English translation of Breton's *Ode to Fourier*.) Conversely, Fourier can be used to counteract some of Nietzsche's failings, especially the cold and lonely aspects of his individualism, his lack of *compassion*. The Situationists proposed a synthesis of Marx and Stirner—why not then of Fourier and Nietzsche?]

ల        ల        ల

Those readers who are about to be seduced by Charles Fourier will no doubt find their own uses for *Theory of Four Movements* and their own favorite passages. If I indulge myself in discussing a few of my own, I do so only to demonstrate one way of reading the book, not to exclude others. Since I've never come across any serious discussion in English of Fourier as a Hermetic Philosopher—(a dimension of his thought already unveiled in *Theory of Four Movements*)—it may serve some purpose for us to browse the text while keeping in mind certain techniques developed by the "History of Religion" (or "histories of religions") in an attempt to elucidate Fourier's later popularity with French Martinists, Illuminists and Freemasons. (In America a similar interest emanated from Swedenborgian circles.) The very name "CHARLES à Lyon" must at once have alerted certain readers, familiar with that city as a hot-bed of late 18th-century occultism and Hermeticism, to be on the alert for mystical hints. And the enigmatic style and cosmic excitements of the text would not have disappointed them.

Fourier reveals that the laws of Social Movement are, "in all points, *hieroglyphs*" of all other movements, such that "if we did not yet know the laws of the Material Movement, determined by modern astronomers, they would be discovered now by their *analogy* with those of the Social Movement which I have penetrated" (italics mine). Fourier proposes a *hieroglyphic science* based on analogies or "correspondences", as they are known in Hermetic theory. He was not referring to the translation of real Egyptian hieroglyphs carried out in the wake of Napoleon's looting of the Rosetta Stone, but to the older "hieroglyphs" of the Renaissance neoplatonists and Hermetic revivalists, as in the Book of Horapollo. The imaginative and fortuitous "mistranslation" of these hieroglyphs supplied an ideological framework for Hermeticism as a "Natural Philosophy" or *science*. As a code which both hid and revealed the archetypal essences of material objects, hieroglyphics could be used to classify, and thus as an epistemological device. Since these essences were able to "act at a distance" (like sight, for example, or gravity), hieroglyphs comprised not only a code of inner natures, a means to "read" Nature itself, but also a *projective semiotics*, a way to influence "reality" by the deployment of images (hieroglyphs, symbols)— *i.e.*, by the deployment of imagination—by "magic".

Fourier followed this tradition, which had of course long ago been "beaten" by other paradigms and "proven untrue"—at least, in the daylight world of early 19th century philosophy and science. For him the "emblem" is not just an allegory (be it of a moral or chemical nature), but a means of praxis. If the lion and the diamond are analogous to the Sun (as he explains in *Passions of the Human Soul*) then to grasp this is not merely to compose a line of poetry, but to deploy the solar characteristics of the lion and diamond for Harmonial purposes (to enhance *luxury* for example, which is also "solar"). According to Fourier, solar light itself could be broken into a spectrum of not seven but twelve colors, each corresponding to one of the twelve Passions. "It should be understood that this ray contains five other rays which are not perceptible to the eye, namely, rose, buff, chestnut, dragon-green, lilac. (I am certain only of the rose and fawn). The white ray then contains, in fact, twelve rays, of which it shows only seven, as the musical octave contains twelve sounds, seven of which only are pronounced." It follows then that colors, sounds, aromas (which play a role of cosmic importance), geometrical shapes ("the properties of love are calculated according to the properties of the Ellipse") and all emblems and sensual symbols exercise real influence on individual and social psychic and material being.

This analogical perception leads directly to the importance of *ritual*, which for Fourier takes the form of festival, of opera, and of religious cult. Presumably the individual might also pursue the benefits of the hieroglyphic science, and Fourier himself is said to have written and carried astral amulets—but here he discusses only social applications of his theory. [Note: I have consulted the article by Adrien Dax, "*A propos d'un talisman de Charles Fourier*"; the talisman there depicted seems suspect if only because it is composed with standard occult symbolism rather than with Fourierist correspondences. The provenance, however, appears soundly attributed. On page 550 of Beecher's biography, notes 37 and 38, several French works concerning Fourier's occult connections are cited.] Opera alone includes all these forms of ritual, and Fourier devotes several pages of *Theory of Four Movements* to its vital role in Harmony. Here we note that Opera will tend toward the condition which the situationists called "the suppression and realization of art"—that is, the suppression of art as a separate category and its realization in "everyday life." For Fourier the audience disappears only to be replaced by a whole society of brilliant artists; art itself disappears, to be replaced by phalansterian life, a constant spontaneous production of Hermetic ritual and aesthetic pleasure. The typically Fourierian performance (aside from the orgy) would be the dramatic procession, whether of a single Series marching off with banners and standards, songs and dance, to pick cherries for an hour in the garden, or of a whole army of operatic knights-errant, arriving ceremoniously at a distant phalanx. As V. Turner might say, the whole of Harmony's social organization is performative.

Fourier's science of analogies was noticed with pleasure by Baudelaire, and later Rimbaud, who made use of it as poetry, and later still by Walter Benjamin, that most crypto-Hermetic of all rogue Marxists. But in *Theory of Four Movements* Fourier seems to want to seduce not poets but Freemasons. In an appendix he launches a typically cryptic appeal, larded with severe criticisms, at Masonry. Its anti-clericalism, vague deism, love of ritual, and (occasional) social radicalism all bear comparison with the Fourierist "religion".

[Note: In America a Fourierist church, shadowy and short-lived, was founded in 1846 by George Ripley and William Henry Channing at Brook Farm (see Guarneri, 54-55). Fourier had defended Jesus as a prophet of pleasure, who multiplied loaves and transmuted water into wine; and Fourier himself was a "demi-messiah". Fourier describes "Hundred Flower altars" dedicated to Harmonial saints, and refers to a priesthood (voluntary and powerless, of course) made up of grand Hierophants and "bonzes". Ripley and Channing were ex-Unitarians, and therefore probably never attempted much in the way of ritual. But part of the happy atmosphere of Brook Farm can probably be attributed to this "lost" religion of celebration and "divine humanity."]

But Masonry failed to realize its potential because it devoted itself (in the Revolution) to a "cult of reason" rather than of pleasure. Fourier is as severe a critic of rationalism as any disciple of Feyerabend could demand; for him it represents only authoritarianism and sterility. Instead he proposes a metarational masonry of "gallantry" and pleasure, which—by the deployment of emblems—would extend its influence into the general culture. It seems improbable that Fourier simply invented this idea, since in fact such societies had existed in the 18th century and might still have existed in 1808. In *The Secret Societies of All Ages and Countries*, by C. W. Heckelthorn, we find a chapter on "Androgynous Masonry", *i.e.*, masonic offshoots which accepted both men and women as members. Using "legends" of gallantry, chivalry, romantic love, and arcadian symbolism, these orders can be traced in Germany and France to about 1788, when the last, the Order of *Harmony*, dissipated after the arrest of its Grand Master, an ex-Jesuit called Francis Rudolf "von" Grossing, for fraud. (Grossing managed to escape, but then disappeared.) [Note: Thanks to Professor Joan Roelofs for this reference.] It would be extremely interesting to know whether any Masonic lodges (perhaps of the Grand Orient) ever responded to Fourier's veiled appeal. The later involvement of some Fourierists in the uprisings of 1848 might be scrutinized in this regard, since that period was much given to "Carbonarism" (even Marx toyed with it). Clearly however no masses of masons ever converted to Harmonialism or attempted to re-organize Freemasonry as a front for the propagation of Passional Attraction.

Fourier's concept of a secret society paving the way for a utopian "uprising" deserves some serious consideration. Bataille and his colleagues in the College of Sociology developed a kind of Nietzschean/revolutionary reading of the secret society which still finds its adherents, and which might usefully be compared with Fourier's chapter on Masonry. The big difference is that violence plays no role in Fourier's "Tong"; it has all been "sublimated" into sexuality (or traced back to sexuality and thus exorcised). This might at first seem like sheer idealism—but Fourier was correct to intuit that such a substitution can in fact be observed "in Nature"—in certain higher primate bands which replace aggression with polymorphous co-sensuality—or in those human groups which M. Sahlins has dubbed "aphrodisian societies" (in opposition to the simple Nietzschean categorization of societies as either Dionysian or Apollonian). Sahlin's example is pre-contact Hawaii, and Fourier's example is Tahiti. In *The Four Movements*, for example, Fourier characterizes true primitive societies by five points: "freedom in Love", first of all; then population-control; nonhierarchization and non-authoritarianism; a low-meat diet; and "the Primitive Beauty of Created Things," i.e., the positive valuation of wild(er)ness. He adds (prefiguring the work of P. Clastres on "primitive warfare") that the "violence" of primitive societies (with their proud sensual capricious men women and children) was actually "the means of social concord," and not the force of disruption which we Civilizees call "war". In short, Fourier's anthropology still holds good and even harmonizes with the radical anthropology of Sahlins and Clastres. Therefore, the secret society (which has its origin in primitive society) cannot be defined simply as a *männerbund* dedicated to violence and death. There exist such things as "aphrodisian" secret societies dedicated to what Bataille himself might characterize as the festal waste of excess social wealth, to fertility, to over-consumption; and to the whole Bakhtinian range of carnivalesque and grotesque material bodily principles—or what might be called the spirituality of pleasure. By definition such societies take on "insurrectionary" implications simply by co-existing with a Civilization based on repression. Fourier's visionary logic here seems impeccable. Such a thing as an Order of Harmony should have existed. If it did not, clearly it was necessary to invent it.

Most modern readers will know Fourier only through Marx, as a "Utopian socialist"; few will have considered him as a religious thinker. But Noyes, Ripley, Channing, Thomas Lake Harris (the astounding Swedenborgian/Fourierist founder of Spiritualism) and other 19th century visionaries had no difficulty in detecting Fourier's theological tendencies. To read Fourier in the light of Paracelsus, Boehme, and German Romanticism, is to read a different Fourier. His "spiritual materialism", his always-astonishing cosmology, his ritual aesthetics, and his messianic "calling", reveal him as nearer to Blake than to Owen or St.-Simon. The aphorisms of *The Marriage of Heaven and Hell* come closer to Fourier's real position than any economic or philosophic reading. Fourier is indeed an "illuminist"—but at the heart of his enlightenment lies the sacred imagination, and the sacred body. It is an almost "Rosicrucian Enlightenment" (in F. Yate's phrase)—not mechanistic, not even rational, but deeply Hermetic. And yet the sunlight has banished the melancholy spookiness that somehow taints the hieroglyphic science (the "grief" of the Emblem Books, noted by Benjamin in his *Origins of the German Tragic Drama*). Instead we are offered a Hermeticism of joy, of Eros and Aphrodite as well as Hermes, of life over death. Fourier purges Hermeticism of its platonic hesitations, urging the primal holiness of the body's pleasure. Fourier's god (who is also the Sun) is precisely this pleasure. And this is the "key" to that Hermetic "riddle", the *Theory of the Four Movements*.

[Note: The original purpose of this essay was to stand as preface to a new reprint edition of the translation of *Theory of Four Movements* by Henry Clapp, Jr., minus the supplementary essay by Albert Brisbane. However, by comparing Clapp's text with the French original in the 1967 edition by Simone Debout (Paris: Jean-Jacques Pauvert), I realized that Clapp's version was flawed by the omission of several important sections. I began to feel that Clapp's version would have to be "improved" by adding new translations of those sections. Luckily, however, I learned that a totally new translation of the work based on Debout's edition would be published in 1996—and it has now appeared: Charles Fourier, *The Theory of the Four Movements*, ed. by Gareth Stedman Jones and Ian Patterson, trans. Ian Patterson.

Oddly enough, Patterson was unaware of Clapp's version until he had finished his own (see p. xxxii). Thus there exists no relation whatsoever between the two versions other than their common source. Clapp's text has the advantage of the flavor of 19th century style (and typography!)—but it also has one other important aspect, missing from Patterson's work. Clapp worked under the direction of Brisbane, who was the leader of the American Fourierists and the Master's chief interpreter in the New World. Thus Brisbane's translations of *key technical terms* became "official" in American Fourierist circles (see Guarneri). Clapp uses the term "Passional Attraction" while Patterson opts for the less technical sounding "Passionate Attraction"; however, the term entered English as "Passional" (also via Doherty's translations, published in England as well as America). I see no particular reason to give up such "accepted" or standard usages.

Aside from that, however, Patterson's version is much to be prefered. He includes sections dropped by Clapp out of prudery (a scabrous satire on cuckoldry; pp. 124ff) or embarrassment (the section on gastrosophy; pp. 158ff). Clapp also dropped the long section on "Insular Monopoly" (*i.e.*, British perfidy; pp. 203ff), and he missed a lot of extra material from later editions and annotations by Fourier, which is added by Patterson (pp. 282-322) including some real gems. Patterson also adds extra material from earlier editions throughout.

The introduction by both editors, Jones and Patterson, is informed and informative, and shows respect for the "Cosmic" Fourier as well as the *sexual* Fourier. While I appreciate their insistence on treating Fourier as Fourier defined himself— as an *inventor*—I see no reason why this should exclude consideration of Fourier as a "precursor of surrealist or modernist poetics" as well (p. xi). After all, he *is* a precursor—an *ancestor*—as I have tried to show in my essays on him. Thanks to Jones and Patterson, the evidence is now easily available again.]

SELECT BIBLIOGRAPHY
(Note: Sources of quotations are identified by the abbreviations used in the text.)

Andrews, Steven Pearl (No date) *The Science of Society; Part 1. The True Constitution of Government*. Bombay: Libertarian Socialist Institute. First published 1848.

Barthes, Roland (1989) *Sade/Fourier/Loyola*, trans. Richard Miller. Berkeley: University of California Press

Beecher, Jonathan (1986) *Charles Fourier: The Visionary and His World*. Berkeley: University of California Press

Breton, André (1970) *Ode To Charles Fourier*, trans. Kenneth White. London: Cape Goliard Press, in association with Grossman Publishers, New York

Davenport, Guy (1984) *Apples and Pears, and Other Stories*. San Francisco: North Point Press

Dax, Adrien "*A propos d'un talisman de Charles Fourier*" in *La Bréche. Action Surréaliste*, 4, February 1963.

Fourier, Charles (1971) *Design for Utopia: Selected Writings of Charles Fourier*, introductions by Charles Gide and Frank E. Manuel, trans. Julia Franklin New York: Schocken Books. First published 1901.

— (1971) HM: *Harmonian Man: Selected Writings of Charles Fourier*, ed. with intro. by Mark Poster, with new translations by Susan Hanson. New York: Doubleday, Anchor Books

— (1967). *Le Nouveau monde amoureux*. Volume X of *Oeuvres complètes de Charles Fourier*. Paris: Editions Anthropos

— (1968) PHS: *The Passions of the Human Soul and Their Influence On Society and Civilization*, two volumes, trans. with intro., commentary, notes, and a biography of Charles Fourier, by Hugh Doherty. New York: Reprints of Economic Classics, Augustus M. Kelly, Publishers. First published by Hippolyte Bailliere, London and New York, 1851

— (1972) "Theory of Four Movements", in *The Social Destiny of Man or Theory of Four Movements*, trans. Henry Clapp, Jr. New York: Gordon Press. First published by: Robert M. Dewitt and Calvin Blanchard, New York, 1857

—(1996) *The Theory of the Four Movements*, ed. by Gareth Stedman Jones and Ian Patterson, trans. Ian Patterson. Cambridge: Cambridge University Press, Cambridge Texts in the History of Political Thought

— (1983) UVCF: *The Utopian Vision of Charles Fourier: Selected Texts on Work, Love, and Passionate Attraction*, trans., ed., and with intro. by Jonathan Beecher and Richard Bienvenu. Columbia: University of Missouri Press

Guarneri, Carl J.(1991) *The Utopian Alternative: Fourierism in Nineteenth-Century America*. Ithaca: Cornell University Press

Heckelthorn, C. W (1965) *The Secret Societies of All Ages and Countries*. New York: University Books

Lieh Tzu (1960) *The Book of Lieh Tzu, A Classic of Tao*, trans. A. C. Graham. New York: Columbia University Press

Noyes, John Humphrey (1966) *Strange Cults and Utopias of 19th-Century America* (original title *History of American Socialisms*), intro. by Mark Holloway. New York: Dover Publications

Stern, M. B (1968) *The Pantarch*. Austin: University of Texas Press

# MARX AND PROUDHON ESCAPE FROM THE NINETEENTH CENTURY

(FOR MARK SULLIVAN)

People used to think History was a nightmare from which we were trying to awaken. But now the CyberCapitalists say that History has indeed come to an end; presumably we are all awake now. And like characters in some bad surrealist novel we wake from horror into a world of pure daylight only to find ourselves trapped in yet another realm of nightmare. Who would have expected that the "End of History" has jackboots of its own?

In a sense the 20th century was just a re-run of the 19th:—same industrial squalor, colonial-imperialism, commodification, alienation, ravaging of the material world, rule of money, class war, etc., etc. The various chief ideologies of the 19th century melted and combined into two opposing camps, "Democracy" and "Communism", corrupt caricatures of the great ideal of the Revolution. The 20th century consisted simply of the struggle between these two 19th century ideas. On the one hand Capital, on the other hand the Social:—the Punch and Judy show of titanic modernism—the "Spectacle".

"History" was identified as the struggle between these two forces, either in a Manichaean-teleological sense, or in a dialectical materialist sense. So naturally, when Capital triumphed over a pathetic post-Stalinist bureaucracy in 1989-91, stamping out all but a few dying embers and buying up the rest in cheap job-lots, the Social came to an end. The world Left—which had defined itself in relation to the USSR (either for or against)—collapsed. The ideological Right (in a shambles since 1945) also lost its focus when "The Wall" came tumbling down. We're already "beyond Left and Right," whether we like it or not. Capital alone remains—but Capital is not "History". Capital *transcends* History, which has therefore ground to a halt.

And we're all ready now for a third repeat of the 19th century—in fact an *ideal* 19th century ("third time's a charm") just as the great bankers and industrialists of the first 19th century envisioned it:—Capital triumphant, unopposed, virtually divine. No need even for Capital-"ism" any more—no more ideology!—just money, pure and simple—the "free market" as perpetual motion machine.

Or better yet:—since 1991 over 90% of all existing money has entered a kind of CyberGnostic heaven or numisphere—thus money bears no relation to production, is not controlled by governments, and virtually never appears as cash. All States and most individuals are "in debt" to this entity that is almost entirely "spiritual" in nature and yet all-powerful in the world. This money does what God could never do: History finds its "Absolute" beyond market forces (which are merely epiphanic manifestations of the Godhead) in a realm of pure Being, metaphysical and metafiscal; ecstatic stasis—end-of-history not as emptiness but fullness, not as cessation but as *telos*.

It's true that the Left also dreamed of an end of history, inasmuch as history is the story of appropriation and separation. The Right dreamed of it also: as a turning-back. Second Coming, end of the Kali Yuga, utopia, romantic reaction…nearly everyone, it seems, would like an end to history, although we obviously disagree on definitions of heaven. In the eschatology of Capital, paradise is reserved for the very few—so post-historical eternity can only be viewed by the rest of us as Hell.

An illusion that attains the status of consensus-reality is still an illusion. This assertion represents *our* brand of "gnosticism":—we are awake to the call of "another reality" that is submerged and all but lost, accessible only in rare and partial circumstances. Now the "illusion" here is precisely the end-of-history as Capital, and the rhetoric (or theology) in which this illusion is masked consists of "Global Neoliberalism", a kind of ultimate expression of the anti-human implications of "political economy"—CyberSpencerian "survival of the fittest" agitprop for CEOs and bank presidents, tricked out with a few crypto-fascist "social planning" concepts such as "security", media saturation, economic discipline, proletarianization of the zones, etc. Behind the illusion of *telos* and realization (propagated by apologists for the profit margin as the bottom line) lies a deeper reality:—a world in which Capital now owes no "deals" to any sector because it no longer needs support in its struggle against the Social. That is, Capital can afford to betray its former allies (e.g., democracy, humanism, religion, the "universal" middle class) because it has triumphed "once and for all" over the Social; and since Capital can "afford" to betray it *will* betray when betrayal promises profit.

Behind even this stark and deep "reality" however lies an expression for which consciousness itself must testify, since the wreckage of all "History" has supposedly obscured even its last vague outline and memory:—the experience of all that *cannot* "move away into representation"—the authentic as realm of the Unseen, if you like—the perceptual ground on which the possibility of resistance finds its root. In other words, in the very moment of the "death of the Social" it is obviously and precisely the Social that is already reborn, just as in the myth of the Phoenix. We are perhaps living in *secret history*, as befits those who already inhabit the Millennium.

It is as if History had stopped around us, yet left us still in motion, still bound to our own becoming. Rats in the ruins of time:—once again, the ancient spectre.

This time around, and starting from zero in some way, the revolution of the 19th century must take another form, a form uncompromised by the failure and futilitarianism, or the cruelty, or the decayed rationalism of the Left. It goes without saying that there will be opposition, that Capital will succeed in rendering the opposition meaningless, and that nevertheless there will be *more* opposition. The question is:—will we simply repeat the mistakes of the first 19th century and of the second 19th century? Or will we get it right the third time, and break the sleeping-beauty spell of the End of History? Capital is ready and prepared now to realize itself in perfection, in its new and absolute post-historical universality and oneness. All-new mutant hyperreal Gnostic Capital is ready for its thousand-year reich—"and more!" (as the advertisements always say). And we—are we ready for utter capitulation to the ecstasy of simulation (eternity at poolside in our mirrorshades, jacked-in, taken up in Capital's Rapture)?—or do we have some *other* proposal to make? Nineteenth Century:—third time around? Or do we snap out of our trance of repetition-compulsion? our nightmare-within-nightmare of perpetual postponement, disappointment, and resentment? "We" have yet to make History—and now they tell us it's too late. Perhaps the question is:—can we *unmake* History? Do we get a *third chance*?

[Note: After writing this essay—and delivering the gist of it to the Libertarian Book Club's Anarchist Forum (NYC, Dec. 10, 1996)—I was told that Jean Baudrillard had propounded a view similar to mine in *The Illusion of the End*. Upon examination, however, it seems that Baudrillard is not proposing a theory of the infinity of the 19th century, but rather suggests that under the sign of "Simulation" history has simply reversed itself. "*It's not even the End of History*," and, "at this rate we may soon return to the Holy Roman Empire." Baudrillard has simply given in to a Cioran-like pessimism; he mocks those who speak of "hope" (presumably he means "revolutionary hope" in E. Bloch's sense of the term). He makes some good points, but essentially his cosmic gloom is a symptom, not a critique, of the psychic sink of triumphant Capital he so disdains. In the end all he has to offer by way of resistance is an ironic capitulation:

> "We have nothing against vice and immorality.... Why not a world society which is entirely corrupt, a single empire which is the empire of confusion, a New World Disorder,..., etc., etc.?"

On this basis Baudrillard despises the utopia of the past (or even the past as epistemological or "subjective" object):

> "Archaeological fetishism condemn(s) its objects to become museological waste... it also betrays a suspect nostalgia.... We have to explore all the vestiges of the path we have traveled, root through the dustbins of history, revive both the best and the worst in the *vain hope* of separating good from evil." (My italics)

Admittedly, rooting though the dustbins of history is an *impure* act, remote from the aesthetic of cyberdandyism that so repels and seduces the exhausted Baudrillard. The garbage of history is the compost of the imagination.]

℘   ℘   ℘

If we do get a third chance, then we can begin by agreeing that Marxism-Leninism had its chance and blew it, in more or less precisely the way the anarchists predicted it would. Does this mean that our "third chance" could or might conform to the structure of an *anarchist* revolution? Anarchism never really had a chance (a few glorious moments but no successes)—why then should we hope that anarchism might provide the counterspell for the malign hex of mutant Capital, a way out of the funhouse of the 19th century? Can we trust anarchism given the fact that historically it shares the 19th century's belief in technological progress, rational planning, and universal post-Enlightenment culture? Is the abolition of government (the one sine qua non of all anarchist theory) still relevant if the power of the State has now been reduced simply to the police force of Capital? The State will not wither away under neo-liberal direction—after all, some entity must exist to empower banks to lend money to the régime, to grant corporate welfare, to facilitate currency exchange (which accounts for a large portion of all "Gnostic Capital"), and to discipline labor and consumption. Government will mediate power for Capital to some extent—but State politics will no longer express the true movement of that power. Money is already more powerful than the State. Can anarchist theory come to terms with this new situation?

If anarchism failed when it attempted to compose itself as ideology and as power, it nevertheless can point to significant areas in which its ideas were transcended in realization:—the paleolithic polity of the hunter/gatherers, and the early neolithic farmers, who avoided the emergence of separation and hierarchy for 99% of the time-span of human existence; and the great counter-tradition of resistance against separation and hierarchy that springs up and renews itself wherever separation and hierarchy appear. These areas are contiguous in ways that both include and baffle such dichotomies as diachronic/synchronic; without speaking of "essence" nevertheless there emerges something like a revolutionary spirit or *esprit*—in non-authoritarian societies it overturns authority *before* it appears—while in the world of separation and hierarchy it *wants* to overturn authority and appropriation. In "failure" or "success", it persists.

In the 19th century anarchism was the manifestation of this "spirit", although not the only one and perhaps not the most important. (It was after all a failure, and a local European/American failure at that, with little or no influence in the rest of the world.) In the 20th century the anarchist critique of Marxism fed into the emergence of a "New Left", Situationism, Autonomia, and other anti-Moscow forms of leftism—but as long as the USSR existed it warped and distorted every effort to reconstruct the Revolution from the left and wrecked every "third way", every neither/nor, every non-authoritarian tendency. The North American anarchist movement, which had begun to grow rapidly and even organize itself between 1986 and 1989, collapsed suddenly and not by mere coincidence around 1991. Like everyone else on the left the anarchists were taken completely unprepared by the surprise implosion of the USSR. After all, Capitalism itself seemed on the verge of Armageddon several times in the 1980s (third-world debt crisis, S&L crisis, junk bond crisis, etc.) while the Soviet empire was still expanding (Nicaragua, Afghanistan).

Of course the New World Order can scarcely be called a triumph of the "Right", since neo-liberalism is not a form of conservatism, nor even of fascism (though it makes use of fascist techniques). The triumph of global Capital has no place for kings or priests, nations, tribes, customs, or rights—no need of religion or state—no need even for the liberal democracy it wore as a mask—no need for wildness, for farms, for conservation (quite the reverse in fact)—no need for authority other than money. Inasmuch as conservatism like leftism implies some theory of the human, so Capital has situated itself beyond left and right because it is beyond the human (hence its rapport with information technology and bioengineering—the markets of the metahuman).

Again—we are "beyond left and right" now, not by choice but necessity. And yet at the same time and paradoxically we are plunged back into an "ideal 19th century", the third and terminal movement of Capital. In our present situation, all manner of ideas and insights from the first and original 19th century might once again seem relevant. "Old" leftist ideas about money for example might throw light on the present, since the early theorists already looked on Capital as triumphant. In the mid-19th century there seemed to exist no real movement of the Social to oppose the over-determined effects of Capital. In a sense, we are in the same position again though presumably sadder and wiser—since we have seen the movement of the Social (which succeeded in delaying the triumph of Capital in the 20th century) culminate in its own betrayal in the form of the USSR. In the final moment of this betrayal, already caught up in the millennium, we are back again (at the point of a spiral?) in about 1844. The movement of the Social, which held back the true and fated development of Capital from 1917 to 1989, has vanished; it is as if, one says cynically and ironically, it is as if it had never been. H. G. Wells' time machine has deposited us back at some past moment—actually a whole series of past moments superinscribed like a temporal palimpsest. We are forced to re-live the past even as Capital prepares for the final take-off into a timeless future.

Well, we could accept the mission. That is, we could look on the past as our domain, and ransack it for whatever we may find useful in our *opposition*, our resistance. In general, this is the project of radical history, and of other disciplines. But we could take a more performative approach to our enforced alienation in history—we could re-visit specific moments, turning-points, key-events—moments especially of failure. We could tamper with those crucial sequences, try to correct them according to our present understanding of how things *should* have happened. In a Sci-Fi story this action would produce the "Time Traveler paradox"—one might change the present by altering the past, or else create alternate realities. In a sense then we can "perform" history in a thought-experiment based on this metaphor, and see if we can recover thereby any light to shed on our present needs. Not just a patchwork or syncresis of past fragments but a new imaginary history, a utopia that might-have-been—or that might possess an unexpected futurity—or indeed an unseen presence.

We could for example return to the time when the social movement was not yet split between Marx and the anarchists. Why? Because we'd like to imagine a movement that would have had the success of Marxism without its betrayal of the Social by authoritarianism;— we'd like to imagine a 19th century that led on to a 20th century of genuine Revolution, rather than to the catastrophe of Hitler and Stalin, and the triumph of Capital. Our imaginary history will be written in an alternate universe where Marx himself became an anarchist—or rather, where the conflict never arose in the first place. The game-world thus constructed will not (we hope) constitute a mere diversion—because in a sense we are really faced here and now with a world in which anarchism and Marxism *never happened*—except as a bad dream from which Capital has at last awakened. We might well learn authentic strategic lessons from our indulgence in make-believe. After all, historiography itself has largely given up the claim to record "what really happened"—and to this degree all history is the history of consciousness, or of the feedback between history and consciousness. If we have to face a situation that parallels and almost replicates the situation faced by "The Revolution" in the mid-19th century, then surely we are in an ideal position to learn from the mistakes of our predecessors, as well as from their most enduring insights.

The split between Marx and the anarchists is usually dated to the struggle in the 1870s between Marx and Bakunin for control and influence within the International, at which time ideological lines were clearly drawn—but more important and decisive was the quarrel between Karl Marx and Pierre-Joseph Proudhon just before the uprising of 1848 (actually in 1846). After the uprising, Marxism and anarchism began to develop along separate paths, though not yet labeled as such. We must go back before the names, and search out the things that the names would later seek to define. In fact, we must go back before the things themselves appear in any form—back to a moment when Marx and Proudhon were part of the same struggle, vaguely known as socialism—and when no sign of a split had yet occurred.

The moment we've chosen begins in a mood of frustration spread by the failures of Utopian Socialism—catastrophic flops, like Owen's New Harmony, the Fourierist phalansteries, or the absurd but colorful cult of St.-Simon's disciples (who at one point vanished into the Orient in search of a Female Messiah). Young radicals like Marx and Proudhon exaggerated their critiques of the Utopians (despite their deep debt to them) in an attempt to define a new socialism, more "scientific", and focused on the working class.

The young Marx had published some journalism but no books yet. Proudhon had published *What is Property?* in 1840 and already had a reputation on the left in

Paris—and Paris was the city of the Revolution. In 1844 the general ferment leading up to 1848 had already begun, Paris was an inspiring place to be, and Marx made the transition from radical democrat to socialist. Perhaps in this he was somewhat influenced by Proudhon. Marx had read his work by 1842, when he called it "penetrating" [McClellan, 54]. Proudhon wanted to learn about recent German philosophy, especially Hegel, but nothing had been translated into French and Proudhon could not read German (although he had taught himself Latin, Greek and Hebrew by setting type in those languages). Marx of course was an outstanding Young Hegelian—someone introduced them—and they spent some long nights in conversation together. Many bitter years later, in an obituary for Proudhon, Marx gave the impression that all the teaching was done by him (and that Proudhon nevertheless failed to grasp Hegel properly); however in 1844 Marx was 25 years old and Proudhon was 35, author of a book that Marx had admired. It is quite possible that Marx learned something from Proudhon's conversation as well as from Proudhon's book.

Marx's opinion in 1844 about Proudhon appeared in Marx's own first book, written in that year, *The Holy Family*. Here he undertakes to defend Proudhon from attacks made on him by Edgar and Bruno Bauer and other German "true" socialists. In later years Marx professed to be embarrassed by certain aspects of *The Holy Family*, and he was probably referring to these paragraphs in praise of Proudhon:

> Just as the first criticism of any science is necessarily implicated in the premises of the science it is combating, so is Proudhon's work, *What Is Property?* a criticism of political economy from the standpoint of political economy. —We need not go further into the juridical part of the book criticizing law from the standpoint of law, since our major interest is the critique of political economy. —Thus Proudhon's work will be scientifically surpassed by criticism of political economy, even of political economy as conceived by Proudhon. This task only became possible through Proudhon himself, just as Proudhon's criticism presupposed the physiocrat's criticism of the mercantile system, Adam Smith's criticism of the physiocrats, Ricardo's criticism of Adam Smith as well as the works of Fourier and Saint-Simon.
>
> All developments of political economy presuppose *private property*. This basic presupposition is regarded as an unassailable fact needing no further examination, indeed even a fact which is mentioned only "accidentally," as *Say* naïvely admits. Now Proudhon subjects the basis of political economy, *private property*, to a critical examination, in fact the first resolute, ruthless, and at the same time scientific examination. This is the great scientific advance he made, an advance revolutionizing political economy and making possible for the first time a real science of political economy. Proudhon's treatise, *What Is Property?* is as important for modern political economy as Sieyès' *What Is the Third Estate?* is for modern politics.

If Proudhon does not grasp the wider forms of private property—for example, wages, trade, value, price, money, etc.—as themselves forms of private property as is done, for example, in the *Deutsch-Französische Jahrbücher* (see F. Engels' "Outlines of a Critique of Political Economy") but uses these economic premises against political economists, this is entirely in keeping with his historically justified standpoint mentioned above.

...

Thus sometimes, as an exception—when they are attacking some particular abuse—the political economists stress the humane appearance of economic conditions, but at other times and in most cases they conceive these conditions precisely in their pronounced *difference* from what is humane, in their strictly economic sense. They reel about within this contradiction, completely unaware of it.

Now *Proudhon* has once and for all put an end to this lack of awareness. He took seriously the *humane appearance* of economic conditions and sharply confronted it with their *inhumane reality*. He demanded that these conditions should be in actuality what they are in conception, or rather that their conception should be abandoned and their actual inhumanity be established. Hence, he was consistent when he presented as the falsifier of economic conditions not partly this or that kind of private property, as other economists do, but private property completely and universally. He accomplished everything a criticism of political economy can accomplish from the standpoint of political economy.

Wanting to *characterize* the *standpoint* of *What Is Property?* Herr Edgar [Bauer] naturally does not say a word about political economy or the distinctive character of this book—precisely that it has made the *essence of private property* the vital question of political economy and jurisprudence. Everything is self-evident for Critical Criticism. For it Proudhon has done nothing new with his negation of private property. He has only divulged one of Critical Criticism's concealed secrets.

"Proudhon," Herr Edgar immediately continued after his characterizing translation, "thus finds something absolute in history, an eternal foundation, a god, directing mankind—justice."

Proudhon's French writing of 1840 does not take the standpoint of German development of 1844. It is Proudhon's standpoint, a standpoint shared by countless French writers diametrically opposed to him, thus giving Critical Criticism the advantage of having characterized the most contradictory standpoints with one and the same stroke of the pen. Further, to deal with this Absolute in history one has only to apply consistently the law set forth by Proudhon himself—the realization of justice by its negation. If Proudhon does not go that far, it is only because he had the misfortune of having been born a Frenchman and not a German.

For Herr Edgar, Proudhon has become *theological* with his Absolute in history and his faith in justice, and Critical Criticism which is *ex professo* criticism of theology can now seize upon him to express itself on "religious conceptions."

"It is characteristic of every religious conception that it establishes dogma in a situation where one antithesis comes out in the end as victorious and the only truth."

We shall see how religious Critical Criticism establishes dogma in a situation where in the end one antithesis, "*the* criticism," comes out victorious over the other, "the Mass," as the only truth. Proudhon, however, committed a still greater injustice in perceiving an Absolute, a God of history, in massy justice, since righteous Criticism had *expressly* reserved for itself the role of this Absolute, this God in history.

...

Proudhon did even more. He demonstrated in detail *how* the movement of capital produces misery.

...

Private property as private property, as wealth, is compelled to *maintain* its *own existence* and at the same time that of its antithesis, the proletariat. It is the *positive* side of the contradiction—private property sufficient in itself.

The proletariat as proletariat, on the other hand, is compelled to abolish itself and at the same time its conditional antithesis, private property, which makes it the proletariat. It is the *negative* side of the contradiction, its internal restlessness—private property dissolved and dissolving.

The propertied class and the class of the proletariat represent the same human self-alienation. But the former feels comfortable and confirmed in this self-alienation, knowing that this alienation is *its own power* and possessing in it the *semblance* of a human existent. The latter feels itself ruined in this alienation and sees in it its impotence and the actuality of an inhuman existence. The proletariat, to use Hegel's words, is abased and *indignant* at its abasement—a feeling to which it is necessarily driven by the contradiction between its human *nature* and its situation in life, a situation that is openly, decisively, and comprehensively the negation of that nature.

Within this antithesis the property owner is therefore the *conservative* party, and the proletarian is the *destructive* party. From the *former* arises action to maintain the antithesis, from the *latter*, action to destroy it.

In its economic movement, private property is driven toward its own dissolution but only through a development which does not depend on it, of which it is unconscious, which takes place against its will, and which is brought about by the very nature of things—thereby creating the proletariat *as* proletariat, that spiritual and physical misery conscious of its misery, that dehumanization conscious of its dehumanization and thus transcending itself. The proletariat executes the sentence that private property inflicts on itself by creating the proletariat just as it carries out the verdict that wage-labor pronounces on itself by creative wealth for others and misery for itself. When the proletariat triumphs, it does not thereby become the absolute side of society because it triumphs only by transcending itself and its opposite. Then the proletariat and its determining antithesis, private property, disappear.

When socialist writers attribute this historic role to the proletariat, it is not, as Critical Criticism pretends to think, because they regard proletarians as *gods*. On the contrary. Because the abstraction of all humanity and even the *semblance* of humanity is practically complete in the fully developed proletariat, because the conditions of life of the proletariat bring all the conditions of present society into a most inhumane focus, because man is lost in the proletariat but at the same time has won a theoretical awareness of that loss and is driven to revolt against this inhumanity by urgent, patent, and absolutely compelling *need* (the practical expression of *necessity*)—therefore the proletariat can and must emancipate itself. But it cannot emancipate itself without transcending the conditions of its own life. It cannot transcend the conditions of its own life without transcending *all* the inhuman conditions of present society which are summed up in its own situation. It does not go through the hard but hardening school of *labor* in vain. It is a question of *what* the proletariat *is* and what it *consequently* is historically compelled to do. Its aim and historical action is prescribed, irrevocably and obviously, in its own situation in life as well as in the entire organization of contemporary civil society.
[*Writings of the Young Marx*, pp. 362-368 *passim*]

Among the aspects of these passages that might later have come to embarrass Marx, the critique of dogmatism, and the defense of Justice as a kind of absolute, are particularly Proudhonian—(in fact, as we shall see, Proudhon will later take Marx himself to task for dogmatizing). But most embarrassing of all:—as Marx outlines Proudhon's views on property and the working class in order to defend them against Bauer's Critical Criticism, it becomes clear that these views are also Marx's views. And as one reads later Marxian treatments of these subjects, it becomes clear that these views *remained* Marx's views. In other words, the most embarrassing aspect of *The Holy Family* was not its incorrectness according to Marx's later line, but rather its correctness. It revealed Marx as something of a Proudhonian, a connection that Marx would come to belittle and virtually deny.

*What is Property?* is a wonderful book and still "reads well" thanks to Proudhon's unique style, which might be called angry sarcasm carried to sublime extremes; to his ability to convey the freshness and originality of his thought by means of vivid paradox combined with passionate openness; and, above all, to its one central and powerful insight into the nature of property as theft.

If I were asked to answer the following question: *What is slavery?* and I should answer in one word, *It is murder*, my meaning would be understood at once. No extended argument would be required to show that the power to take from a man his thought, his will, his personality, is a power of life and death; and that to enslave a man is to kill him. Why, then, to this other question: *What is property?* may I not likewise answer, *it is robbery*, without the certainty of being misunderstood; the second proposition being no other than a transformation of the first?

I undertake to discuss the vital principle of our government and our institutions, property: I am in my right. I may be mistaken in the conclusion which shall result from my investigations: I am in my right. I think best to place the last thought of my book first: still am I in my right.

Such an author teaches that property is a civil right born of occupation and sanctioned by law; another maintains that it is a natural right, originating in labour,—and both of these doctrines, totally opposed as they may seem, are encouraged and applauded. I contend that neither labour, nor occupation, nor law, can create property; that it is an effect without a cause: am I censurable?

...

*Property is robbery!* ... What a revolution in human ideas! *Proprietor* and *robber* have been at all times expressions as contradictory as the beings whom they designate are hostile! all languages have perpetuated this opposition. On what authority, then, do you venture to attack universal consent, and give the lie to the human race? Who are you, that you should question the judgment of the nations and the ages?

...

Nevertheless, I build no system. I ask an end to privilege, the abolition of slavery, equality of rights, and the reign of law. Justice, nothing else: that is the alpha and omega of my argument: to others I leave the business of governing the world.

[*What is Property?*, pp. 37-39, *passim.*]

As Marx notes, the insights of *What is Property?* are not yet fully developed—but as he also says, Proudhon has made further developments possible on his own terms. Proudhon himself of course spent a lifetime developing the idea—as in a sense did Marx as well—that property as capital is the sum of expropriation (of "surplus labor" as Marx would express it). Each came to feel that the other had failed, and Marx was to devote a whole book to the "overcoming" of Proudhon—but we are getting ahead of the story.

Marx wrote another work in 1844 but never published it or even finished it. When it appeared in 1932 as *Economic and Philosophic Manuscripts* it caused a great stir in Marxological circles. To some critics it seemed that a Marx before Marx had been revealed, a "Young Marx" somehow very different from the later political and "dialectical-materialist" Marx. Other critics were at pains to deny this impression, arguing that no break in "epistemology" separated Marx from Marx (or more importantly, Marx from Marxism!), that the *Manuscripts* contained nothing that the later Marx failed to re-use or develop—including the concepts of "alienation" and even "humanism". The argument is historically important because the champions of "Young Marx" tended toward unorthodox and specifically anti-Stalinist interpretations, while the defenders of a more single Marx appear often as Party liners or traditionalists of some sort.

Here we are more interested in the *Manuscripts* as a text written in 1844 rather than as a text rediscovered nearly a century later. What does it tell us about Marx's reading of Proudhon? We find that Marx is already carrying out the project of extending and correcting Proudhon's basic insight. He adjusts Proudhon's thesis on wages for example, quite logically. He says (154) "that Proudhon is to be criticized and appreciated." In other words the *Manuscripts* contain *constructive* criticisms of Proudhon, and one can imagine that Proudhon would have been capable of understanding and making use of such useful "attacks" (since his own motto was *Destruam et aedificabo*, "I destroy to build"). He might also have appreciated the visionary intensity—even the poetry—of the *Manuscripts*. Certainly he would have approved "anarchistic" statements like this:

> To be avoided above all is establishing "society" once again as an abstraction over against the individual. The individual *is* the *social being*. The expression of his life—even if it does not appear immediately in the form of a *communal* expression carried out together with others—is therefore an expression and assertion of *social life*.
> [*Young Marx*, p. 306]

Proudhon would have found Marx in agreement with him in his critique of "crude" communism (based on "envy" as Marx says, pre-empting Nietzsche). Marx goes on briefly to develop the idea of political communism, either "democratic or despotic" on the one hand, or on the other hand, having overcome the State—that is, social democracy, dictatorship of the proletariat, and "withering away of the State."

> In both forms communism already knows itself as the reintegration of or return of man to himself, as the overcoming of human self-alienation, but since it has not yet understood the positive essence of private property and just as little the *human* nature of needs, it still remains captive to and infected by private property. It has, indeed, grasped its concept but still not its essence.
>
> (3) *Communism a~ positive* overcoming of *private property* as *human self-alienation*, and thus as the actual *appropriation of the human* essence through and for man; therefore as the complete and conscious restoration of man to himself within the total wealth of previous development, the

restoration of man as a *social*, that is, human being. This communism as
completed naturalism is humanism, as completed humanism it is naturalism. It is the *genuine* resolution of the antagonism between man and nature
and between man and man; it is the true resolution of the conflict between
existence and essence, objectification and self-affirmation, freedom and
necessity, individual and species. It is the riddle of history solved and
knows itself as this solution.

    [*Young Marx*, pp. 303-304]

But even at this point Marx has not reached the end of his exposition of communism. Communism itself, it seems, is a condition to be overcome:

Since for socialist man, however, the *entire so-called world history* is only the
creation of man through human labor and the development of nature for
man, he has evident and incontrovertible proof of his *self-creation*, his own
*formation process*. Since the *essential dependence* of man in nature—man for
man as the existence of nature and nature for man as the existence of
man—has become practical, sensuous and perceptible, the question about
an *alien* being beyond man and nature (a question which implies the unreality of nature and man) has become impossible in practice. *Atheism* as a
denial of this unreality no longer makes sense because it is a *negation of
God* and through this negation asserts the *existence of man*. But socialism as
such no longer needs such mediation. It begins with the *sensuous perception, theoretically and practically,* of man and nature as *essential beings*. It is
man's *positive self-consciousness*, no longer attained through the overcoming
of religion, just as *actual life* is positive actuality no longer attained through
the overcoming of private property, through *communism*. The position of
communism is the negation of the negation and hence, for the next stage
of historical development, the necessary *actual* phase of man's emancipa-
tion and rehabilitation. *Communism* is the necessary form and dynamic
principle of the immediate future but not as such the goal of human development—the form of human society.

    [*ibid.*, p. 314]

It is quite clear that Marx sees no role whatsoever for the State in such a future,
and in this he and Proudhon were still much closer than their later followers might
conceive possible.

    The more powerful the state and hence the more *political* a country is,
the less is it inclined to seek the basis and grasp the *general* principle of
*social* ills in the *principle of the state* itself, thus in the *existing organization
of society* of which the state is the active, self-conscious, and official expression. *Political* thought is *political* precisely because it takes place *within* the

bounds of politics. The more acute, the more vigorous it is, the more it is *incapable* of comprehending social ills.

…

The principle of politics is *will*. The more one-sided and thus the more perfected *political* thought is, the more it believes in the *omnipotence* of will, the blinder it is to *natural* and spiritual *restrictions* on the will, and the more incapable it is of discovering the source of social ills.

…

*Revolution* in general—the *overthrow* of the existing ruling power and the *dissolution* of the old conditions—is a *political act*. Without *revolution*, however, *socialism* cannot come about. It requires this *political act* so far as it needs *overthrow* and *dissolution*. But where its *organizing activity* begins, where its *own aim* and *spirit* emerge, there socialism throws the *political* hull away.

[*ibid.*, pp. 349-350, 357]

These were the climactic words of the *Manuscripts*. Marx seems to imply that the revolution will be "political" but that as soon as it takes power the State will disappear. This would contradict later Marxian concepts of a *proletarian State*, succeeded only at some vague and distant era in post-History by a gradual "withering away" rather than an abrupt casting-off of the political "hull". The Marx of the *Manuscripts* cannot be very easily distinguished here from his later anarchist admirers like Bakunin, who even called him "master". His passionate analysis of alienation (too complex to go into here) would certainly have influenced later anarchist readers—if they'd been able to read it. By 1932 no anarchist would have been able to read the *Manuscripts* outside the historical context of the existence of the USSR—and of Stalin. It is only now after 1989-91 that anti-authoritarians can at last approach this text and make the acquaintance of a Young Marx who was … almost … an anarchist.

In order to understand what happened next, it's necessary to admit that by all accounts Marx and Proudhon were not the easiest fellows in the world to get along with. Marx in particular had a strong authoritarian streak in his personality and impressed many as a man who would tolerate no disagreement. He regularly imputed base motives to his opponents (sometimes justly, of course) but could be extremely unpleasant about it. Proudhon for his part constructed for himself (or realized in himself) the character of a self-described prickly stubborn peasant. He was a prim moralist (hence the fascination and revulsion he felt for Fourier) and had absurd petit-bourgeois crochets about women and Jews. He was working-class, self-educated, and sensitive about it; Marx was bourgeois in origin and superbly educated. Marx was a Jew—albeit completely secularized, and even a bit of an anti-Semite himself. And he has certainly not escaped criticism by feminists as one of the patriarchal pantheon (he once said he admired women for their "weakness")—so perhaps we could score Marx and Proudhon evenly-matched on the level of their 19th century failings and superstitions. In any case, Marx and Proudhon were not fated to be friends. In an alternate universe they might have hit it off—two radical curmudgeons united in struggle against private property. It's not mere fantasy to imagine this, since a certain warmth is implied by the all-night Hegelian bull sessions—and more importantly, a philosophical compatibility is demonstrated in their texts—a certain harmony. But it was not to be.

The quarrel between Marx and Proudhon was a nexus-point in the history of the 19th century and thus of our world as it is now—a failure to connect, to synthesize, that influenced the subsequent course of the movement of the Social, and hence of Capital as well. The Marxists, who would eventually monopolize the Social and win for it a whole "second" world, did so on the basis of an implacable hatred for Proudhonian anarchism, its only significant rival within the movement. As for the anarchists, although they can be faulted for many things, their critique of Marxism proved flawless. No one can take that away from anarchism:—everything it predicted for Marxism came true. Capitalism never understood Marxism or developed a theory capable of opposing it *as theory*; anarchism did so, however. Tragic irony.

In 1845 when  Marx left Paris (pursued by bad debts, a frequent pattern) he believed himself still on good terms with Proudhon. The next year, living in Brussels, Marx conceived the idea of forming a Committee of Correspondence to link Socialists in Europe together in an information exchange network (nowadays it would be a Web page, I suppose). He decided to invite Proudhon to join. Their exchange of letters is the only correspondence between the two men and is crucial for an understanding of the quarrel, so we must include the whole of both texts.

> Marx to Proudhon
> Brussels, May 5, 1846
> My Dear Proudhon,
>
> I very often intended to write to you since I left Paris, but circumstances independent of my will have hitherto prevented me from doing so. Let me assure you that the only reason for my silence has been that I was overwhelmed with work and kept busy by the troubles involved in a change of residence, and the like.
>
> And now let us jump in *medias res*! Together with two friends of mine, Frederick Engels and Philippe Gigot (both in Brussels), I have organized a continuous correspondence with the German Communists and Socialists, which is to take up both the discussion of scientific questions and the supervision of popular publications as well as socialist propaganda, which can be carried on in Germany by this means. It will be the chief aim of our correspondence, however, to put the German Socialists in contact with the French and English Socialists; to keep the foreigners posted on the socialist movements that are going to take place in Germany, and to inform the Germans in Germany of the progress of socialism in France and England. In this way it will be possible to air differences of opinion. An exchange of

ideas will ensue and impartial criticism be secured. It is a step which the social movement should take in its literary expression in order to free itself of its national limitations. And at the time for action it is certainly of great benefit to everyone to be enlightened on the state of affairs abroad as well as at home.

Besides the Communists in Germany our correspondence would also embrace the German Socialists in Paris and London. Our connections with England have already been established; as for France, we are all of the opinion that we could not find a better correspondent there than you. As you know, the English and Germans have up to the present appreciated you more than your own fellow countrymen.

So you see, it is only a question of initiating a regular correspondence and of assuring it the facilities for following the social movement in the various countries, a question of making it interesting, meaty and varied, which the work of a single individual can never achieve.

If you accept our proposal, postage for the letters sent by us to you and by you to us will be paid for here, the money raised in Germany being intended to cover the expenses of the correspondence.

The address we would ask you to write to here is that of M. Philippe Gigot, 8, rue Bodenbrock. He is also the one to sign the letters from Brussels.

I need not add that the utmost secrecy must be maintained by you with regard to the whole of this correspondence; in Germany our friends have to act with the greatest circumspection to avoid compromising themselves.

Send us an early reply and believe in the sincere friendship of
Your humble servant,
Karl Marx

Brussels, May 5, 1846
P.S. Let me here denounce M. Grün in Paris. The man is nothing more than a literary swindler, a charlatan, who would like to deal in modern ideas. He tries to cover up his ignorance with high-flown, arrogant phrases, but he has only succeeded in making himself look ridiculous through his pompous nonsense. Moreover, the man is dangerous. He abuses the relations that his impertinence has enabled him to establish with well-known authors, using them as a ladder and compromising them in the eyes of the German public. In his book on the French socialists he dares to call himself Proudhon's tutor (*Privatdozent*, an academic rank in Germany), claims to have revealed important principles of German knowledge to him, and jokes about his writings. Therefore beware of this parasite. Perhaps I will mention this individual to you again later.

I am happy to have this opportunity of telling you how pleased I am to enter into relations with someone as distinguished as yourself. Meanwhile, allow me to sign myself,

Your humble servant,

Phillippe Gigot

For my part I can only hope that you will approve of the project which we have just proposed to you and that you will be obliging enough not to deny us your cooperation. May I say that your writings have left me with the greatest respect for you and that I remain

Your humble servant,

Frederick Engels

જ

Proudhon to Marx

Lyon, May 17, 1846

My dear Monsieur Marx,

I willingly agree to become one of the stages of your correspondence, whose aims and organization appear to be most useful. However, I do not propose to write to you either at length or often since my various occupations as well as my natural laziness do not allow me to make these epistolary efforts. I will also take the liberty of making several reservations which have been prompted by various passages in your letter.

Firstly, although my ideas on matters of organization and realization are at the moment quite settled, at least as far as principles are concerned, I believe that it is my very duty, and that it is the duty of all socialists, to maintain for some time yet an attitude of criticism and doubt. In short, I profess with the public an almost total anti-dogmatism in economics.

By all means let us work together to discover the laws of society, the ways in which these laws are realized and the process by which we are able to discover them. But, for God's sake, when we have demolished all *a priori* dogmas, do not let us think of indoctrinating the people in our turn. Do not let us fall into your compatriot Martin Luther's inconsistency. As soon as he had overthrown Catholic theology, he immediately, with constant recourse to excommunications and anathemas, set about founding a Protestant theology. For three hundred years Germany's whole concern has been to destroy Luther's hodgepodge. Let us have a good and honest polemic. Let us set the world an example of wise and farsighted tolerance, but simply because we are leaders of a movement let us not instigate a new intolerance. Let us not set ourselves up as the apostles of a new religion, even if it be the religion of logic or of reason. Let us welcome and encourage all protests, let us get rid of all exclusiveness and all mysticism. Let us never consider any question exhausted, and when we have used our very last argument, let us begin again, if necessary, with eloquence and irony. On this condition I will join your association with pleasure, otherwise I will not.

I must also make some observations about the phrase in your letter, "at the time for action." Perhaps you still hold the opinion that no reform is possible without a helping *coup de main*, without what used to be called a revolution but which is quite simply a jolt. I confess that my most recent studies have led me to abandon this view, which I understand and would willingly discuss, since for a long time I held it myself. I do not think that this is what we need in order to succeed, and consequently we must not suggest revolutionary action as the means of social reform because this supposed means would simply be an appeal to force and to arbitrariness. In brief, it would be a contradiction. I put the problem in this way: How can we put back into society, through some system of economics, the wealth which has been taken out of society by another system of economics? In other words, through Political Economy we must turn the theory of Property against Property in such a way as to create what you German socialists call community and which for the moment I will only go so far as calling liberty or equality. Now I think I know the way in which this problem may be very quickly solved. Therefore I would rather burn Property little by little than give it renewed strength by making a Saint Bartholomew's Day of property owners.

My next work, which at present is in the middle of being printed, will explain this to you further.

This, my dear philosopher, is my present position. I may be mistaken, and if that happens and you give me the cane, I would cheerfully endure it while waiting for my revenge. I must add in passing that this also seems to be the feeling of the French working class. Our proletarians are so thirsty for knowledge that they would receive us very badly if all we could give them to drink were blood. To be brief, it would in my opinion be very bad policy to use the language of extermination. Rigorous measures will come right enough; in this the people are in no need of exhortation.

I sincerely regret the minor divisions which would appear to exist already in German socialism and of which your complaint against M. Grün gives me proof. I am rather afraid that you may have seen this writer in a false light, and I appeal, M. Marx, to your well-balanced judgment. Grün is in exile with no fortune, with a wife and two children and with no source of income but his pen. What else besides modern ideas could he exploit in order to make a living? I understand your philosophic wrath and I agree that the holy writ of humanity should never be used as a bargaining counter. But in this case I must consider the misfortune, the extreme necessity, and I excuse the man. Ah yes, if we were all millionaires things would be much better. We should all be saints and angels. But we must *live*, and you know that this word is still far from meaning what is expressed in the pure theory of association. We must live, that is to say, buy bread, fuel, meat, and we must pay our rent. And good heavens! a man who sells ideas about society is no less meritorious than one who sells a sermon. I know nothing about Grün's having made himself out to be my tutor. Tutor in what? I am only concerned with political economy, a subject about which he knows practically nothing. I regard literature as a plaything for little girls, and as for my philosophy, I know enough about it to be able to make light of it on occasion. Grün revealed nothing at all to me, and if he claims to have done so, he has been presumptuous and I am sure he regrets it.

But what I do know, and value more than I condemn a slight attack of vanity, is that it is to M. Grün and also to his friend Ewerbeck that I owe my knowledge of your writings, my dear M. Marx, and those of M. Engels, as well as of Feuerbach's very important work. At my request these gentlemen have been good enough to make several analyses for me in French (for unfortunately I am quite unable to read German) of the most important socialist publications. And it is at their entreaty that I have to make some mention (as I would have done of my own accord in any case) in my next work of the works of Mssrs. Marx, Engels, Feuerbach, etc.... Lastly, Grün and Ewerbeck are working to keep alive the sacred flame among the German colony in Paris, and the respect that the workers who consult them have for these gentlemen seems to me to be a sure guarantee of the honesty of their intentions.

It would give me much pleasure, my dear M. Marx, to see you reverse a judgment resulting from momentary irritation, for you were in an angry frame of mind when you wrote to me. Grün has told me of his wish to translate my present book. I realize that this translation more than any other would be of help to him. I would therefore be grateful, not on my own account but on his, if you and your friends would aid him on this occasion by helping to sell a work that, with your help, would doubtless benefit him more than myself.

If you would assure me of your assistance, my dear M. Marx, I will send my proofs to M. Grün immediately. I think that notwithstanding your personal grievances, on which I do not intend to pass judgment, this course of action would be a credit to all parties.

Your humble servant,

Kindest regards to your friends Messrs. Engels and Gigot.

[Proudhon, *Selected Writings*, pp. 147-154]

At first glance these letters would seem to form a reasonable basis for further correspondence. Proudhon agrees to join the Committee under certain conditions—but apparently these conditions could not be met, since Marx never replied—except in his scathing attack on Proudhon's next book, *The Philosophy of Poverty*. Marx had already expressed himself on the subject of dogmatism in terms not unlike those of Proudhon's letter, but apparently he took Proudhon's remarks personally. As for the disagreement about violence, this might appear more serious. In the 1870s in the International, Marx and his followers were willing to collaborate with Proudhonians who eschewed all recourse to electoral politics or violent revolution (they were evolving the concept of the General Strike). Of course Marx finally succeeded in purging the International of all anarchists—but he was at least willing to consider a united front at one time. In 1846 however he apparently balked at cooperation with Proudhon, and perhaps he might have explained his revulsion at Proudhon's "conditions" on the ground of a principled rejection of Proudhon's non-violence. Since Marx cut off the correspondence, however, we can only assume this, not prove it. The issue does not seem to have been brought up in later polemics—though I might well have missed it, since my reading for this essay has been superficial.

Did Proudhon mean to offend Marx? Perhaps unconsciously he did. But Proudhon was as much a 19th century ink-slinging polemicist as Marx, and not afraid to make enemies. If he'd wanted to offend he could have done so without such contradictory signs of esteem as a promise to quote Marx in his next book! Even so, Proudhon's letter has a slightly superior air about it, and one can understand why Marx was annoyed.

Both Marx and Proudhon were later to take part in the revolutions of 1848. Proudhon still rejected violence but gave his whole support to the working class of Paris, even going so far as to allow himself to be elected to office—which he later regretted as a bad mistake. Marx in Cologne found himself working for a bourgeois revolution, which he believed was a necessary precursor to any successful proletarian revolution—even though it involved some strange bedfellows for a self-professed communist. In other words, in 1848 both Marx and Proudhon compromised with the reality of revolution. In theory, at any rate, they could have compromised on the theoretical issue of revolutionary violence in 1846.

Why did they quarrel? Marxists and anarchists are alike convinced (if they think about it at all) that the deepest of issues must have divided the two founders, that their disagreements were profound, unbridgeable, that fate had decreed the split, that there was no choice. But we have seen (or at least suspected) that the philosophical chasm might not have been so vast as Afterthought has believed. And in any case, if Marx and Proudhon disagreed on basic principles, what precisely *were* those principles? If we analyze Marxism and anarchism in, say, 1921 or even 1880, we can identify distinct disagreements about specific things. But was this also really true in 1846?

Later that year, Proudhon's next book came out: *Système des Contradictions Economiques, ou Philosophie de la Misère*, in two volumes (of which only the first was translated into English as *The Philosophy of Misery*. I have preferred to call it *The Phi-*

*losophy of Poverty* in order to contrast it directly with Marx's reply, *The Poverty of Philosophy*.) Proudhon, like Marx, had been devouring the classical economists, and now he attempted to re-think his discoveries about property in the light of economic categories. It is a disappointing book to read after *What is Property?*; it definitely falls apart at the seams, although it is shot through with plenty of passages of good Proudhonian rhetoric and paradox which lighten the load of political economy.

For example—in his introduction and conclusion to Vol. I, Proudhon treats religion in a very unusual way. Beginning with the "hypothesis of God" and even with a critique of vulgar atheism, he ends in a position that can only be called an anarchist theology—an attack on God.

> And for my part I say: The first duty of man, on becoming intelligent and free, is to continually hunt the idea of God out of his mind and conscience. For God, if he exists, is essentially hostile to our nature, and we do not depend at all upon his authority. We arrive at knowledge in spite of him, at comfort in spite of him, at society in spite of him; every step we take in advance is a victory in which we crush Divinity.
>
> Let it no longer be said that the ways of God are impenetrable. We have penetrated these ways, and there we have read in letters of blood the proofs of God's impotence, if not of his malevolence. My reason, long humiliated, is gradually rising to a level with the infinite; with time it will discover all that its inexperience hides from it; with time I shall be less and less a worker of misfortune, and by the light that I shall have acquired, by the perfection of my liberty, I shall purify myself, idealize my being, and become the chief of creation, the equal of God. A single moment of disorder which the Omnipotent might have prevented and did not prevent accuses his Providence and shows him lacking in wisdom; the slightest progress which man, ignorant, abandoned, and betrayed, makes towards good honors him immeasurably. By what right should God still say to me: *Be holy, for I am holy?* Lying spirit, I will answer him, imbecile God, your reign is over; look to the beasts for other victims. I know that I am not holy and never can become so; and how could you be holy, if I resemble you? Eternal father, Jupiter or Jehovah, we have learned to know you; you are, you were, you ever will be, the jealous rival of Adam, the tyrant of Prometheus.
>
> [...]
>
> Your name, so long the last word of the *savant*, the sanction of the judge, the force of the prince, the hope of the poor, the refuge of the repentant sinner,—this incommunicable name, I say, henceforth an object of contempt and curses, shall be a hissing among men. For God is stupidity and cowardice; God is hypocrisy and falsehood; God is tyranny and misery; God is evil.
>
> [...]

> *God* in religion, the *State* in politics, *property* in economy, such is the
> triple form under which humanity, become foreign to itself, has not ceased
> to rend itself with its own hands, and which today it must reject.
> [*Philosophy of Misery*, 448-457 *passim*.]

It's interesting to note that Proudhon when younger had considered writing a
book on Christian heresies, and that he showed particular fondness for revolutionary Gnostic Dualists such as the Cathars. For the Gnostics the Jehovah of religion
was an evil demiurge—actually Satanic—while the true unknown God was utterly
removed from any material creation and utterly opposed to all becoming. Proudhon
saved the idea of an evil God, but banished the notion of pure spirituality, thus
approaching sheer nihilism. The Proudhonians became known as atheists, and
Bakunin was echoing Proudhon when he later declared that if God existed we
should have to kill him. For the Church, Proudhon was a type of the Anti-Christ.

A year after Proudhon's book appeared, Marx took his revenge (a bit cold), and
launched the "caning" that Proudhon had wryly predicted in his letter—a whole
book devoted to attempted slaughter, and called *The Poverty of Philosophy*. Marx was
finished with constructive criticism; he intended to demolish Proudhon and add
him to the already-growing list of successful hits, such as the Bauer brothers, or his
former comrades the Young Hegelians (*The German Ideology* disposed of them nicely, although Marx failed to get it in print), or his former fellow-socialists. Marx had
already begun his life-long strategy of defining Marxism by excluding, traducing,
and even misrepresenting its "enemies"—a strategy that tainted all of Marxism-to-
come with the odor of the denunciation, the Purge, and the betrayal of potential
allies on the left. Some Marxologists consider *The Poverty of Philosophy* a good and
important work, but again, except for a few passages where Marx wanders off the
subject, I found it a difficult—in fact unpleasant—read. Having actually slogged
through Proudhon's book, which I suspect is more than most Marx-scholars have
done, I was continually annoyed by Marx's slanted and sometimes downright twist-
ed presentation of Proudhon's position. For example, he begins with this:

> M. Proudhon's work is not just a treatise on political economy, an ordinary
> book; it is a bible. "Mysteries", "Secrets Wrested from the Bosom of God",
> "Reveleations"—it lacks nothing. But as prophets are discussed nowadays
> more conscientiously than profane writers, the reader must resign himself
> to going with us through the arid and gloomy erudition of "Genesis", in
> order to ascend later, with M. Proudhon, into the ethereal and fertile realm
> of *super-socialism*.
> [*Poverty*, p. 26]

Here Marx clearly implies that Proudhon is some sort of religious socialist, and
since most French socialists of the period were religious this would not surprise the
reader. Either Marx missed the irony of Proudhon's use of the "hypothesis of God"

or else he simply skipped the introduction and conclusion of the book—or else he is engaged in deliberate misrepresentation.

In short, these two books, the *Philosophy of Poverty* and *The Poverty of Philosophy*, should make clear for us the real grounds for the quarrel between anarchism and Marxism (the supposed abyss)—but instead they do nothing of the kind. Proudhon indulges in some unclear thinking about economics, and Marx is able to correct him. For instance, where Proudhon thinks he has discovered some principle Marx is able to show that some other earlier economist thought of it first—so that where Marx must hide from the reader his essential agreement with Proudhon he does so by hurling accusations of plagiarism, or ignorance, or (a Marxian favorite) suspect motivations. Here Marx develops a means of character assassination that would become a perennial favorite on the left:—So-and-so claims to be a revolutionary. But look:—So-and-so's ideas about (say) the equality of wages are incorrect. If such ideas were implemented they would only fail and thereby help Capitalism. *Therefore* So-and-so is not a revolutionary—he's a bourgeois traitor to the proletariat, and must be purged. Intentions count for nothing—the Party Line is above the individual will. Proudhon, for example, is "bourgeois" (p. 164) and even worse, "petty bourgeois" (p. 167). Never mind that Proudhon wants to *abolish property* (strange behavior for a bourgeois); "Let us put it another way: M. Proudhon does not directly state that *bourgeois life* is for him an *eternal verity*; he states it indirectly by deifying the categories which express bourgeois relations in the form of thought." And never mind that Proudhon was born a peasant and made his living as a worker (typesetter)—he is nevertheless petty bourgeois. His attitudes toward women and sexuality prove it.

Does this then turn out to be the huge gulf that divides anarchism and communism? No, clearly there must be something more. But one will study these two works in vain to discover it. I don't want to make light of the argument about economics, which for the most part I cannot understand—but it seems clear that Marx could have attempted a constructive criticism (as he was willing to do in *The Holy Family* and the *Manuscripts*) rather than a destructive blitzkrieg. Disagreements over questions about political violence and strikes were clearly important but not sufficient reasons for enmity (Marx after all had already known Proudhon's opinions on these issues when he invited him to participate in the Correspondence Committee). In short, we must look elsewhere for the real split between anarchism and communism. Proudhon, deeply hurt by Marx's surprise attack, annotated his copy of *The Poverty of Philosophy* and apparently intended a formal response. However, he was distracted by the events of 1848 and never returned to the project. A study of these annotations would undoubtedly further our inquiry but unfortunately cannot be carried out; a few examples however are given in W. Pickles' article "Marx and Proudhon" (1938). From these it becomes clear that at least one topic of utmost importance emerges from the controversy:—the question of the materialist concept of history. According to Marx (and later Marxists), Proudhon was not a materialist but introduced "religious" or ethical categories or "absolutes" such as "Justice" to bolster his interpretation of history. Marxism however makes no use of absolutes because absolutes are nothing but representation, where Marxism concerns itself with real materiality—with "scientific" objectivity. However,

> Proudhon himself, in one of the marginal notes to his copy of Marx' *Misère*, argues that even where he appears to reason from abstract principles he is in fact not denying the validity of the materialist conception. "Voilà donc," he says, à propos of one of Marx' attacks on this point, "que j'ai eu le malheur de penser encore comme vous! Ai-je jamais prétendu que les principes sont autres choses que la représentation intellectuelle, non la cause génératrice des faits?"
> [Pickles, p. 251]

And Pickles adds that "it is undoubtedly possible to quote innumerable passages from Proudhon's works in which the materialist conception is eloquently stated," giving several examples from *The Philosophy of Poverty*. Of course, he goes on to say, materialism for Proudhon becomes in effect a moral category, so that in a sense, Marx's criticism is not meaningless. But here we could interpose a more interesting question. Does the "Young Marx" himself not also treat materialism in the same way, *i.e.*, as a moral category? Turning back to the *Manuscripts* we find such passages as this:

> The *human* essence of nature primarily exists only for *social* man, because only here is nature a *link* with *man*, as his existence for others and their existence for him, as the life-element of human actuality—only here is nature the *foundation* of man's own *human* existence. Only here has the *natural* existence of man become his *human* existence, and nature become human. Thus *society* is the completed, essential unity of man with nature, the true resurrection of nature, the fulfilled naturalism of man and humanism of nature.
> [*Young Marx*, pp. 305-306]

Thus it would appear that in 1844, nothing truly separated Marx and Proudhon on the issue of the materialist theory of history. In 1846 Marx claimed that a difference existed, but Proudhon could not see it ("I have the misfortune to think like you!"). Later, however, a true difference arose, or was at last clarified (depending on your view of the "young" Marx), and this difference led to a very distinct disagreement between Marxism and anarchism that manifested, for example, in opposing views about the "inevitability" of revolution. In the view of dialectical materialism, the revolution is impossible until Capital itself is perfected, in a sense, and thus succumbs to its own inherent contradictions. Proudhonian anarchists like Gustav Landauer argued, however, that revolution is a response to the condition identified by Young Marx as the misery of alienation, that this misery is real and present, and that Capitalism might just as well be eternal for all the satisfaction we can derive from a theoretical crisis in its future. This issue came to a head for my generation in 1968, when the French Communist Party tried to suppress the uprising in May. It's true that the Paris "events", which encapsulated the whole project of the 60s, ended in failure. But Stalinism ended in failure too. The entire movement of the Social ended in failure in 1989-91. The purpose of this essay is to ask whether that failure had anything to do with the terms of the quarrel between Marx and Proudhon in 1844, and our interest in an answer is more than academic. In a sense we stand where Marx and Proudhon stood in 1844—all the same issues are alive for us again. We've come to suspect that their theories were not irreconcilable; perhaps they were even complementary. We've come to suspect that the quarrel was a big mistake.

We could test our suspicions in several ways. For instance, we could try a Sci-Fi thought experiment, and ask what might have happened if Marx and Proudhon had not quarreled, but instead had overcome their differences. Proudhon would have accepted Marx's points about economics, and would have mastered the Hegelian dialectic. Marx would have renounced dogmatism, and developed his theory of alienation instead of abandoning or distorting it. United in the Committee of Correspondence the two geniuses would have entered the fray of 1848 as comrades-in-arms, and the revolutionary failure would not have shaken them as badly as it did. The Committee would have blossomed into the International much sooner, and by 1871 the International would be in a position to dominate the Commune with Proudhono-Marxian ideas. Seizing the Bank in Paris, the Communards would have established a democratic republic and treated directly with Prussia for peace. Thenceforth Europe would move inexorably toward the Social Revolution—first Germany, then Russia, Italy, Spain, etc. By the end of the 19th century this federated Europe would oppose the imperialism and colonialism of England and the USA in the Middle East, Asia, Africa, and South America; consequently all these areas would be liberated for the movement of the Social. By the mid-20th century civil war or revolution would engulf the UK and USA and lead to a final war against Capital from within and without—and Earth would be won for the Social. At this point (round about 1999) I suppose the UFOs would really finally arrive and invite Terra to join the Galactic Federation, to struggle against Capitalism somewhere beyond the spiral nebulae…it's impossible to avoid the *ad astra, ad absurdum* syndrome when indulging in such fantastic speculation.

It might prove more useful to follow the ramifications of what actually happened rather than the forking paths of an alternate universe. The real and actual disagreement between Marxism and anarchism crystallized around the question of the State—more abstractly, the problem of authority. Whether by revolutionary or legislative means, the Marxists determined to take political power, although they seemed unclear as to whether this seizure would constitute the condition or simply the sign of the overcoming of Capitalism. The anarchists, however, argued for the immediate destruction of the State as a pre-condition for the Social Revolution, although they disagreed about whether these ends could be obtained by revolutionary war or by revolutionary but peaceful economic means. The Marxists viewed the anarchists with some justice as wrong-headed and ineffectual; the anarchists viewed the Marxists as authoritarian machievellian schemers, and predicted that Communism in power would prove even worse than Capitalism in power. And they were correct.

Despite Marx's dogmatism, innumerable Marxist sects arose each claiming the mantle of orthodoxy (including one Trotskyite groupuscle in England that actually believes in the UFOs and the Galactic Federation!). The Social Democrats emphasized legislative means, the Bolsheviks emphasized vanguardism and the *coup de main*. The anarchists were anti-dogmatic on principle, and Proudhon was constitutionally incapable of systematization or even consistency—as a result many different political ideas and movements owe something to Proudhon, from the mainstream anarchists and syndicalists to various revolutionary anti-Capitalist monarchists and fascists. (Fascism, of course, can adapt any philosophy to its purposes—including Marxism, as we can see from the "Red/Brown Alliance" in Russia and on the "New Right" in general today.) Proudhon himself tried to adjust his theory for this dissipativeness in his later work on federalism, as we shall see. But all this is subsequent to 1844 and therefore only tangentially relevant to our question. Perhaps it would be useful to put aside the whole diachronic question (what could have happened, or what did happen) and concentrate instead on a synchronic view of Marx and Proudhon, a view which need not be limited to their coincidence in time and space in 1844 or to their divergence thereafter. After all we're not looking for the Judgement of History here. We feel ourselves in a desperate situation; we're looking for *help*.

It seems to me that the one really basic and important agreement between Marx and Proudhon concerns the nature of property or private property. Since we live in a time when over 90% of all property has no existence except as money, and where some 430 people "control" more of that money than half the population of the globe, we might expect to find the views of Marx and Proudhon a bit out-dated. But on the contrary they seem if possible more fresh than when they were expressed in the middle of the (first) 19th century. A synthesis based on Proudhon's *What is Property?* and Marx's *Economic and Philosophic Manuscripts of 1844* would serve as an admirable basis for a critique of Too-Late Mutant Gnostic Capital in 1996. Probably this is because "everything" that came between 1848 and 1991 (*i.e.*, the whole movement of the Social) has been swept away by "the End of History". Capital which was potentially triumphant in 1844 is now finally actually triumphant in 1996. What Proudhon and Marx detected as the inner essence of this Capital has now been exteriorized as real form. The ecstatic realization of simulation, in media for example, or in bioengineering technology, is already inherent in the alienation analyzed by Marx and Proudhon. In their later writings, if we put aside those passages which divide them, we can find plenty to add to our synthesis; we need not limit ourselves to texts written before 1844. In general we will find Marx most useful for understanding economics and money, but will be far less interested in his ideas about authority and organization. As for Proudhon's later economic doctrine of Mutualism, we might have a great deal to learn from it—but on the whole we shall take more interest in Proudhon's ideas about authority and organization—if only because we know where Marxist organization leads, but we do not know where anarchist organization might take us. The synthesis implied by such a study would demand at least a whole book to develop, and we can only offer a few tentative beginnings.

We might start by asking if Capital, in the very moment of its universal hegemony, is not finally poised on the very brink of that terminal crisis so often predicted by Marx. The moment of the death of the Social is by definition the moment of the re-birth of the Social; like the Phoenix, it arises from its own ashes. But what caused the conflagration in the first place? Capital has exploded in five years, filling a vast South Sea Bubble with hot gases, expanding till it englobes the earth in a fragile membrane, stretched thin as soapy film, a kind of money-weather that encapsulates the world. Capital is "free" (for example as migratory or nomadic Capital) but at the same time Capital is entirely self-enclosed. The ruins of the USSR may not provide the new market Capital needs for its infinite expansion as a closed system. Cyberspace is not really a "market" at all, but simply the conceptual space of Capital as a totality, together with all its representations. Today the Stock Market is still soaring, while all over the world (even in the former "first world"), zones of depletion come into being as Capital simply abandons them and moves on. Some of these zones are non-geographical but include demographic groups (e.g., the homeless), or ethnic groups, or whole classes of people. Others include geography and even entire nations, such as in certain parts of Africa. The IMF and World Bank (probably as close as we can get to the institutionalization of power) can do nothing to salvage these depleted zones except impose punitive discipline and provide pools of cheap labor for institutional neo-liberalism. In order to combat Communism, Capitalism once had to cut deals with various potential allies:—the deal with the labor-aristocracy for example, or the deal with democratic reform, or the deal with organized religion. But Capital in power no longer needs any of these deals—or so it believes—and is now in the process of betraying all its former allies. Is there a human being in the world who is not in debt to Capital? Outside of the remnants of the left, or the shattered fragments of "third world" neutralism, is there any global force of resistance against Capital worth taking seriously? (Islam, perhaps?) What would happen if a giant meteor came close enough to Earth to "wipe the tape" of every computer on the planet—what would happen to all the *pure* money? What kind of catastrophe could tip the balance and upset the Capitalist *imaginaire*? A series of Bhopals and Chernobyls? A radical populist uprising in Mexico or Indonesia? Or how about that perennial favorite—a crisis of overproduction, carried to obscene extremes—bankruptcy, world depression? But—could mere production (10%) survive the collapse of money (90%)? Some of these questions might be answerable through a study of Marx. CyberMarx.

Both Proudhon and Marx discussed alienation; Marx's more philosophical analysis remains more useful than Proudhon's, although he himself perhaps failed to develop it. Neither thinker could have foreseen the extent to which alienation would be exacerbated by media, in which more and more autonomy has been leached from "everyday life" (where some direct relation between subject and object remains possible), and has "passed into representation" where words and gestures are always intercepted by things, by "dead Capital". As the nation-state and the community are alike reduced to a spectacle of control, acting as enforcers or shills for Capital but stripped of real power, alienation emerges as the true and most forceful manifestation of the power that is not ours, and that confronts us directly with our own depletion and belatedness. Alienation itself mediates for us with power. This has been called the problem of Work, since alienated labor is the force that takes the place and assumes the face of the hierarchy of immiseration for most of us most of the time. But we also "work" at the diminution and dilution of authenticity in leisure and in all relations defined by exchange as well as "on the job"—and this sphere has expanded through mediation till it has come to occupy all individual and social space save a few corners of unconsciousness and nihilism. Mediation in principle acts against presence and for separation, which explains why it becomes in itself the principle of the Totality. The modality of this power depends on separation (as hierarchy, division of labor, alienation, etc.) and simultaneously on sameness; global culture is exactly analogous to monoculture as depletion of variety—cognitive poverty (*misère*). Restricted to an infinity of "choice" within a single universe of discourse (mediation), subjectivity is "enclosed" in monotony and anomie just as communal fields were once enclosed on behalf of monoculture and Capital. With the collapse of the spectacle of opposition (the USSR) the spectacle of sameness is inflated to global proportions ("obscenity", "simulation") in a mediated discourse of separation.

In this sense, Capital will achieve the single rational world-consciousness that was the stated goal of the Enlightenment. This goal was shared by all the heirs of the *philosophes*, including democrats, capitalists, Marxists, and anarchists. The entire project of colonialism was justified from this perspective, even by Marx himself; in fact, Communism had as much to do with the emergence of this "single vision" as Capitalism—neither system could "spread" unless *different* consciousnesses were replaced by *same* consciousness. Hence the inherent imperialism of both systems. Anarchism, which denounced the politics of separation, nevertheless appealed to the same single "scientific" form of consciousness to realize itself in theory and praxis. All progressive forces agreed that progress follows the homogenization of consciousness. Difference was relegated to the diminishing sphere of reaction, superstition, prejudice, and ignorance.

Capital has already nearly achieved the goal of all religion, since money is now almost completely "spiritual" and yet contains and exercises all power in the world. Now Capital will carry out the entire anti-religious project (disenchantment of the universe) as well, since it will "evolve" a unified, all-pervasive, flat, self-reflexive, and successfully alienated consciousness—the world's representation of itself to itself as rational, illumined, free—and yet somehow completely one-dimensional. Now if we can believe for a moment in our Phoenix of revolution, and in the re-appearance of authentic opposition, we might well ask whether the progressive scientism of the old left can serve in resistance against the progressive scientism of Capital—or whether we need a new concept of consciousness altogether. The problem is to avoid falling into the paradigms of the old right and its anti-progressive anti-scientism, rooted in theocratic feudalism, simply out of our disgusted reaction against the monoculture of globalism. In a way this project (which might be called the reenchantment of the universe) constitutes a great deal of the philosophy, anthropology, and political theory of the last 50 years. Plenty of effort has gone into an epistemology that is both anti-Capitalist and anti-Communist (or perhaps post-Capitalist and post-Communist). These philosophies were seen under the rubric of "neither/nor", or "Third Way". But now there is no third way, because the first and the second have both imploded into the One World of transcendent Capital. How, for example, can we still speak of a "Third World" when there is no more Second World or even First World? The third-way philosophies had some theoretical success in defining a consciousness that escaped the Enlightenment/anti-Enlightenment dichotomy, and thus the authoritarianism of both Science and anti-Science. But the political assumptions of the Third Way were based on the "reality" of the Iron Curtain, and the hegemony of the spectacle of opposition. Now the situation has changed, and the political analysis based on third way thinking must be adjusted to meet the new conditions. The old "international proletarian solidarity" of the left was based on Enlightenment rationality no less than the international bourgeois solidarity of Capital. But now we are precipitated into a world where the unification of ideals has been realized, and where we are "beyond left and right" whether we like it or not. Global Capital is neither (or both!) left and right—so we must be… something else. Not another synthesis of left and right, but perhaps making use of both radical and conservative perspectives (as Paul Goodman called himself a "neolithic conservative"!).

Global Capital depends on a paradoxical fusion of *sameness and separation*. If we are to oppose it, we must explore the contradictions called into being by such a paradox—namely, *difference and presence*.

In this part of our project Proudhon may be of more use than Marx. Although Proudhon made the same obeisance to scientific consciousness as every other 19th century progressive, he was not consistent in his worship. He realized the importance of different; for example, he very much appreciated his own regional difference as a peasant of the Franche-Comtois. Unlike the Jacobins and Communists he was always opposed to centralization (thus his denunciations of bureaucracy ring more sincerely than those of the Marxists), and he sympathized with peasants and petty-bourgeoisie as much as with proletarians (although his last book elevated the working class to a primary position in the Revolution).

In his later writings he even abandons the dialectic (with its culmination in synthesis) in favor of a view of reality based on contradiction. He believed that contradiction was eternal, and that it should be harmonized and balanced rather than reconciled and eliminated. On this basis he was able to combine his Mutualist economics with a political system that could be called anarcho-federalism, although he called it simply Federalism (*The Principle of Federation*, 1863). In this system, groups formed for whatever reason (economic, cultural, regional, etc.) could affiliate in a federation based on economy and administration rather than on political unity. Each group must be considered autonomous in the sense of preserving its right to secede. [Note: The Soviet Constitution lifted this anarcho-federalist idea when it guaranteed the right of secession to all "Autonomous" republics within the USSR—a right that was never granted.] Property as possession succeeds property as Capital, leading to rough economic equality (with scope for talent and energy, but with a guaranteed living). Within the group all matters not pertaining to federated relations are left to the group to manage, and there even remains potential space for the autonomous individual (thus the appeal to individualist anarchism). Obviously one could belong to several groups simultaneously (labor syndicate, consumers' coop, neighborhood alliance, peoples' militia, etc.)—the possibilities for difference ("contradiction") are innumerable, as are the possibilities of presence. The empire of representation is shattered, both politically and culturally. Unlike Marxism, this social-federalism allows for more than one consciousness—a true plurality rather than a mediated pluralism. Unlike capitalism, Proudhon's system allows and even demands presence ("solidarity") since mediated relations cannot meet the exigencies of the federal economy, much less encompass the unmediated pleasures of the federal culture.

In other words, Proudhon's system offers us a theory of revolutionary difference and revolutionary presence—and therefore it should offer some guidance in constituting our opposition to Capital's sameness and separation. Proudhon's federalism was most thoroughly developed by the anarchist Gustav Landauer, who tried briefly to implement these ideas in the Munich Soviet of 1919 (and was killed by proto-Nazis when the Soviet fell on May 2). Particularity was precious to Landauer, who had no wish to see culture homogenized by either capitalism or Marxism; to be different was to be free. He envisioned a socialism of the *Volk* in opposition to the *volkisch* authoritarianism of the right. Although anti-religious, Landauer understood enough about "spirituality" to realize the reality and value of non-ordinary consciousness. Here I want to look at Proudhon's federalism though Landauer's version of it, and see if it has any use in our project.

Contemporary leftism (what's left of it) is experiencing great anguish over the question of particularity. Deleuze and Guattari, for example, were willing to consider the "molecularity" of the revolution and the "heterogenesis" of resistance in such examples as the gay/lesbian movement, children, the insane, oppressed minorities, etc. But most leftists have a very hard time extending this open-mindedness to (say) a tribe of native Americans interested in shamanism and radical conservation—or even worse, to a group of poor whites interested in Christianity. In other words most leftists can accept particularity only when it appears as embedded or replaced within the monolithic consciousness of "scientific rationalism" that defines the progressive project of the 19th century. For instance, most leftists are utterly incapable of seeing Islam as opposed in principle to Capital's monoculture and thus potentially a revolutionary force, since they have been nurtured on a view of Islam as "irrational", "fanatic", and "backward"—a view that owes everything to Enlightenment chauvinism and nothing at all to a shared humanity. Most leftists would support the Zapatistas because they represent a valid continuation of leftist ideas into the post-Communist world of struggle—but the same leftists would express themselves as "worried" by the fact that the Zapatistas are Mayan Indians who want to be Mayan Indians rather than secular socialist illuminati like "us". Perhaps "we" should start to learn how to act as if we really believed that more than one consciousness (hence more than one identity) can flourish in a movement devoted to "empirical freedoms". We should stop boasting about giving up our eurocentric unidimensional bourgeois *weltanschauung*, and actually do it.

What about Serbian nationalism and ethnic cleansing?! Isn't that particularism with a vengeance?

No. That is old-fashioned ethnic chauvinism manifested as imperialist aggression, completely complicit with Capital, and impossible to confuse with the anti-hegemonic particularism of the Zapatistas, or of women, or of gays and lesbians, or of Afro-Americans.

But—since Capital has succeeded in unifying consciousness, shouldn't we congratulate ourselves that it has done our work for us and prepared the Revolution that Marx predicted?

No—because even if unified consciousness were a Good Thing, it has not been attained by Capital, which is responsible only for a homogenization (or homogenesis) of consciousness, a vicious parody of the Enlightenment project, not its true realization. Our attack here is not on rationality per se. As a mode of consciousness we might even say that it's in short supply and that we could use *more* of it, not less. The attack is on rational*ism*. Historically rationalism has appeared as the hegemonic particularity of "Western Man", who may be left or right, but is always *right* by comparison with lesser breeds outside the law (women, children, "natives", etc.). Western Man takes his own alienation as Nature's Plan for *homo sapiens*—even if it makes him a bit triste at times—even if it makes him violently irrational at times—still, it is the one and only true consciousness of the world. If that were so, I would beg (like Baudelaire's soul), "Anywhere! Anywhere, so long as it out of this world!" But I don't believe it. I believe in revolutionary difference—and in revolutionary presence.

Thus it would seem that on the point of *organization* we have less to learn from the centralized model of Marxism than from the decentralized models of Landauer and Proudhon, because organization or praxis is the natural concomitant of consciousness or theory. In fact, Proudhon's system is of less interest as a "utopia" or plan for the future than as a model for resistance, a strategy for the present. The federal system in struggle would amount to a kind of "united front" without an ideological head; but more importantly it would be able to work on the construction of a different economic order "within the shell" of the capitalist world order. The quote is from the IWW Preamble, and it is possible that some of the ideas of the anarcho-syndicalist movement inspired by Proudhon may once again have a certain utility. (In the USA, for example, labor has been "pushed back" to about 1880, and certainly has a lot to re-learn about such concepts as sabotage, the General Strike, etc.) The problem is that the labor union or syndicate is only one out of a myriad organizational forms needed to constitute the resistance movement of "revolutionary federalism". Even work itself (such as the reproduction and housework of women or the "schooling" of children) cannot easily be organized in a labor-union model, much less vital areas of "non-work" such as the production of the festal, pleasure of creativity, or pride of identity. The appeal of the federal concept for an anarchist is that it makes possible coalition or cooperation with every movement and tendency that opposes Capital, whether they are "anarchistic" or not, while the structure of such a coalition (the organization by which presence is achieved) remains an essentially anarchist structure. As an anti-ideologist the anarchist doesn't especially care if someone else wants to be a Mayan, or a Moslem, or a rationalist, provided that anyone at any time is free to secede, and that everyone at all times respects individual autonomy as well as social solidarity. On the single condition of anti-hegemonism any person or group can affiliate with the anti-Capitalist federation. "After the Revolution" no doubt the struggle will continue and begin to extend these freedoms into the deepest structure of society—but we can worry about that day when it dawns.

At present, we have not even begun to organize a federation for resistance. The remnants of the left continue the "franchising of issues" common to the period of "post-modernism"—unless they remain committed to even older models. The resulting fragmentation of consciousness (separation) plays into the "invisible hand" of Capital, or rather into the mediated simulation of "pluralism" and "democracy" that still make up Capital's construction of social reality. Everything is exhausted in representation—all resistance can be commodified as "resistance" and all life can be fetishized as "lifestyle". In this situation that approaches total atomization, the power of the monoculture seems absolute. Since nothing can escape it, the only alternative to the happiness of the consumer appears as the morbid bitterness of the defeated. When Bush said during the Gulf War that "there is no peace movement" in the USA, he might simply have said that there is no *movement*. Nine-tenths (at least) of the world have been excluded from the Rapture of Capital and have been left behind in this hell of the infinitely-repeated 19th century. But there is no movement. Nothing is happening. Not only has "History" been snatched out of the grasp of people like you and me, we might wonder whether any human being, no matter how "rich and powerful", can still *make history*. Global neo-liberalism claims that it is not an ideology, and this is true—or rather, it is an ideology that relinquishes all ideas to the machine of Capital, to the "bottom line" of profit, to the judgement of the "free" market, to the oracle of the computer. No one is in control. Power still exists, but control is missing. 432 zillionaires don't really constitute a "ruling class". The nation-state survives only to provide discipline for labor and corporate welfare for Capital. "God is dead—and I'm not feeling so good myself", as the bumper sticker says. But God is reborn as Money. What will *my* resurrection be?

This state of affairs cannot last, obviously—which means at least that we occupy a "point" of history which is objectively transitional. Either we capitulate, or else we re-imagine ourselves as the opposition—either way, we must move out of the Slough of Despond. If we choose the task of re-imagining, then we must make the best possible use of the Past to which we have been consigned. If Science Fiction seems bankrupt, it is because the future has been hijacked into cyberspace—and we're still stuck in the 19th century. Marx, Proudhon, Fourier, Nietzsche—these are our contemporaries. The Mayan Elders who inspired the communiqués of the Zapatistas—these too are our contemporaries: men and women of a primordial past. And the past is interesting because it is always changing, whereas the future (at least the future of the One World of Capital) is boring because it is still-born, dead, never-changing. This past we inhabit is unknown, unmapped, unexplored. Our task constitutes a kind of migration through the fabric of time, in a search for the space we have been denied. And perhaps from this nomadic drift will arise a discovery, a key, a thread for the labyrinth—a way out of the 19th century.

Saturnalia 1996
NYC

BIBLIOGRAPHY

Baudrillard, Jean (1994) *The Illusion of the End*, trans. C. Turner. Palo Alto: Stanford University Press

Hyams, Edward (1979) *Pierre-Joseph Proudhon: His Revolutionary Life, Mind, and Works*. London: John Murray

Jackson, J. Hampden (1962) *Marx, Proudhon, and European Socialism*. New York: Collier Books

Marx, Karl (1955) *The Poverty of Philosophy*. Moscow: Progress Publishers

—(1964) *The Economic and Philosophic Manuscripts of 1844*. Ed. and intro. by Dirk J. Struik, trans. by Martin Milligan. New York: International Publishers

—(1967) *Writings of the Young Marx on Philosophy and Society*. Trans. and ed. by Loyd D. Easton and Kurt H. Guddat. Garden City, NY: Anchor Books

Marx, Karl and Frederick Engels (1959) *Marx and Engels: Basic Writings on Politics and Philosophy*. Ed. by Lewis S. Feuer. Garden City, NY: Anchor Books

McLellan, David (1973) *Karl Marx: His Life and Thought*. New York: Harper and Row

Pickles, William (1938) "Marx and Proudhon". *Politica* 3:13. London School of Economics and Political Science

Proudhon, Pierre-Joseph (1888) *System of Economical Contradictions: or, the Philosophy of Poverty*, Vol. I. Trans. Benj. R. Tucker. Boston: Benj. R. Tucker. (Original French publication 1845)

—(1923 [1969]) *General Idea of the Revolution in the Nineteenth Century*. Trans. John Beverley Robinson. New York: Haskell House. (Original French publication, 1851)

—(1969) *Selected Writings of P.-J. Proudhon*. Ed. by Stewart Edwards, trans. by Elizabeth

Frazer. Garden City, NY: Anchor Books

—(1979) *The Principle of Federation*. Trans. and intro. by Richard Vernon. Toronto: University of Toronto Press. (Original French publication, 1863)

—(no date) *What is Property?*, Vol. I. Trans. by Benj. R. Tucker. London: William Reeves. (Original French publication 1840; Tucker's first edition Princeton, 1876)

Woodcock, George (1956) *Pierre-Joseph Proudhon: A Biography*. London: Routledge and Keegan Paul

# THE SHAMANIC TRACE

(For the Dreamtime Avocational Archaeology Group)

"In the Big Rock Candy Mountains,
the jails are made of tin,
And you can walk right out again
as soon as you are in."
—Harry K. McClintock, "The Big Rock Candy Mountain"

"Where there is still a people, it does not understand the state and hates
it as the evil eye and the sin against customs and rights."
—Nietzsche, *Thus Spoke Zarathustra*, I.

## 1. BIRTH OF A NOTION

The emergence of the State seems revolutionary in terms of *la longue durée*,
but appears gradual in terms of human generations. The State emerges slowly, even hesitantly, and never without opposition.

"State" stands for a tendency toward separation and hierarchy. Is "capital" a *different* force? At the level of *custom* in the non-authoritarian tribe, the two are not
necessarily distinguished. Accumulation of goods, for example, is seen as usurpation
of power; the *chief* in such a case will be virtually powerless because the chiefly function is *redistribution* ("generosity"), not accumulation.

Where does the State emerge? In Sumer or Egypt? But separation and hierarchy
must have already occurred long before the "sudden appearance" (as archaeologists
say) of the first ziggurat or pyramid. We should look "back" to the first moment
when the durable but fragile structure of the non-authoritarian tribe is shattered by
separation and hierarchy. But such a moment leaves no trace in stone or written
record. We must reconstruct it on a structural basis making the best use we can of
"ethnographic parallels". We should investigate whether myth and folklore contain
"memories" of such a moment.

Now the great contribution of P. Clastres was to point out that no such thing as a "primitive" society exists or ever existed, if we mean a society that is *innocent* of the knowledge of separation and hierarchy.[1] The problem proposed by Rousseau to the Romantics:—how can one *return to innocence?*—is a non-problem. The actual situation is much more interesting. The "savages" are neither ignorant nor unspoiled. Every society, if it is a society, must have already considered the problem—the catastrophe—of separation. Humans are not blank slates, to be "spoiled" by some mysterious outside force (—where would it come from? outer space?). Separation is inherent in the very nature of consciousness itself. How could there ever have existed a time when it was *unknown*, since "to know" is already to separate?

The problem for "primitive" society therefore is to prevent separation from reaching catastrophic proportions and manifesting as hierarchy—eventually as "State" (and/or "Capital"). Normal humans want to preserve autonomy and pleasure for themselves—the whole group—and not give it up to a few. Therefore normal society is defined by *rights and customs* that actively prevent catastrophic emergence. The question whether any given individual or group is "consciously aware" of the purpose of such structures is far less important than the operative existence of the structures themselves. If "rights" allow for fair redistribution of goods, for example, and "customs" (including normative mythologies) succeed in preventing the accumulation of power, then these structures must be seen as efficient modes of reproducing non-authoritarian society, no matter what "explanation" may be given by the "ethnographic subject" or informant.

Society opposes itself to the "State":—that is the Clastrian thesis. Its motive is clear and unambiguous, provided we understand the life of the non-authoritarian tribe not as "nasty, brutish and short" but as a process of maximizing autonomy and pleasure for the whole group. This process is closed to separation and hierarchy, so the individual maximizing of pleasure, for instance, is limited by the requirement of a rough equality of condition, and the autonomy of the individual (though it may be extreme) is limited by the autonomy of the group. The hunter/gatherer economy, dependent on small groups in ecological balance with nature, is ideally suited to this non-authoritarian structure. And as Sahlins made clear in *Stone Age Economics*, the hunter/gatherer economy—even in ecologically disadvantaged areas like deserts, rain forests, and the Arctic—is based on abundance and leisure.[2] (The hunter can know *starvation* of course—but not "scarcity"—because scarcity is the opposite of surplus or *accumulation*, and opposites cannot exist without each other.) In Paleolithic times, when humans occupied the richest ecologies of Earth, the hunter's "subsistence" must have been rather idyllic. No wonder *hunting* survived well into the era of agriculture under the sign of a kind of magical freedom from work and routine; at one point hunting was supposed to be the privilege of the aristocracy, and resistance to authority took the form of poaching. Even in medieval times the elaborate rules for dressing game can be seen as prolongations of the essential act of the

1. Clastres, P. (1977), (1994)    2. Sahlins (1972). See also Lee and Devore (1968) and Barclay (1982/1990)

primordial hunter:—the *just distribution* of the kill. (This is also one of the origins of animal sacrifice.)

The non-authoritarian hunter/gatherer tribe seems to have been the universal form of human society for 99% of its existence. We have legends of lost and pre-diluvian "civilizations" like Atlantis, but no archaeological evidence for them. Perhaps we should take them seriously, however, as mythic reminders of the fact that separation and hierarchy *could have* emerged at any point in that longest of long durations we call "prehistory". Once tools were developed by *homo erectus*, implying the existence of full consciousness (since tools represent a prosthesis or "doubling" of self), presumably the potential for emergent catastrophe was already complete as well. But it "failed" to emerge. The anti-authoritarian institutions analyzed by Clastres *prevented* it from emerging.

From a certain point of view agriculture is the one and only "new thing" that has ever happened in the world. We are still living in the Neolithic, and industry (even "information" technology!) is still a prolongation of agricultural technology— or rather agriculture *as* technology. If we could eat information, we might speak of a "revolution" and an end to the Neolithic. Who knows? it may happen. But it hasn't happened yet. Civilization itself—the "culture" of cities—our conceptual world—was formed at Çatal Hüyük or Jericho (or somewhere similar) less than 10,000 years ago. Not very impressive in terms of the Long Haul!

Moreover, since Sahlin's paradigm-shift, a great mystery hovers around the question of agriculture. Namely:—What on earth could induce any sane person to give up hunting and gathering (four hours daily labor or less, 200 or more items in the "larder", "the original leisure society", etc.) for the rigors of agriculture (14 or more hours a day, 20 items in the larder, the "work ethic", etc.)? The "first farmers" had no idea of the glories of Sumer or Harappa to spur them on in their drudgery— and if they could have foreseen such glories, they would've dropped their seed-sticks in despair and disgust. Babylon was not destined for *peasants* to enjoy, after all.

A study of myths and folk tales about the origin of agriculture reveals over and over again that it was the invention of women—a logical extension of womens' gathering, of course—and that the establishment of agriculture somehow entailed violence to women (sacrifice of a goddess, for example). The link between agriculture and ritual violence is strong. Not that hunters are ignorant of ritual violence (e.g., "primitive warfare")—not at all. But human sacrifice, head-hunting, and cannibalism, for example, seem to belong much more to agriculturalists (and to "civilization") than to the hunter/gatherers. Offhand I can't think of one hunting tribe that practiced such customs—all the cannibals, etc., were "primitive agriculturalists", or advanced agriculturalists such as "us", who disguise our human sacrifices (in an "electric chair" no less!) as legal punishments. No doubt exceptions will be found—I simply haven't read enough anthropology to make any categorical statements—but I will stand by my intuitions about the "cruelty" of agriculture ("raping the body of our Mother Earth", as hunters often call it). Intense anxiety about the calendar, the seasonal year, which must be adjusted to "fit" the astral year (the image of divine perfection), leads to a view of time itself as "cruel". The smooth time of the nomadic hunter (unstriated, rhizomatic, like the forests and mountains, like "nature") is replaced by the grid-work, the cutting of earth into rigid rows, the year into layers, society into sections. "Division of labor" has really emerged; separation has emerged. Hence there must be cruelty. The farmers who work 14 hours a day instead of four are being cruel to themselves; logically then they will be cruel to each other.

The hunter is violent—but the farmer is cruel.

So we might expect to find the moment of emergence of the "State" somehow associated with the "Agricultural Revolution". For some time after reading Sahlins (and misinterpreting him) I looked for a direct link between the catastrophe of agriculture and the catastrophe of State-and-Capital. But I couldn't find it. True, separation has occurred. But separation does not appear to lead "all at once" to hierarchy. In fact "primitive" farmers are just as staunchly non-authoritarian as the hunters. Perhaps we need to revive the old idea of a "stage" of *horticulture* as opposed to agriculture *per se*. The gardener works hard, but also still hunts, both for meat and for pleasure (and for the sake of preserving an actual and ritual relation with "nature"). Even free peasants are fiercely independent, and horticulturalists are quite "ungovernable". Hard work is seasonal for the gardener, with plenty of time left for laziness and feasting. The Dyaks, gardeners and headhunters, have an extreme zero-work mentality, and spend as much time as possible lying about drinking and telling stories (see *Nine Dyak Nights*.[3]) The gardeners' chief has the most yams or pigs, but is also obliged to beggar himself by giving feasts—his "power" is constantly deconstructing itself in potlatch. Warfare is still "primitive", in that it still operates to diffuse and centrifugalize power and wealth rather than accumulate it. The war chief is still a temporary appointment; his power ends with the end of war. Custom and right still protect group autonomy, and still prevent the effective emergence of the State. It may still prove to be the case that the State is an epiphenomenon of agriculture; but the key would not lie in the crop-growing process itself, since cultivation of the earth can be carried out without accumulation. The key is the invention of *surplus and scarcity*. The whole thrust of the "Clastrian machine" (if I can use this term to describe *the entire system of rights and customs that resists State-emergence*) is not aimed at any economic technique, and in fact can survive even the great transition from hunting to horticulture. It is aimed against the accumulation of wealth and power, which must be resisted by keeping wealth and power in maximum (potential) movement. Accumulation is stasis—stasis is scarcity. Scarcity implies surplus (opposites cannot exist without each other)—and surplus implies appropriation. Agriculture makes surplus possible—but not necessary. The State begins with the breakdown of the "Clastrian machine".

Fine. But *where* did it happen? And *when*, and *how*?

It might be interesting to consider the possibility that it never really happened at all. If we are all still living in the Neolithic, then it must be true that we are all

3. Geddes (1957)

somehow still living in the Paleolithic as well. We still have our immemorial rights and customs (i.e., customs "older than memory") that preserve for us the remnants of our autonomy and pleasure. These fragments are not "lost" but perhaps severely reduced in scope and scale, limited to secret corners and cracks where the monolithic power of State-and-Capital cannot penetrate. I believe this to be the case *in a sense*, and this paper will be devoted to tracing those rights and customs as they appear out of prehistory, so to speak, and enter into history, and *persist*. History itself can be viewed as a process of Enclosure, a fencing-in and reduction of the area ruled by "custom" in our sense of the word (which we owe to E. P. Thompson).[4]

Yet this process remains (by definition?) incomplete. Autonomy and pleasure have failed to disappear; the rule of State and Capital depends in part on a spectacular delusion, and *pretense* of the erasure of customs. And even when autonomy *does* disappear, it is sustained by a kind of secret tradition, rooted in the Paleolithic, that guarantees its *re-appearance*. (Again: the "tradition" need not be *conscious* to be "real".) The "Clastrian machine" never breaks down—entirely.

Nevertheless, something happened! We have the evidence at Uruk. I saw evidence myself at Aztalan in Wisconsin, the site of the farthest-north extension of the Mississippian or Cahokian culture of pre-Columbian North America, where agricultural city dwellers killed and ate hundreds of human beings (some archaeologists speak of the "Southern Death Cult"). The ziggurats, mounds, and pyramids reveal the very structure of these catastrophic societies:—hierarchy has burst its ancient bonds, freed itself of the restraints of "right and custom", and triumphed over a beaten class of peasants and slaves. The strictures of the old tribal laws and myths of equality and abundance and against separation and hierarchy have proven so weak as to seem non-existent, never existent. State and/or Capital has triumphed. Autonomy and pleasure have become *property*.

We may never be able to track down the "moment" of the State. But one thing we can be sure of:—it didn't just happen, on its own, spontaneously, and according to some law of evolution. No climate change or population growth pushed an innocent and unresisting mass of humans *into History*. Humans were involved. The State (as G. Landauer said) is a human relation, a relation amongst humans and within humans.[5] It is always possible. But so is *resistance*.

In a sense the State can be seen as a revolt against the old rights and customs. We cannot call it the revolt of a "class" because non-authoritarian societies have no classes. But it does have roles, functions, divisions. Hunter/gatherer, men/women, chiefs/people, shamans/non-shamans. One or more of these divisions must have revolted against the others. If the shamans revolted we would expect the emergence of a "priestly" State; if the chiefs or warriors, a "kingly" State; if the women, a "matriarchy"—and so forth. Unfortunately we can find examples of all these, and mixtures as well. An analysis of primitive institutions cannot provide us with an answer, because each of these institutions in itself is designed to *prevent* the State, not to facilitate it. As Blake would say, each of these institutions possesses its *emanation* or

4. Thompson (1993)    5. Landauer (1919/1978)

*form* and its *spectre*; the former holds the latter in check. The revolt we're looking for would be a *spectral emergence*, therefore, and thus perhaps impossible to see.

In order to throw light on this problem we need two things: a more complete definition of the "Clastrian machine" (Clastres himself dealt mostly with primitive warfare); and a number of examples of how it works not only in "primitive" societies but also and especially in "historical" societies, where it operates as opposition to separation and hierarchy. Once we can view the mechanism more clearly perhaps we can "read it back" and see where catastrophe would be most likely to occur. Of course we must avoid any "mechanistic" interpretations—our "machine" is organic, complex, even chaotic. But some generalizations may prove feasible, even so. Our hope lies in the continuity of the institutions in question, their "traditions", their cohesion toward meaning. Rather than seeing "rights and customs" merely as Paleolithic survivals or extrusions of non-authoritarian *mores* into a later and more-developed authoritarian totality, we should see them as representing the *consideration of catastrophe* that society has always already made, and that resists all corrosion despite its infinite mutations, regressions, compromises, and defeats—a consciousness that persists, and finds expression.

In order to define more clearly the "Clastrian machine", then, we need to name its parts—which, for the sake of brevity, we will limit to three: "primitive warfare", the "Society of the Gift", and shamanism. We might examine any customs of non-authoritarian peoples in the expectation that all of them will harmonize (however indirectly) with the double function of realizing autonomy and pleasure and suppressing separation and hierarchy. But these three areas of custom are *directly* concerned with the social economy or dialectic we want to examine. Do we have a problem of categorization here, in trying to compare three such "separate spheres" under the rubric of some apparently unified or universal force? But Society itself has already done so:—it combines war, economy, and spirituality within its "universe". Admittedly the world of ethnographic discourse is not a clearly-bounded pure and impermeable abstraction; nevertheless we would be unable to sociologize or anthropologize to any extent whatsoever if we could not assume that a given society experiences itself on certain levels as a *whole*. We have located the "Clastrian machine" on such a level; our demonstration will depend on comparing our examples according to this hypothesis. In order to suggest the persistence of the "machine" through history we shall have to expand our search beyond the "perfect case" of the non-authoritarian hunter/gatherer or horticulturalist tribe (which in any case exists for most of us only in ethnography, archaeology, folklore, etc.); we need to examine cases from eras in which Society is losing or has already lost power to the State (and/or Capital), and in which the "machine" now acts as an oppositional force, or for the facilitation of autonomous zones within the space of Power.

## 2. Machinations

According to Clastres, "primitive" warfare and "classical" warfare are radically different phenomena. Warfare as we know it, from Sun Tzu to Clausewitz, is waged on behalf of separation, appropriation, hierarchy, accumulation of power. In this sense we are still waging classical war, despite its supposed apotheosis into the "purity" of instantaneity and cyber-spectacle ("information war"). For us, warfare is *centripetal*, drawing power towards the center. Primitive war, however, is *centrifugal*—it causes power to flee the center. First, warriors have no (political) power except on the warpath. Second, war is considered an affair of personal glory ("immortal fame"), not a means of acquiring property, slaves, or land. The rare prisoner is either killed or adopted into the tribe; there is no "surplus of labor". Third, in fact, and most importantly, any booty must be shared out with the whole tribe—the warrior acquires nothing for himself alone, nor does the warband enrich itself as a sodality at the tribe's expense. Fourth, actual death is rather rare in such war; there is no "excess manpower" to spare. Honorable wounds (or even symbolic wounds, as in "counting coup" among the Plains Indians in North America) and clever thefts are more highly valued than martyrdoms. But the primitive warrior soon comes to understand that a life devoted to war can end only in a glorious death, or in a miserable old age of poverty and powerlessness—since the tribe is very careful to see that he accumulates neither wealth nor authority.[6] Hence the well-known "melancholy" of the primitive warrior, so often noted in the literature. The "uncleanness" of the warrior, frequently expressed in ritual and myth, represents the anxiety about his role shared by the tribe as a whole. If the warrior revolts against tribal custom and seizes power and wealth for himself (an obvious temptation), he has committed what G. Dumezil called "the sin of the warrior"[7]—in effect, the creation of "classical warfare".

Thus for Clastres primitive warfare was the perfect model of rights and customs institutionalized as a force for the dissipation and centrifugality of power as separation. Primitive war serves precisely the purpose of Society in resisting the emergence of the State. It is not really "primitive" in the sense of being a crude and imperfect foreshadowing of classical war; in fact, it is a highly sophisticated complex evolved for distinct "political" purposes. Violence, which appears as a "natural" human trait, must not be allowed to cause separation within the tribe. Violence must be used to protect and express the egalitarian structure of the non-authoritarian group, not to threaten it. Violence is the price of freedom, as the 18th century revolutionaries might have expressed it—but not of appropriation and slavery.

The idea of the Economy of the Gift as a "stage" in social development was clarified by M. Mauss and refined by G. Bataille and others.[8] Here it would be misleading to speak of "primitive exchange" or "primitive communism", since it is not a matter of property-in-movement or property-in-common but of the failure of property to emerge. The *potlatch* of the Northwest Amerindian tribes, as we know it from ethnographic literature, is perhaps not the ideal model for elucidating the "Gift"; its "classical" form of "conspicuous consumption" is now seen as perhaps

6. See, for example, Fadiman (1982)   7. I no longer remember where Dumézil uses this phrase; in general, see Littleton (1966). See also Dumézil (1969), especially Part II, "Fatalités: Les trois péchés du guerrier"   8. Mauss (1950/1980); Bataille (1988)

owing too much to pressure from an encroaching money-economy to be considered as an organic expression of the economy of reciprocity. Potlatch in this form might better be considered in the light of Bataille's "Excess"—the necessity for *non-exchange* in a society of "primitive abundance". The original "pre-Contact" form of potlatch would perhaps have included a wider system of smaller but more numerous and frequent ceremonies, in which the essentially *redistributive* nature of potlatch might be seen more clearly. If we accept an historical development from the economy of the Gift to the economy of redistribution to the society of exchange, then potlatch would belong to the second "stage", not the first. And this would make ethnographic sense, since the Tlingit, Haida, and other tribes were in fact highly civilized town-dwellers with authoritarian chieftaincies, hereditary usages, division of labor, monumental architecture, etc.—more comparable to Çatal Hüyük or even pre-Dynastic Egypt than to, say, the Inuit, Australian Aborigines, rain forest pygmies, or even "primitive" horticulturalists. The true economy of the Gift is to be found among such non-authoritarian peoples. It originates in the equal sharing-out of game and gathered food, and is anything but arbitrary or "spontaneous". Every person has a "right" to the Gift, and knows exactly what will constitute reciprocity. But nothing "enforces" the Gift except "rights and customs" (and the possibility of recourse to violence). The Gift is "sacred"—and generosity is "divine"—because the very structure of the social depends utterly and absolutely on the free movement of the Gift. The Gift in turn is related to the Sacrifice, in which the spirits that provided the game (and who in effect *are* the game) are included in the kinship structure of the tribe by the gift of a portion of the kill (usually blood or smoke) in return for the gift of life's very sustenance. This structure also holds for plants and the "lesser mysteries" of gathering—which will evolve into the grand sacrificial ideology of the Neolithic. The Gift is the voluntary sacrifice that "atones" for the violence of the hunt or the cruelty of agriculture, and "at-ones" the fabric of society by including everything (animals, plants, the dead, the living, the unseen) in symbolic unity and renewal. Property fails to appear in such a society because everything that *might be* property is *already* Gift; the possibility of exclusive possession has been pre-empted by usage and by donation, or *donativeness*, to coin a term.

In reality however, the three "stages of economic development"—gift, redistribution, and exchange—cannot be seen as a crude linearity or conceptual grid or diachronic fatality. Each is overlaid, super-inscribed, contaminated, magnetized, and compromised with the others in a palimpsestic permeability of cross-definitions, paradoxes, and dialectical violence. The economy of the Gift is also obviously an economy of redistribution and exchange, in broad general terms. We somewhat arbitrarily reserve the term *redistribution* to refer to the chiefs (and later the States) in their function as ritual conduit of wealth for the people—it flows to the "top" and is redistributed "justly" and as widely as possible. As we've seen, in some tribes this means the chiefs are periodically bankrupted by the custom of excessive generosity they must honor—and even the "classical Civilizations" of Sumer, the Indus Valley, Egypt, or the Mayans experienced ceilings or upper limits on their power of accumulation, due to the ancient rights and customs of redistributive justice. In a sense, then, the structure of redistribution is a *prolongation* of certain aspects (or "survivals") of the structure of the Gift; the Gift is still embedded in the economy that now overcomes or (at least) absorbs it. The imperative of redistributive justice, to which even the most despotic of despots must pay lip service, if not true devotion, consists in fact of the "Clastrian machine" at work within the authoritarian structure of the ancient kingships and theocracies. Not even king or priest must interfere with this justice, which is (therefore) cosmic in nature—an eternal truth—a morality.

Now the mystery of the third stage of economic development—"exchange"—as K. Polanyi pointed out[9]—is its *failure to appear*. In the ideal terms of Classical Economics, exchange was always the purpose and telos of any "earlier" or "more primitive" economic form. Property was inherent in these forms as the flower in the seed, and only needed to "evolve" toward the dawn of "the Market" eventually to be born as full-fledged 19th century Capital. The assumption is that all societies are based on greed and competition, but that we moderns have at last realized a rational system to maximize the positive (wealth-generating) aspects of this eternal law of nature while suppressing the negative aspects by legislation. But Polanyi, as an *economic anthropologist*, was able to prove that no known human society ever based itself or its economy on the presumption of greed and competition as laws of nature. On the contrary, the economics of the Gift and of Redistribution are based on a *deliberate refusal* of such a possibility. They represent the "Clastrian machine" at work against the emergence of "pure exchange", which has always already been foreseen and suppressed by the Social for itself and in itself. The one and only social system based on "exchange" is that of 18th and 19th century European capitalists and their class-allies among the intelligentsia. Even in the 20th century, the "Market" still failed to emerge, thanks to the redistributive ideologies of Roosevelt, Hitler, and Stalin—who for all their evil still paid lip service to the immemorial ideal of economic justice. In fact "exchange" really only emerges in 1989 with the collapse of the movement of the Social, already hopelessly betrayed by its own leaders and thinkers. For the first time in history, the Market today rules unopposed. Or so it believes. In fact, of course, the "earlier" economies of Gift and redistribution are still present "under" the inscriptions and prescriptions of the Capital State. They cannot be erased, and they cannot be considered as "failed precursors" to the triumphalist Market. If they have been forced underground into a "shadow economy" of barter, "black work", fluid cash and alternative forms of money, etc., they nonetheless persist and find expression. The totality of Capital remains illusory—and in fact has its true being in "virtuality" and "simulation". The very completeness of its victory, which seems to culminate a long, drawn-out process of gradual encroachment, ever-tightening enclosure, and relentless erosion of "empirical freedoms", presents Capital all at once with the *question* posed to it by its very universality.

This question could perhaps best be expressed in terms of *money*.

9. Dalton (1968); see also Finlay (1985).

Symbolic exchange already exists within the economy of the Gift. Malinowski's Pacific Argonauts, who trade splendid but useless works of ritual art over thousands of miles of open sea, practiced a closed system in which symbols could only be exchanged for symbols, not for "real wealth". In fact the process was a kind of Bataillesque Excess, not a form of money. The extremely important but little-studied trade in ceremonial polished-stone axe-heads that pervaded all of late Paleolithic and early Neolithic Eurasia and Africa, may offer another example. Earlier axe-heads tend to be full-sized and utilitarian, while later ones move toward delicacy, miniaturization, and aesthetic perfection. The axe-heads had an obvious spiritual value for numerous and wide-spread cultures, ranging from Neanderthal to Minoan Crete. It's interesting to note that an early form of Chinese coinage took the shape of small axe-heads. It's possible that the Paleolithic axe-heads were not merely traded for *other symbolic goods*, but also for "real wealth", in which case they could be considered "money". If so, however, it must have been a money hedged around with taboos in order to prevent its becoming an opening to separation and hierarchy through "primitive accumulation", because we have no evidence that the ceremonial axe-heads changed society the way money changes society. No doubt these objects took their place in a complex system based on reciprocity rather than the "profit motive"!

A most persuasive argument was made by the German scholar Bernhard Laum and his followers, who assert that the origin of money is in the Sacrifice.[10] Each part of the animal in venery and in sacrifice has its designated recipient as gift. Incidentally this constitutes a kind of pecking order, a potential form of separation that must be "rectified" by the concept of rights and customs. This rectification holds good within the intimacy of the hunting band or horticultural village—but when the group becomes too large to share in a single sacrifice (for example, in a typical agricultural Neolithic town of 500 or so), then *tokens* must be distributed among the whole group, while the sacrifice itself is reserved to the "priests" (a custom that survives into Greece and Judea, of course). These tokens eventually take the shape of "temple souvenirs", which are later traded (because they have "numinous value" or *mana*) for real wealth. Hence the first coins, from 7th century BC Asia Minor, are issued by temples, stamped with numinous symbols, and made of symbolic metal (*electrum*, a mixture of solar gold and lunar silver). The idea of money as numismatic *numina* explains how money will be able to reproduce itself even though it is not alive (money is the sexuality of the dead). When "money begets money", the old rectified egalitarianism of the sacrifice is shattered by the possibility of accumulation and appropriation ("*usury*"). Religion has in a sense inadvertently let loose the demon of money in the world, which explains religion's ambiguous relation to the stuff. For religion, *all exchange is usury*—and yet religion is the very fountainhead of money itself. Jesus of Nazareth, for example, is said to have felt this paradox with particular poignancy.

10. See, for example, Desmonde (1962). On religion and money in general I have consulted Weber (1958), Tawney (1952), Angell (1929), Le Goff (1990), Merrifield (1987), Shell (1982)

The temple-token theory of money's origin is instructive but not conclusive—since in fact money makes a much earlier appearance—(somewhere in the proto-Sumerian millennia of the mid-to-late Neolithic)—as *pure debt*. Its pre-history can be traced in the rubbish-heaps and tells of archaeological digs in the Near East, in the form of clay tokens representing units of material wealth (we can guess this because some of them have the obvious shapes of hides, animals, containers, plants, etc.). Later on one finds clay envelopes containing sets of clay tokens, with *symbols of the tokens* pressed into the clay to record the envelope's contents. At some point around 3100 BC in Uruk, some clever accountants realized that if you have symbols of tokens on the outside of the envelope you don't need actual tokens inside the envelope. You can manage much more easily with a clay tablet impressed with symbols. Thus writing was invented.[11]

Now the clay tokens can only have been symbols of exchange—but obviously not money in the way coins are money. They were *records of debt*. It's easy to see that the token-system developed along with the Temple cult, since the tokens are found in or near Temple storehouses. We can guess that the primitive tokens represent *promises to pay*, and we can surmise that the Temple was the focus of accumulation and redistribution for the whole community. We can presume this because the earliest cuneiform tablets that can be deciphered seem to show such a system (or State!) already long established and taken for granted. There are promises to pay the Temple, and there are "cheques" issued by the Temple—in effect, "money". Once again we see money emerging from a religious matrix.

Money can be defined as a symbolic medium of exchange—although on the basis of the "sacrificial" origin-theory it might be more accurate to call money a medium of symbolic exchange. In Sumer however these perhaps complementary definitions can be subsumed into a much older and deeper definition:—*money is debt*. As soon as debt begins to circulate, credit appears—since opposites cannot exist without each other. Your debt is my credit, just as your scarcity is my surplus, and your powerlessness is my power. Just as *mana* once seemed to adhere to the temple souvenir and made it more valuable than the "cost" of the useless symbolic metals that composed it, so also "wealth" now seems to adhere to money itself, even to mere paper, despite the fact that the "medium" is strictly imaginary (a consensus-hallucination), and that the "wealth" in question is nothing but debt, "promise to pay", sheer absence. The anarchist P.-J. Proudhon once hypothesized that money must have been invented by "Labor"—the poor—as a clever means of forcing primitive accumulation into motion, so that some wealth might flow at least as "wages".[12] It's an intriguing notion, because it reveals that money in interest-free and immediate circulation—"innocent" money, so to speak—can appear as a form of empirical freedom. But Proudhon was wrong about the origin of money, if not about a certain aspect of its fate. Money originates and emerges in history as debt. But it has a "pre-history" as appropriation. The egalitarian economy of the Gift—which does not

11. Schmandt-Besserat (1992). My inadequate summary cannot do justice to this extremely important work.   12. Proudhon (1888); I've lost the exact reference.

know money—can be shattered only by the economy of surplus and scarcity. Now these terms can have meaning only for human beings:—some few will enjoy surplus, the rest must experience scarcity. Slavery, tribute, and debt are all forms of scarcity. Without writing and even without arithmetic, sophisticated systems of surplus/scarcity accounting are quite possible—but writing succeeds not merely in accounting but in *representing* surplus and scarcity, a form of control that appears as "magical" because it emanates from the Temple, and because it effects action-at-a-distance. At this point the Temple became a Bank, a moment that can still be traced in the architectural details of modern banks—and at the same time, it became a bureaucracy (or perhaps we should say *the* bureaucracy, since all bureaucracy is somehow the same bureaucracy).

Money is still today heavily inscribed (almost "overdetermined") with religious and heraldic symbolism, an obvious clue to its true "origin". But once the idea of money is born into the world (with writing as midwife, not mother), the link between money and writing can be broken. Anything can be money provided people believe it to be money:—cows, cowrie shells, huge stones, gold dust, salt. All that need be grasped is the notion of representation—the notion of separating wealth from the symbol of wealth and then simultaneously (and "magically") recombining them as "money". This kind of separation and paradoxical thinking can only be achieved by a society already split by separation and hierarchy, surplus and scarcity. Money does not create the State, though it may serve to mark the border between a "primitive State" and the full-fledged genuine article.[13] In clashes between a money economy and a non-money economy (say between Europeans and Natives in 16th century America), money itself inevitably acts as an opening wedge into the psyche of the infected people, since it bears with it all the "interest" that animates the society of separation. The Cargo Cults serve as modern-day examples of this process, as do millenarian cults with the opposite objective of *refusing* money and "White Man's goods".[14] Money reveals its true nature in such borderland situations where it comes into conflict with gift economies and non-authoritarian tribes, or even with quite sophisticated (but essentially moneyless) civilizations such as the Aztecs, Incas and Mayans. The "Clastrian Machine" goes into overdrive in an attempt to ward off catastrophe not from within its own society but from outside it. Both the beautiful ideals of the millenarians and their violence are attempts to construct a theory and praxis of resistance out of a "way of life" that had always already considered the catastrophe of its breakdown into separation and hierarchy. Once the economy of the Gift is destroyed and then even its memory is effaced (except in folklore and custom), resistance must take other forms. But the ideals, secretly enshrined in tradition, never die out entirely. They may come to take quite bizarre and superstitious forms, fragmentary, unconscious, ineffable—but they persist. Peasant revolts, bread

13. For stages of State development, see Mair (1962/1964) and Krader (1968)
14. From the immense bibliography on this subject, I will mention only Worsley (1968) and Thrump (1970); Martin (1991) offers a good case history, and Adad (1979) is especially useful for its economic analysis and excellent bibliography.

riots, the cloud-cuckoo-lands of mad heretics and rebels, forest outlaws and poach-
ers—thus for example did the primordial tradition of resistance find expression in
medieval Europe.[15] The ideal of reciprocity, and (failing that) the ideal of redistribution, can never be entirely effaced and replaced by the idea of *exchange*. The very
moment of the apparent triumph of the Market—of exchange—will inevitably call
forth the old, old dialectic once again (like the phoenix reborn from its ashes)—and
the re-appearance of the cause of the Gift.

    Like primitive warfare and the economy of reciprocity, shamanism is a part of
the "Clastrian machine" and an almost-inevitable feature of hunting and gardening
societies. (Obviously I'm using the word "shamanism" quite loosely.) The important
thing to note about the shaman is that he or she is not a *priest*. The line of demar-
cation may grow quite fuzzy, but on either side of the line one can discern quite distinct realities. The priest serves separation and hierarchy and the shaman does not.
The shaman is not paid a salary and is not a "specialist", does not necessarily receive
a "line of succession" from teachers, and does not "worship God".[16] The shaman
must hunt or keep a garden like anyone else. In many tribes, "everyone shamanizes"
to some extent, and "the" shaman is simply a first-among-equals, not at all comparable to a modern "specialist". Initiation for the shaman may or may not be mediated by other shamans, but inevitably it consists of direct unmediated contact with
spirits or "gods". No succession is involved, and no *faith*. The shaman does not look
on "worship" as a one-way street, or as debt to be paid; the shaman works with the
spirits and even compels them. Great shamans are even greater than great spirits.
Even so, the shaman has no "authority" except that of the successful practitioner. In
many tribes a shaman who fails too often (or even once!) may be killed. Shamans
may be chiefs or warriors or advisors to chiefs and warriors, but in the end possess
no more political power than chiefs or warriors. In non-authoritarian society everyone shamanizes a bit, and is also a bit of a chief and a warrior—even the women and
children (who have mysteries and sodalities of their own, and perhaps also voices in
the assembly). Thus although shamanism as an institution fulfills Durkheimian
functions of social cohesion, it also serves as a dissipative or centrifugal force in relation to accumulation of power. Most significantly, the shaman does not *represent* the
spirits but makes them *present* (either with entheogenic plants, or by becoming possessed, or by the "trickery" of sucking out witch-objects, etc.). Spirits that are *present* are experienced by "everyone", not just by the shaman. The priest by contrast
may no longer be capable even of an exclusive "experience" of presence, much less
able to facilitate it for his entire congregation. Among the Huichol of Mexico only
the shamans see and communicate with the "Great Spirits" while eating peyote—
but everyone else on the Pilgrimage also eats peyote, and *witnesses* the shaman com-
municating with the Spirits. But with or without entheogens, shamanism is *experi-
ential* and *therefore* "democratic" (or rather, rhizomatic)—while priestcraft is based
on mediation and faith, and is *therefore* separative and hieratic.

15. See Cohn (1970) and Hobsbawn (1959)    16. See Lewitsky (1988)

The shaman is directed by the "Clastrian machine", so to speak, inasmuch as he or she is prevented from acquiring unjust accumulations of power—but the shaman also directs the machine, inasmuch as the spirits always vote for the supremacy of "rights and customs" that guarantee or at least safeguard autonomy for society. It's interesting to consider the shamans as not only the visionaries of their societies but also as the intellectuals. They "think with" plants, animals and spirits rather than with philosophies and ideologies. Shamans are "outsiders" in many ways and yet they occupy a kind of "center" of their societies, a focal-point of social self- and co-definition. In societies of separation the intelligentsia are "insiders" (priests, scribes) but *displaced*, out of focus, and finally powerless.

Thus we have named at least three parts of the complex of rights and customs that expressed Society against the State—war, economics, and spirituality. They are a unified entity inasmuch as society itself is "one", first in its opposition to the emergence of the State, and then (later) in its resistance against the hegemony of the State. In the former case, their unity is effective; in the second case, it is shattered and even fragmented—but still on some level a recognizable whole. For instance, even the classical and modern societies still harbor "survivals" of reciprocity and redistribution, or shamanic experience, or violence as a defense of autonomy. But even in such fragmented conditions there persists a deeper "substructure" in which a living connectedness among these *parts* can be experienced. For example, on one level war, reciprocity, and spirituality all have to do with death and the Dead, and with the relation between the Dead and the Living. Since classical and modern social paradigms cannot "speak to the condition" of the Dead with the same directness and unity as the "ancient ways", we still live with vestiges, shreds, hints, and unconscious apprehensions of those old ways—we still live "in" the Paleolithic.

It seems that only in some relation with the primordial "rights and customs" can we hope to resist the totality of separation and strive for the degree of autonomy and pleasure our imaginations can encompass. Of course the paradigm of hierarchy has long ago proven itself adept in the appropriation of opposition; it makes shamans into priests, chiefs into kings, warriors into an instrument of oppression; and the spectrum of human potential it transmutes into caste and class. But once all the old roles have seemingly been appropriated, somehow they re-appear outside the bounds of control or even definition. Shamanic talents crop up in salesmen and housewives (especially after the re-emergence of ceremonial entheogenism in the 1960s); non-authoritarian structures suddenly appear within institutions:—the "facilitator" and the "talking stick" replace *Robert's Rules of Order*. The courage of the warrior deserts the hi-tech battlefield and manifests in gangs of young criminals; and the old slogan of the peasant revolts—"Land and Liberty!"—refuses to go away.

My contention is that the "Clastrian machine" goes on manifesting itself long after its original non-authoritarian social matrix has been destroyed and seemingly lost in the amnesiac obsessions of "History". Writing, which serves power, has only deepened the amnesia with its deliberate lies and its perpetuation of stupidities. History *as writing* must be circumvented and evaded in order to come at the truth.

What truth? For example: that the "nomadic war machine" subverts the very centripetality of classical war, and is always veering off into chaos. That there are whole
economies that know nothing of money or exchange (economies of emotion, of language, of sensation, of desire). That there exists an unbroken underground tradition
of spiritual resistance, a kind of hermetic "left" that has roots in Stone Age shamanism, and flowers in the heresies of the "Free Spirit". We must now turn to tracking
the traces of that spirit—the "Clastrian machine"—through the tangled thickets of
historiography, ethnography, *-graphia* itself.

### 3. WILD MAN

In the search for exemplary cases I will focus on shamanism more than on warfare or economics. All institutions of right and custom can be visualized as pillars
holding up the edifice of non-authoritarian society; and even when the house is in
ruins, reduced to the slums or margins of Civilization, the unity of the original
structure can still be discerned. Of all the pillars, however, shamanism claims for
itself a certain centrality:—*axis mundi,* in effect—conceptual focus of the whole
social construction. And even in the decay and ruination of the Social, shamanic
"remnants" still appear in axial positions in the geographic or conceptual spaces of
exile, dispossession, and depletion. In other words, as the field of rights and customs
is gradually enclosed, the spirit of resistance "loses its body" and is deprived of its
geographical, tactical, and economic materiality, till only "spirit" remains. A defeated or enslaved people will be reduced to tales and memories of former glory; till one
day the people, spurred by those memories, rise to re-embody them in material resistance. And as shamanism is precisely that which pertains to spirit (*ésprit*), we must
look to shamanism, or to its fragmented survivals, or even to its "trace", in order to
see the continuity of the "Clastrian machine" in History.

Hélène Clastres (wife of P. Clastres) has provided us with vital epistemological
tools for our search in her *Land-Without-Evil*, a study of the mysterious mass migrations of the Tupi-Guarani of South America in search of an earthly utopia, the
"Land-without-Evil".[17] Urged on by visionary shamans, the tribes would wander off
after signs and wonders, abandoning their fields and villages in defiance of the chiefs
and elders, and often come to grief through starvation or enslavement by another
tribe, or be turned back by impassable mountains or oceans. H. Clastres shows that
these remarkable movements began well *before* any contact with Europe, and in fact
took another form in the post-Contact era. Originally it appears that the migrations
occurred as a result of a struggle between the shamans and the chiefs. Perhaps under
the distant and indirect influence of the Incas or other High Civilizations, the chiefs
were asserting more and more power within the tribes, upsetting the egalitarian and
non-authoritarian structures of Tupi-Guarani society. The migrations involved leaving agriculture behind and "reverting" to hunting and gathering. The new nomadic
way of life, which was far from normal for these people, was interpreted by the
shamans as a shamanic quest involving the entire people, not just the shamans.

17. Clastres, H. (1995)

Chiefly power was disestablished simply by walking away from the chiefs. The Land-without-Evil was an image of the tribe as it should be and once was, according to proper right and custom. If the strategy failed because the Land-without-Evil could not be found (since it was an ideological construct and not a real place), nevertheless the shamans succeeded for brief periods in revivifying the old autonomy and inspiring the people with visionary fervor. The quests occurred over and over again for generations and were still going on when the repercussions of the Conquest were beginning to be felt. Gradually the migrations assumed a new form in response to these different forces, and began to resemble the sort of millenarian movements familiar to the student of the colonial process. Shamans and others emerged as military leaders, and "primitive warfare" was added to shamanic power in uprisings and rebellions—all doomed to fail. The "Clastrian machine", already out of balance in pre-Contact times, struggled against dissolution with drastic means, even with a kind of mass suicide—but against the money-economy and technology (and germs) of the Europeans these "embodied" forms of resistance were simply crushed.

But shamanism was not erased by colonization in South America—in fact, it has renewed itself again and again, and still persists today. Indeed, it may even be experiencing something of a renaissance. To understand how shamanism continues to serve as (at least) a conceptual space of resistance, even after "Contact" with monotheism and capitalism, we may turn for instruction to M. Taussig's brilliant study of ayahuasca healing cults, *Shamanism, Colonialism, and the Wild Man*.[18] On the one hand, Taussig points out, the conquerors always regard the conquered (the "natives") as radical Other, despised sub-humans, devoid of culture, better off dead, etc., etc. This is the daylight or conscious side of colonialist "racism", so to speak. But it has a night side as well—because, on the *other* hand, the natives retain some advantages that the conquerors would rather not think about too clearly, lest their superiority should begin to appear to them as less than absolute. For instance, the conquerors are strangers in a  strange land, but the natives are at home. They are "wild men", but this implies a connection with locality that the colonialist cannot share. They know where to find animals and plants—often the early colonists would starve unless the natives fed them, and this momentary dependence still rankles in the collective memory of the colonial gentry [e.g., "Thanksgiving" as a festival of guilt in North America]. Above all the native knows the spirit of place and possesses a magic that appears uncanny, ambiguous, or even dangerous to the colonist—depending on degree of credulity, in part, but also on a general background of Christian imagery, fear of the unknown, and the genuine bad health of the colonists. Sooner or later the conquerors come to believe that for certain afflictions only the Natives possess a remedy. Catholicism, which is already open to "superstition" at the popular level, is perhaps more open to such influences than Protestantism. New England Puritans were not known to consult Algonkin medicine-men, but in South America such situations could arise more easily. In the case of the Ayahuasca cults,

---

18. Taussig (1987); see also his (1980). Taussig's latest work (1997) came to hand only after this essay was written, and is very relevant to my thesis.

the natives possessed a distinct advantage in their knowledge of an "efficacious sacrament" in the form of an entheogenic plant mixture used in shamanic healing. Structurally and to some degree actually the cults pertain neither to the world of the pure-blood colonists nor the pure-blood forest Indians, but to the mixed-blood Mestizos who belong to both worlds and to neither, who are both a bridge and a chasm between cultures. But the axis of the cults, so to speak, tips toward the Forest, and traces itself to aboriginal shamanism. Here it is the Colonists who are outsiders—and yet the Colonists are among the enthusiastic patrons of the healing cults. (And nowadays the expanding Ayahuasca *religions* like Unio Vegetal are made up almost entirely of "Whites".) The fact is that shamanism has effected a curious reversal of colonial energies, in which elite anxiety gradually turns into a kind of romanticism ("noble savages", etc.) and then into an actual dependence on "native" sources of power. Perhaps no one thinks of this situation as "revolutionary"—and certainly Ayahuasca shamanism can do little to disestablish actual elite power—but it must be seen as a kind of mask for subtle forms of resistance.

Taussig's thesis represents a major break-through in the consideration of shamanism as a system interacting with the whole world, and not as a "pristine", remote, exotic, and self-enclosed object of analysis without any relevance outside the sphere of anthropology or the history of religions. In short, he has given us a *politique* of shamanism to match in importance Clastres' *politique* of primitive warfare. The model of the hidden power of the oppressed, which is so frequently a shamanic power, prepares us to perceive even subtle models in which the overt signs of shamanism and resistance may be muted almost to the point of invisibility. In fact, since Taussig makes creative use of W. Benjamin in constructing his thesis, we might borrow and adapt Benjamin's phrase "the utopian trace" and speak of a *shamanic trace* that may be present even in institutions or images lacking all open connection with shamanism *per se*. In the ayahuasca cults the links with "pristine" shamanism (assuming it exists as other than a structural model) are quite clear. But in other examples we might examine, the "trace" will be obscured to the point of unconsciousness, just as the trace of "utopia" is obscured by the advertisement in which it is embedded as an image of promise. The difference between utopian trace and shamanic trace is that the former is often deliberately "put into" the advertisement in order to exacerbate commodity fetishism by raising unconscious hopes that cannot be fulfilled; whereas the latter intrudes itself in certain phenomena, so to speak, as an unconscious welling-up or manifestation of "direct experience". This authentic or valid or veridical experience is the keynote and *sine qua non* of shamanic re-appearance. In this sense the shamanic trace is also "utopian", since it may involve the *desire* for such experience rather than the experience itself. The desire may take "perverse" forms but even at its most attenuated we can still recognize it as a movement of the "Clastrian machine", and as a sign that autonomy and pleasure still claim their right and custom.

*Shamanism, History, and the State*, a collection of essays edited by N. Thomas and C. Humphrey, is dedicated to Taussig and is largely devoted to exploring the opening he has made to shamanism as a "political" form.[19] On the back of the book a statement by Taussig himself appears, speaking of the ways in which "it shows 'shamanism' to be a multifarious and continually changing 'dialogue' or interaction with specific, local contexts.... This collection tries to demonstrate through 'case studies' just how different 'shamanism' becomes if seen through a lens sensitive to the history and the influence of institutions, such as the state, which seem far removed from it." In the whole of this excellent volume, however, there is not one mention of the work of P. Clastres or H. Clastres. I cannot imagine why this should be so, unless perhaps a certain post-Marxist slant of the Taussig "school" has prejudiced it against Clastres, who was an anarchist, and polemicized against Marxist anthropology. Perhaps mistakenly, it seems to me that Taussig's findings (and those of his "school") are complementary to those of Clastres. What Clastres demonstrated is that "primitive" society constructs for itself a "machine" (my term) to resist the emergence of the State. Taussig shows that one part of this machine, shamanism, goes on resisting the State even after the appearance and apparent triumph of separation and hierarchy. *Shamanism, History and the State* clarifies Taussig's work in a number of ways. For example, Peter Gow in "River People: Shamanism and History in Western Amazonia," examines certain ayahuasca healing cults (not the same ones discussed by Taussig) and finds that although they proclaim themselves to have originated with Forest Indians, in fact they were spread historically by Mestizos and geographically by the Christian missions and the rubber industry in the late 19th century. These cults too belong not to "the Forest" in reality but to the periphery or border between town and wilderness—and not so much to some "pristine" paganism as to resistance against official Christianity. It seems to me that Gow has nicely illustrated both Taussig's thesis and Clastres' thesis. On one hand the cults represent a turning-back or even a "reversion" (however romantic and unrealizable) to more primordial *customs*; on the other hand they represent a "going-forth", a resistance, a demand for *rights*.

In an attempt to harmonize the two schools, we should look for examples that have not been treated by either, and attempt analyses based on both. The first theme I want to examine is "reversion", and the example I've chosen has never (so far as I know) been discussed by anyone.

## 4. EMBLEMATICK MOUNDS

The idea of "reversion" is in the air, anthropologically speaking. In brief, the conviction is growing that many supposedly pristine examples of "primitive" societies studied by ethnographers may in fact be drop-outs from History—that is, they may have *reverted* to a more primitive state from a more "advanced" one at some point (usually unknown). In an evolutionist view of society this reversion must appear unnatural or perverse: why would anyone give up the benefits of, say, agriculture and revert to hunting and gathering? Or the benefits of rational monotheism for backward shamanic cults? Obviously such reversionary peoples must be infe-

19. Thomas and Humphrey (1996)

rior, unless they simply had no choice in the matter. But this old progressivist view is no longer so popular. The new orthodoxy implies that because of reversion all "primitivity" is suspect. The pristine ethnographic subject does not exist as an object of cognition. The neo-conservative version of this orthodoxy goes on, therefore, to critique all positive evaluations of "primitive" as mere romanticism or special pleading. The views of such anthropologists as Sahlins and Clastres are under attack as out-moded 60s hippie hot air. There are no "primitives" at all, much less "good" primitives. Any enthusiasm about the original leisure society, the economy of the Gift, or shamanic spirituality, is only a leftist illusion covering up the real reality of "eternal Market values" and the preordained triumph of technology, etc., etc.

A great deal of this new orthodoxy depends on certain presuppositions it makes about "reversion". The old evolutionist prejudice is still at work, to the point where reversion can be seen as a nullification of all meaning. The word "reversion" is used to end a discourse that it should instead inaugurate. In Clastrian terms, reversion can be interpreted as a *victory* against the emergence of "higher" forms of separation and hierarchy.

To illustrate this contention I must first begin by describing the Effigy Mounds of Wisconsin. The following section consists of a number of quotations from my own unpublished field-notes, based on two summers (1993-94) during which I saw perhaps a hundred of these mounds.[20]

The "Driftless Region" consists of a large chunk of Southern Wisconsin, with slivers in Iowa, Minnesota and Illinois. It's called the "driftless" because during the last Ice Age (ironically known as the "Wisconsin Glaciation" since it was first studied by geologists in the northern part of the state), the glaciers passed around this region, encircling it but not touching it, so that the earth was not flattened and stretched as in the rest of the northern part of the continent, but retained its primordial pre-Pleistocene form, gradually eroding into a landscape of "hidden valleys" and low hills, a mixture of prairie and climax forest. This region coincides precisely with the area in which the effigy mounds are found. The whole eastern half of North America is littered with mounds of various kinds, but most of them are architectural (temples, forts) or funerary tumuli. Effigy Mounds, by contrast, are built in shapes, mostly of birds or animals but also of humans and objects; they are very obviously neither military nor architectural, and only about half of them contain burials. Because they are so different from all other prehistoric American mounds, they remain baffling, mysterious, and even a little bit embarrassing to orthodox archae-

20. A dossier was compiled, and a xerox copy of the entire work can be acquired from Xexoxial Endarchy, Route 1 Box 131, La Farge WI 54639. My notes and books are still in Wisconsin and I may not have every reference at hand. I would like to thank Jan Beaver, Adrian Frost, Merlin Redcloud, James Scherz, Ernie Boszhardt (the State Archaeologist in La Crosse), Brad Thales, John Kilis, John Ward, Merton Everline, Robert The, Soren Sorenson, Fly, Brad Will, Eddy Nix, Patrick Mullins, Miekal And, Elizabeth Was, and the Dreamtime Avocational Archaeological Group. However, I must emphasize that my interpretations are my own.

ology. As a result, they remain almost unknown outside the Driftless region itself— no glossy coffee table books, no prestigious museum exhibits; they are ignored even by most afficionados of "Mysterious America", UFOlogy, pre-Columbian contact theories, and the like. Since the 19th century, almost no interpretations of the Effigy Mounds have been propounded, either by archaeologists or occultists. In effect, the mounds have not yet "appeared" except as curiosities in a few state parks, or as the subject of a few obscure academic monographs.

This non-appearance of the mounds constitutes one of their great mysteries. Why are they not seen? Leaving aside the problem of interpretation, the immediate and most striking aspect of the mounds is their great beauty. Considered simply as "earth art" they assume at once a timeless and exquisite power; and the more one sees of them the more one realizes (despite the ravages of time, of agriculture, of archaeology, and of sheer wanton destruction, which have erased perhaps 80-90% of the mounds) that the entire Driftless region is a work of art, a worked geomantic landscape in which wilderness and culture have achieved a dialectical unity and aesthetic/spiritual cohesion. What does it all mean?—an interesting question—but not the essential question. First and foremost, the "meaning" of the mounds is not mysterious at all, but rather completely transparent:—the total enchantment of the landscape. This is not to say that the mound builders were "artists" in the modern sense—"mere artists"—or that the mounds have no other significance than the aesthetic impact of their actual physical presence. Indeed, if we consider the totality of the Effigy Mound "project" as a single art work, or as the transformation of the Driftless region itself into art, we must admit that aesthetics alone could not have animated such a vast vision. Spirituality, economics, and the "social" must have acted synergistically to create the "religion" or way of the Effigies, an entire culture (lasting from about 750 to 1800 AD) centered on mound creation as its primary expression.

As soon as we begin to investigate this culture with the epistemological tools of archaeology, however, the "mystery" of the Effigy Mounds deepens rather than dissipates—and this helps to explain the baffled silence or dull muttering of the academics in the face of such strange evidence. The Effigy Mound culture was preceded, surrounded, invaded, and superseded by "advanced" societies which practiced agriculture, metallurgy, warfare and social hierarchy, and yet the Effigy Mound culture rejected all of these. It apparently "reverted" to hunting/gathering; its archaeological remains offer no evidence of social violence or class structure; it largely refused the use of metal; and it apparently did all these things consciously and by choice. It deliberately refused the "death cult", human sacrifice, cannibalism, warfare, kingship, aristocracy, and "high culture" of the Adena, Hopewell, and Temple Mound traditions which surrounded it in time and space. It chose an economy/technology which (according to the prejudices of social evolution and "progress") represents a step backward in human development. It took this step, apparently, because it considered this the right thing to do.

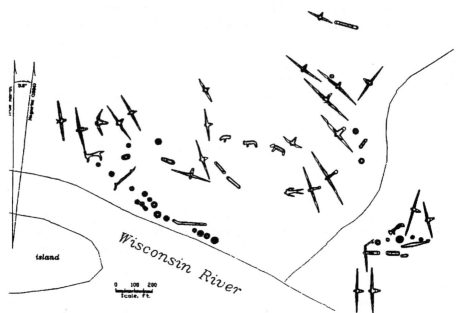

"Ghost Eagle Nest", Muscoda, surveyed 1886 by T.H. Lewis, re-surveyed 1993 by Jan Beaver, James P. Scherz, and the Wisconsin Winnebago Nation. Note Calumet pipe mound at lower right.

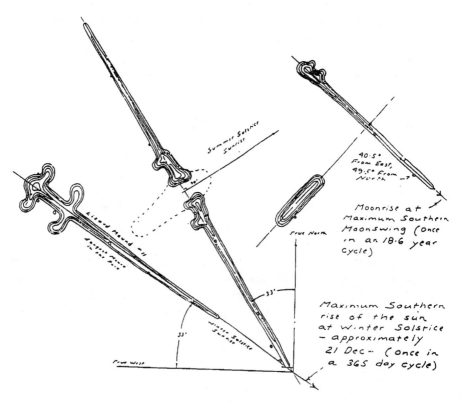

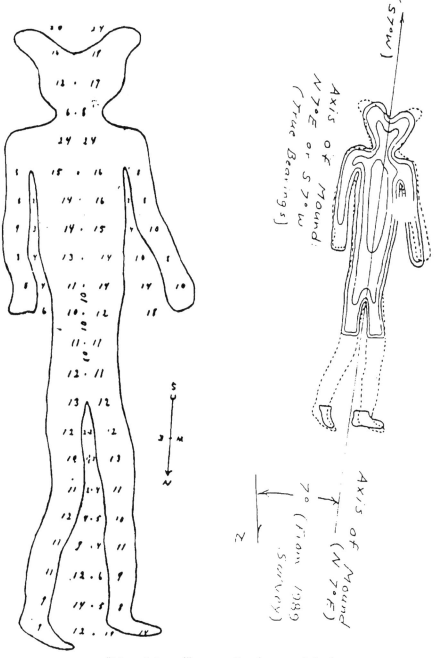

"Man Mound" near Baraboo, original
etching and 1989 survey showing damage.

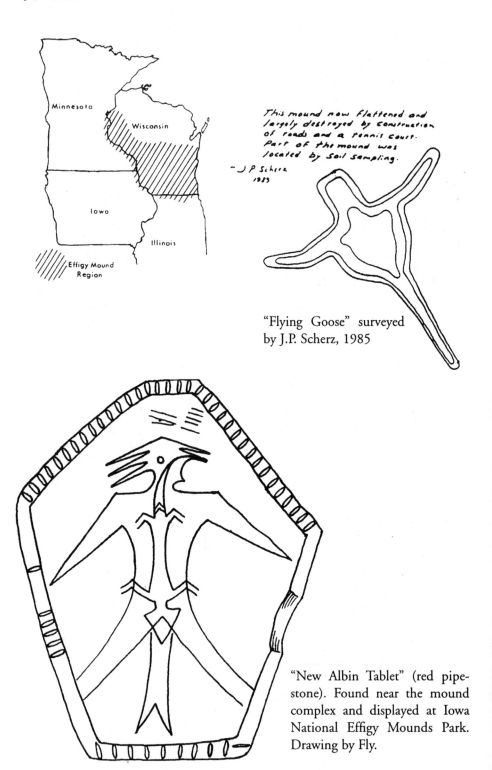

This mound now flattened and largely destroyed by construction of roads and a tennis court. Part of the mound was located by soil sampling.
— J.P. Scherz 1985

"Flying Goose" surveyed by J.P. Scherz, 1985

"New Albin Tablet" (red pipestone). Found near the mound complex and displayed at Iowa National Effigy Mounds Park. Drawing by Fly.

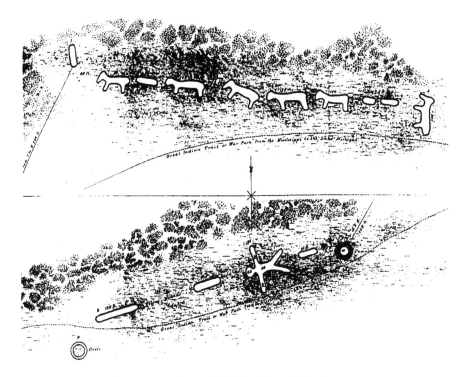

Above: Bear mounds at Iowa National Effigy Mounds Park.
Below: Monuments surveyed by Squier and Davis, 1848, no longer extant

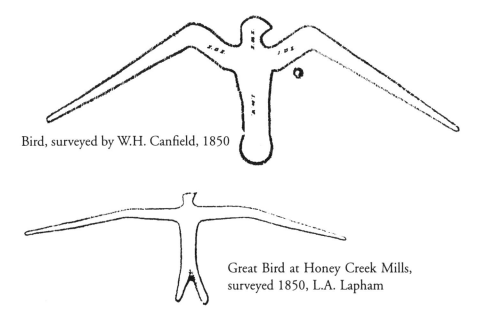

Bird, surveyed by W.H. Canfield, 1850

Great Bird at Honey Creek Mills,
surveyed 1850, L.A. Lapham

Most archaeologists lose interest in Effigy Mound culture as soon as they realize this "reversion". As *grave robbers*, they are disappointed by the poor or non-existent "grave goods" of the Effigy Mounds; and as *civilized scientists*, they are shocked and offended by the deliberate "primitivism" of a society that seems to have turned its back on the blessings of agriculture, architecture, work and war.

Since the 1960s, however, concepts have developed within *anthropology* which offer new epistemological tools for the interpretation of prehistoric *archaeology*. Marshall Sahlins, in his masterpiece *Stone Age Economics*, presented the first revisionist defense of hunter/gatherer societies as economies of excess (as opposed to the imposed scarcity of agricultural economics) and of immense "leisure" (as opposed to the endless work of the peasant). In the light of such an "anarchist epistemology" (to quote P. Feyerabend), we can now interpret hunter/gatherer cultures in the light of an actual *resistance* to social hierarchy and the emergence of "The State". This dialectic was traced by the brilliant French post-Structuralist anthropologist P. Clastres in his classic *Society Against the State*, and in his unfinished (posthumous) essay on "primitive" warfare, *The Archeology of Violence*. The point made by Sahlins, Clastres, *et al.* is that Hunter/Gatherer societies know very well what "progress" implies for the *victims of progress* (as opposed to the winners, the priest-kings and their house-slaves)—and they reject it by means of their very social organization. Hunters know, for example, how to limit population to ecologically appropriate numbers, and they *institutionalize* this knowledge. Later the knowledge is deliberately suppressed by agriculturist "nobles" who desire more and more shit-workers and peasants to support them. Agriculture is not the result of any "population explosion"—it is the cause.

The Effigy Mounds apparently have something to say (that is, to show rather than to tell) about the proper technique for humans to relate to "Nature", to the wild(er)ness, to the "Beauty Way", as some Native Americans put it—the way of harmony and guardianship. As one sees more and more of the mounds, the initial appreciation of them as "art" broadens and deepens into more subtle and complex categories—not only aesthetic but also spiritual and even "political". As these levels unfold, the "mystery" only intensifies, of course—and eventually evades all categorization.

The earliest commentators were so impressed by the Mounds of America that they invented an entire "mysterious race of Mound Builders" to account for them—people who couldn't be Indians—because how could the wicked degenerate Indians have created such great monuments? This racist hogwash has long since been dissipated. Whoever the Builders were or weren't they were certainly "Indians", and the Effigy builders were clearly ancestors of such tribes as the Winnebago. But why did they build? What do the mounds mean? All this remains a mystery—so much so that almost no serious interpretive work has been done on the mounds—as if they constituted an embarassment to "Science"! (Is "Science" easily embarrassed? Well, I've seen no mention in any archaeological text of the very obvious phallic mounds. And at the Effigy Mounds National Monument Park Museum in Iowa we saw an astounding tablet carved out of red pipestone, the so-called "New Albin Tablet", which has apparently never been published—because it depicts a shaman with an erection! (See page 97) This work is vital for our thesis—but scientific prudery has placed it on a high shelf, out of the view of children, and even adults have to stand on tip-toe to see it.)

Some "facts" about the Builders have been determined. They are said to constitute a recognizable culture or group of cultures, associated with distinctive pottery, tool-kit, grave-goods, etc. They built from around 500/600 AD to 1600/1800 AD, and flourished around 1000 AD. They were limited to the Driftless Region and a few outlying areas. They got the idea of mound-building from a culture which preceded theirs and overlapped with it in time, called "Hopewell". The Hopewell mounds however are all conical burial mounds, not effigies. Moreover, the Hopewell was a highly stratified society which produced a lot of luxury items and buried them along with their aristo owners in a kind of death-potlach—an archaeologist's delight. The Effigy Mound Builders however did not build their mounds only as burial sites, and did not indulge in "rich" burials at all. Many of the linear, compound, and effigy mounds contain no burials. The Builders seem to have adopted a consciously-maintained lifeway of "voluntary poverty", at least as far as technology was concerned. An egalitarian hunter/gatherer society by choice, they put their creative ability into the communal art of the mounds—not into luxury goods for an elite. However, they need not be seen as a "poor" people in terms of comfort. They inhabited an area which must have been a total paradise for hunter/gatherers—the whole region was their collective larder, and they moved around in it by season, hunting and feasting—and working on the mounds.

A. Clark Mallam, one of the few archaeologists to attempt an interpretation of the mounds, sees them as serving the function of border-markings and meeting-places between separate social groups, who thus symbolized their agreements to share the wealth of the Driftless Region. He calls the Mounds a system of social integration. He suggests that this thesis is supported by demonstrable differences in style among the various mound-complexes—*i.e.*, that they were built by different groups. He believes that this kind of contractual behavior must account for the obvious peacefulness of the Builders' society, the lack of evidence for slavery, cannibalism, social hierarchy, or any emphasis on war.

Stylistic variations within the Effigy Mound Culture as a whole are indeed discernable—but might also be accounted for by differences in function. Of course the Builders were divided into clans and phratries, secret societies, perhaps even language groups. But what if different mounds served different purposes? Would this account for some of the observable stylistic variation? I find Clark Mallam's hypothesis thought-provoking but limited.[21] It may be a grave error to think of the mounds as symbols of "ownership" of various territories defined by "boundaries". These are very European ideas. Utilization is not the same thing as "ownership". The Driftless

21. Mallam (1976); see also Hurley, *The Journal of the Ancient Earthworks Society*, and Lapham (1855). After writing this essay I learned that Clark Mallam, before his death,

Region was so rich in game and plants that the few thousand or so Builders could easily share. The Mounds undoubtedly served an integrative function, but I suggest that the integration could have gone much deeper than the level of mere contracts. I believe we're looking at an integrated culture, sharing what may be called (for convenience) a "religion of Effigies". No doubt this "religion" began and continued as a "congeries of cults" rather than a centrally-organized and dogmatic "Church". This would help to account for the stylistic variation, just as it helps to account for stylistic variation in the temples of Taoism and Hinduism. The mound-complexes however were obviously not "temples", not buildings where deities were worshipped, but something else altogether.

In terms of spatial orientation the mounds have a certain quality of "aboveness"—that is, they might best be appreciated from above, a bird's-eye or spirit's-eye view. Moreover many of them are placed high, typically on bluffs overlooking water. The Wyalusing and Effigy Mound National Monument complexes command vast views and far-distant lines of sight. (This would be more apparent in an old-growth forest setting or prairie where trees would have been farther apart than now, thus opening up more views. Moreover the Builders could easily have cleared away all

---

changed his mind about the Mounds. Clearly he had been talking with "Native informants":

> A more encompassing view has recently emerged. Focusing on ideology, this new approach uses elements from the other interpretations, but relies heavily on information derived from historic Native American belief systems. Essentially, it stresses relationships. Its proponents believe that the mounds are not only burial sites and territorial demarcators, but actually are metaphorical expressions that stress the idealized state between nature and culture—harmony and balance.
>
> This theme of balance, recurrent throughout Native American cultures, emphasizes the tenuousness of order in the universe and the reciprocal relationships that exist among humans, uniting them as a people with those life forces upon which they depend. In this sense, the effigy forms are cosmic representations of these life forces— structured messages about a people's cosmological conviction graphically displayed across the landscape.
>
> The ongoing practice of mound building dramatized the cosmological conviction and reaffirmed the relationships. To participate in it strengthened human bonds and contributed toward order and balance in the universe. Mound building, then, functioned as a ritual of lifeway reinforcement and world renewal. To these hunting and gathering peoples, it represented the social means for insuring the continuation of the annual cycle of life, expressed in seasonal regeneration of plants and animals. Perhaps this explains why the effigies appear to be integrated with the earth while they simultaneously emerge from it—the mounds symbolize the cyclical regularity of life itself, ever-changing, always the same, constantly being reborn.

See Mallam (1995). Thanks to Ron Sakolsky for lending me this pamphlet.

view-obstructing vegetation using controlled fire or selective cutting, to create Mound-parks with tremendous vistas. Needless to say, this would not have been an exercise in "pure aesthetics", but would have had specific ceremonial and spiritual purposes.) Some of the most severely eroded or plowed-under effigies have been rediscovered by aerial photography. Many mounds depict birds.

If the mounds are related to sky events then perhaps the most important such event is the shaman's flight into the sky, or "cloud-walking".

Clark Mallam makes a useful contribution by suggesting that the mound-complexes served as ceremonial and festal sites, linked to areas of intense seasonal hunting/gathering activities (where large groups could feast together on whatever was in season). It appears that people who died in the winters stayed unburied (as bundles of bone) until the clan arrived at one of the mound-complex meeting-places in the spring or summer. Perhaps the mounds were seen as doorways for the spirits of the dead to enter the Other World of the stars. Undoubtedly, however, life was served as well as death. Some of the complexes have been interpreted as initiatic sites. Contemporary Winnebago shamans, for example, have identified at least part of the "Ghost Eagle Nest" group (the mounds in the lower right-hand corner of the outline map) as the setting for a kind of initiatic procession, which would pass between the wings of the two parallel eagles in order to arrive at the calumet-pipe. (See figure, page 92.)

Some of the most convincing interpretations of the Effigy Mounds come from precisely the people whom one would expect to possess authentic knowledge about them, *i.e.*, the real "locals", the original inhabitants of the mound area, the Winnebago—who in fact claim that their ancestors built the Effigies. Unfortunately, since they are no longer building mounds, the anthropologists (like P. Radin) have largely ignored their interpretations, which in any case are closely guarded as secrets by the tribal elders. Most archaeologists ignore the Winnebago for the same reason. Luckily, I was able to meet a Winnebago man of knowledge, Merlin Redcloud, who not only showed or directed me to many important and obscure sites, but also shared with me his interpretations to the extent he deemed possible, given his deep attachment to a tradition that cannot be fully revealed to outsiders. The following notes record our first meeting, at Lila's Cafe in Muscoda, WI, with my friend Eddy Nix, and Merlin's relative John Ward:

> Merlin Redcloud gives us too much information! He goes through the Wisconsin atlas with us page by page pointing out unpublished sites.
>
> Merlin and his nephew John explain their commitment to Winnebago (Ho-Chunk) spiritual paths. John mentions a woman relative who had four religions including Christian, traditional, and Peyote (Native American church), and practiced each one in its own context. They believe that in order to get along they must "walk with one moccasin in each world." They feel the Winnebago have a head start at this because they have never had a reservation. Lacking the cocoon, they went through their "white-ification" process early and learned how unsatisfactory it was....hence the

enthusiastic return to tradition even among the young. The Winnebago who got a reservation in Nebraska have only one medicine bundle and appear to have forgotten most ritual. Jo Anne Funmaker, the tribal chairperson, bridges the gap between the elders—whom she respects and consults—and the official tribal government. (Her "reign" was apparently predicted by the elders.)

According to an interesting pamphlet by Chuck Kingswan, *Ho-chunk History = A Glimpse: Notes to America = Word's Straight From the Source's Mouth = From the Ice Age to the Nuclear: Thoughts for All Ages*:[22]

Ho-chunk are here to stay.

The Great Lakes region has hosted Ice Age glaciers no less than eight times in the past million years, each living glacier scouring and moulding the countryside, gouging fingerprints of giants as a legacy to fill the legends of people yet to come. As the ice fields fled north for the last time their tracks soon felt footprints of a people of that day. Where they came from, no-one knows. Where they went is hard to say, except that their kind went from the ice age to the future. However it may have been, Hochunk words today still echo of ice age days: The short faced bear, dead and gone for these 10,000 years, lives on in name, "hoonch ah se lech". An archaic name for the Mississippi, draining the giant glacial lake far to the north, that once covered parts of what are today Minnesota, North Dakota, Ontario and Manitoba. And the equally archaic derivitive of that name, "nee goo sak hoo xhoon noomp", given to the Wisconsin River, which means, "Swift Drain River #2," maybe reflects that river's history as a secondary route for glacial waters streaming the seas.

"Hoonch ah se lech, nee koo sak hoo xhoon", "nee koo sak hoo xhoon noomp", these names speak ties to when ice fields were recent and the lands were still fresh. Glaciers have come and gone. Hochunk names have come and stayed.

*In other words, "Winnebago" language is coded with memories of the Ice Age.*

The Elders apparently agree with some archaeologists on the dating of the mounds, 750 or 1000 AD up to 100 years ago, but I couldn't get Merlin to discuss why they started and why they stopped; I got the distinct impression this was a "secret". The Elders can interpret the mounds according to oral tradition, sometimes in great detail. Some mounds are historical markers (wars, treaties, migrations, etc....), some are maps of journeys, some are calendrical. (Merlin mentioned a Winnebago solar clock based on a 20 hour day, key to many alignments, he says.) The wonderful thing about the Elders' interpretation is its *complexity*, which feels like a sign of its authenticity. Some single mounds are territory markers

22. Kingswan (1990)

(clan hunting grounds). About 50% are funerary. Large groups of conicals often mark battle site burials. Effigy burials are often of high initiates, sitting position at heart or head of effigy. The "altars" may be fireplaces for sweat lodges to prepare the worker/artists. When I asked Merlin if mounds were exclusively the work of men (i.e. as opposed to women) he misunderstood me to mean "mortals" and said, "No, some were built by spirits." (A shaman is told in vision that he will see such and such a spirit in person at such and such a place...goes there and finds newly built effigy.) Some mound groups are ceremonial, initiatic, celebratory (such as Eagles Nest near Muscoda) or agricultural (astro-alignments for planting) or downright magical. A "Religion of Effigies", complex as any true religion, organic, accretionary, multivalent.

...

Despite the fact that it was still pouring rain we left the cafe and drove over the Wisconsin River bridge to Eagle Township where Merlin showed us the newly-discovered (by him and Adrian) Eagle mound, just inside a copse of woods near Eagle Mill Creek, near a mowed field. The mound was in excellent shape, but overgrown with trees which seem *older* than surrounding trees including a triple trunked tree on the head.

Very beautiful and moving in the rainy woods. We talked about eagle mounds and agreed that some could be actual sites for meditation/fasting to acquire "cloudwalking" power. He told some tales of cloudwalking in the old days (e.g. a war party with two shamans travels in two days to Southern Iowa; an 80 year old shaman arrives at the journey's goal two days before the young men, etc....). He spoke of training others, including his own children, how to fast, how to "meditate" (my term) by inner spontaneous prayer, how to not get "scared half to death" by certain events, how to become fully adult, how to increase fasting period from two to four days on to longer periods, how to bear up under harsh conditions. (Merlin told a funny story of his own experience bitten by millions of gnats. I called it his "gnat quest!") He spoke of trying to recover cloudwalking wisdom at Eagle's Nest. I replied that even if the technique was lost, the *vision* of it was still alive.

[Note: the "Eagle's Nest" is a group of mounds near Muscoda which is now the property of the Winnebago people, who hope to restore it and use it as a tribal center. An amazingly huge eroded eagle-mound was identified here by aerial photography. I was introduced to Eagle's Nest—and to obsessive mound-viewing!—by Jan Beaver, a Native American woman who played an important role in publicizing the site, and who died in a tragic accident in 1993. The "Adrian" mentioned in the notes is her husband, the British artist Adrian Frost.]

The "silence of interpretation" that surrounds the Effigy Mounds owes something to embarrassment, since the 19th century indulged in orgies of speculation on the "mysterious Mound Builders" and propagated notions that now appear quite absurd. Interestingly, however, the old moundophiles showed very little interest in the Effigy Mounds, instead reserving their admiration for the architectural and funerary mounds of the Cahokian/Mississippian culture. An entertaining book on the history of 19th century mound-mania, R. Silverberg's *Mound Builders of Ancient America:—The Archaeology of a Myth*,[23] records that

> A certain J. W. Foster, writing in 1873 about the ancient mounds of America, subscribed to the current theory that the "Red Man" had nothing to do with such monuments.
>
>> His character, since first known to the white man, has been signalized by treachery and cruelty. He repels all efforts to raise him from his degraded position: and whilst he has not the moral nature to adopt the virtues of civilization, his brutal instincts lead him to welcome its methodical labor; he dwells in temporary and movable habitations; he follows the game in their migrations; he imposed the drudgery of life on his squaw; he takes no heed for the future. To suppose that such a race threw up the string lines of circumvallation and the symmetrical mounds which crown so many of the river-terraces, is as preposterous, almost, as to suppose that they built the pyramids in Egypt.

The author of the official History of Richland Co. (1884) projected such proto-eugenicist attitudes onto the builders of the Effigy Mounds when he wrote,

> The historian, looking back away down the dim corridor of time, perceives faintly in the mythical light of that far off, pre-historic period, before the red man's foot had desecrated its soil, the traces of a race who evidently peopled these hills and valleys of Richland County; a race who lived in semi-barbaric civilization, akin to that of the Aztec that Cortez found on the plains of Mexico; a race who lived and died and left no trace of their existence except the mysterious mounds and ridges that they have built that mark the site of their ruined buildings; a race of whom no tradition even exists from which their history can be written; a people of mystery, and probably ever to remain so—the Toltecs or Mound-builders.

Silverberg does a good job of showing how the myth of the Mysterious Lost Race of Mound Builders was finally debunked and trashed by official Smithsonian archaeologists such as Cyrus Thomas. Silverberg also describes how a good deal of interesting bath water got thrown out along with the mysterious but bogus baby. Mound Builder mythology was not entirely or simply racist; it also embraced a plethora of "damned" facts and theories (as Charles Fort would say) some of which might have been worth saving.

Silverberg has a lot of fun with one William Pidgeon and his remarkable book: *Traditions of De-coo-dah and Antiquarian Researches: Comprising Extensive Explo-*

23. Silverberg (1968)

*rations, Surveys, and Excavations of the Wonderful and Mysterious Earthen Remains of the Mound Builders in America: the Traditions of the Last Prophet of the Elk Nation Relative to their Origin and Use; and the Evidences of an Ancient Population more Numerous than the Present Aborigines* (1852). Pidgeon claims to have acquired a Native informant in the person of De-coo-dah, last of the Elk Nation, the original mound builders. A great deal of Pidgeon's book can be dismissed as pure hooey; apparently he had a technique of measuring mounds with some kind of hallucinometer. As for De-coo-dah (if he existed) he clearly enjoyed a vivid dream life as well. However, however...Pidgeon's eye is not always cocked. In Muscoda, for example, he spotted mounds, "some resembling redoubts or fortifications, others resembling the forms of gigantic men, beasts, birds wild reptiles among which may be found the eagle, the otter, the serpent, the alligator, and others pertaining to the deer, elk, and buffalo species." Some of these mounds may have been missed by the (much more scientific) T.H. Lewis in his later survey of the region, and are only now being "re-discovered" again around the Ghost Eagle area. As for De-coo-dah, his technique of mound interpretation seems in some ways structurally similar to that of, let's say, the Winnebago Elders quoted by Merlin Redcloud, even though the actual *content* of De-coo-dah's versions may differ widely from any known Native traditions. For example:

> "My great-grandfather," De-coo-dah told Pidgeon, "had a great reverence for mounds; and said that a new mound was erected at each national festival; the national festivals were frequently attended and held in union by several nations; at the place appointed for these union festivals, each nation erected a national monument significant to their number and dignity."
>
> Pidgeon now sets forth, via De-coo-dah, a symbology of the mounds, that for all its incoherence has about it the fascination of lunacy, like some monstrous bridge constructed of toothpicks. The revelation begins with an account of the so-called Amalgamation Mound, on the Wisconsin River about fifty miles above its junction with the Mississippi. This, according to Pidgeon, is a group of effigy reliefs and conical mounds stretching several hundred feet, presenting in outline the forms of two gigantic beasts, together with a well-delineated human figure. It was constructed, he asserts, "as a national hieroglyphic record, to commemorate an important event in the history of two great nations. These nations, once great and powerful, had become greatly reduced in numbers and resources by the adverse fortunes of war against a common enemy. Being no longer in a condition to maintain separately their national existence they resolved to unite their forces, subject to one great head or Sovereign ruler. And this earth-work was constructed as the great seal and hieroglyphic record of their

union and amalgamation." De-coo-dah interprets the hiero-glyphs. ("Horns appended to effigies represent warriors. One horn being longer than the other, shows one nation to have been the stronger of the two; and one horn having more prongs than the other, represents one nation having more celebrated chiefs than the other, while some prongs, being longer than the others, represent some of the greater and more distinguished chiefs.") Truncated mounds were sacrificial altars; the figure pointing to the west symbolized the setting sun of the amalgamating nations; the human figure looking up at the noon sun stood for the great-ness of the united powers. A stately oak firmly rooted in the bosom of the mound told Pidgeon that at least four centuries had gone by since its construction; but, he adds sourly, "The tree has since been removed and converted into shingles, and, in 1844, it formed a canopy over the drunken revels of Muscoda."

According to De-coo-dah, one earthwork is a "mound of extinction," marking the end of the nation symbolized by the buffalo effigy; for the Buffalo nation was uniting with the Elk nation when this mound was erected. The left forelimb of the buffalo is connected with the foot of the elk effigy. Nearby are "seven truncated mounds running east from the national mound." They are "matrimonial memorials" recording the inter-national marriages of seven chiefs, which occurred during the construction of the work. And so on, for many more pages of detail about amalgamation monuments, in which two or more animal effigies are joined. Three small mounds extending from the third matrimonial memorial denote the birth of three chil-dren; the great length of the arms of the human figure represent immense territorial domination; the even elevation of both arms signifies the equal status of the Buffalo and Elk nations in the merger. "Thus aided by tradition," comments Pidgeon, "we read in the hieroglyphical mounds of the earth, the dignity and des-tiny of nations unknown to written history," and he hopes that "a comparatively small portion of the funds expended in superficial surveys" of the mounds will go instead to "the acquisition of Indi-an traditions from the more secluded sons of the forest."

There are those who would call Mr. Pidgeon the Carlos Castaneda of the 19th century (or Castaneda the Pidgeon of the 20th!). Both of them are practitioners of some kind of anthropo-mythopoesis. Let's admit that Castaneda's *value* is not for "science", but for...something else. Perhaps then we can admit that some *value* can be salvageable even from Pidgeon and other "Mound Builder" theorists. Not every crackpot is an evil racist; the very word *crackpot* is a double-edged sword in hands such as ours. And a "crank" (as E. F. Schumacher used to say) is a small device that causes revolutions.

Like most *science*-fiction writers of the Old School, Silverberg fetishizes modern orthodox scientific dogma. Thus having cleared away the cobwebs of superstition in the first half of his book, he devotes the second half to the "actual facts" uncovered by "real" archaeologists. (As a writer of science-*fiction*, of course, Silverberg can't help confessing to a "warm understanding" of the myth-makers [p. 337], even though he must sadly reject their work as mere "fantasy".) In fact, his summary of the current (1968) theories of Adena/Hopewell/Temple Mound development is as clear and concise as anything I've seen…a good deal *more* clear than most archaeology texts. Maybe *too* clear.

According to this view, at about the time of the emergence of the Effigy Mound culture in the Driftless region, the Hopewell/Temple Mound development had climaxed in a great "empire" which covered most of the southeastern portion of North America, including the Mississippi Valley as far north as Aztalan in Wisconsin (and possibly the Great Lakes copper mines). Mesoamerican influence can be felt clearly in the great artistic attainments of the Temple Mound culture, even though (according to Silverberg) very few specific Mexican motifs can actually be traced in North America. Many people experience a frisson of dark weirdness in contemplating Temple Mound art, a sensation akin to that evoked by a certain blood-thirsty formalism in Mayan and Aztec motifs. In effect, Mississippian culture seems to have devoted its entire creative energy to a potlatch of death in which a peasant class labored to produce vast amounts of art, including personal ornament, for the sole purpose of burying it all along with the corpses of kings and noble families in vast and elaborate conical mounds. Human sacrifice is strongly indicated, also cannibalism. Vast fortifications testify to the development of genuine (as opposed to "primitive") warfare. Some archaeologists interpret all this as a religious movement, rather than as a political "empire", and call it the "Southern Death Cult".

The Effigy Mound builders certainly inherited and learned a great deal from the Hopewell/Temple Mound culture. For one thing, they continued to build Hopewell style conical mounds, and to use at least some mounds (both conical and effigy) for burials.

However, if the Effigy Mound builders accepted and used some Mississippian concepts and motifs, we should remember how many things they *refused*. The Effigy Mounds reveal no archaeological evidence for agriculture, class hierarchy, human sacrifice, or even warfare. If the Effigy Mound people practiced warfare, it could only have been "primitive" low scale, almost playful, and (as Clastres points out) a "centrifugal" social force acting against the centralization and institutionalization of power.

Temple Mound warfare, by contrast, must be called true classical warfare, since it apparently involved the permanent subjugation of enemy people, and constituted a *centripedal* process of power centralization. No doubt it would be going too far to suggest that the "Religion of Effigies" represents a kind of "Protestant Reformation" in its relation to the "High Church" of the Hopewell or the Southern Death Cult. But it begins to appear that the Effigy Mound builders deliberately rejected the death obsession, cruelty, and oppression of the Temple Mound culture, in favor of a "return" to an "earlier" way of life, perhaps viewed as a "purification." The Hopewell/Temple continuum demonstrates a religion based on "animal totems"; perhaps the Effigy builders proposed a radical return to such "roots", to an "oldtime religion" that would appear utopian, egalitarian, and life-oriented by comparison with the "decadence" of the Southern Death Cult. Above all, the Effigy Mound religion would be a spirituality of wild(er)ness, as opposed to the civilization of Temple Mounds. It would thus constitute a return to "nature".

Some remnants of the Southern Death Cult apparently survived into the "historical" (post-1492) period in America. Most notably (according to Silverberg) the Natchez of Mississippi:

> The Natchez government was an absolute monarchy. At its head was a ruler called the Great Sun, who was considered divine and had total power over his subjects. "When he [the Great Sun] gives the leavings of his dinner to his brothers or any of his relatives," wrote one of the French observers, "he pushes the dishes to them with his feet...The submissiveness of the savages to their chief, who commands them with the most despotic power, is extreme...if he demands the life of any one of them he [the victim] comes himself to present his head."
>
> The Great Sun's foot never touched the bare earth. Clad in regal crown of swan feathers, he was carried everywhere on a litter, and when he had to walk, mats were spread before him. He and a few priests were the only ones permitted to enter the temple atop the mound, where an eternal fire burned, and the bones of previous Great Suns were kept. When a Great Sun died, his entire household—wife and slaves—was killed to accompany him in the afterlife.
>
> The immediate relatives of the Great Sun were members of a privileged class called "Suns." All of the important functionaries of the tribe were chosen from the ranks of the Suns, who were regarded with the greatest deference by the lower orders. Beneath the Suns in importance was a class called the "Nobles." Beneath them were the "Honored Men," and below them were a large

body of despised and downtrodden commoners known by the uncomplimentary name of "Stinkards." The class divisions were sharply drawn and there was no social mobility; once a Stinkard, always a Stinkard.

The unusual feature of this class system is the way it revolved from generation to generation. All Suns, including the Great Sun himself, were required to chose their mates from the Stinkard class. Thus every Sun was the offspring of a Sun and a Stinkard. The children of female Suns married to Stinkards were Suns themselves, but the children of male Suns were demoted to the Noble class. The son of the Great Sun, therefore, could never succeed his father, for he would only be a Noble. The Great Sun's successor was usually the son of one of his sisters, who, since Sun rank descended through the female line, had to belong to the highest caste.

The children of Nobles also had to marry Stinkards; the offspring of female Nobles were Nobles also; the children of male Nobles were demoted another class and became Honored Men. It worked the same way among them: the children of male Honored Men became Stinkards. Since there were always a great many more Stinkards than members of the three upper classes, most Stinkards married other Stinkards, and their children, of course, were Stinkards too. But a good many Stinkards were selected as mates for Suns, Nobles, and Honored Men, and so their children rose in class structure. The ones whose lot was least enviable were the Stinkard men who married Sun women. Although their children were Suns, these men had no power themselves, and were regarded simply as stud animals. They could not eat with their Sun wives, had to stand in their presence like servants, and might at any time be executed on a whim and replaced with another Stinkard.

As with many Indian tribes, the men ruled, but the power of descent was matrilineal. Female Suns elected the new Great Sun; females alone could transfer their rank to their children. It was an intricate and clever system which guaranteed a constant transfusion of new blood into each of the four classes. Whether this unusual arrangement was common to all Temple Mound peoples must forever remain unknown; but it seems safe to say that some sort of class system was found among them all, and probably an absolute monarchy as well. It could be that the Natchez, the last survivors, evolved this extremely specialized social structure independently, as a manifestation of a decadent culture's last surge of creativity.

The Natchez rebelled against the French in 1729. In a pro-
longed and bloody campaign, they were nearly wiped out; the
survivors were scattered among other Southeastern tribes, who
looked upon them as gifted with mystic powers.

This gives, I imagine, a very clear picture of just what the Effigy Mound
builders were refusing when they rejected the "High Civilization" of the
Temple Mound culture. Perhaps the Effigy Religion can even be interpreted as a "revolt of the Stinkards". Another way of tracing the "origins" of
Effigy Mound culture might be to view it as the axial point of a meeting
space between the vast spiritual sphere of Mesoamerican culture and that
of "Arctic shamanism". Until recently, orthodox archaeology has maintained that humans first arrived in the New World across the Bering Sea
Land Bridge shortly after the end of the last Ice Age (about 12,000 BC).
By now, however, this theory has begun to collapse under the weight of
problems and contradictions. For instance, if the first incursion took place
in Alaska, then Alaskan archaeological remains (such as the "fluted" flint
arrowheads of the Paleo-Indian period) should be *older* than comparable
material excavated to the south (such as the fluted arrowheads of California and the Southwest). Such, however, is not the case. In its way, the
Bering Strait Theory is as "racist" as the old Mound Builder myth, since it
implies, in effect, that the "Red Man" has only been here a few thousand
years longer than the Europeans, and consequently has no better claim to
"indigenous" status. (This theory usually also blames the Bering Strait
immigrants for wiping out the megafauna of the New World, including
the Mastodon, as if to say "these Indians were even worse ecologists than
we Europeans!" Palpable nonsense, of course.) In *The Quest for the Origins
of the First Americans* (1993), the Alaskan academic archeologist E. James
Dixon proclaims his conversion to the revisionist theory: that the Bering
Strait migration was the *second-to-last* arrival of humanity in the New
World. The *first* arrivals probably came island hopping across the Pacific to
South America and were here by 40-33,000 BC. This theory is based on
"hard" radio carbon dating and careful stratigraphical analysis from South
American sites, evidence which has been unjustly ignored by North American orthodoxy. A rock shelter as far north as Pennsylvania has been dated
to 17,000 BC. The Bering Strait monopoly has been broken. Even the Ho-
chunk Elders' theory, that the Driftless Region was inhabited *during* the Ice
Age, must be seriously reconsidered. The *long chronology* of American pre-
history once championed by such 19th century "heretics" as F. W. Putnam
(see Silverberg pg. 197ff) must be re-envisioned.

Because Silverberg follows so closely the party line of American academic archaeology, it's interesting to note his assessment of the Effigy
Mounds, as opposed to the Hopewell/Temple Mound cultural artifacts he
so much admires:

In some of these fringe areas of what is known as the Burial Mound II Period, mounds shaped in animal effigies and other odd forms were constructed. The link connecting these effigy-mound people to Hopewell is exceedingly tenuous. Most of the Northern effigy mounds which so excited Pidgeon were built quite late, maybe even in the Seventeenth or Eighteenth century, a thousand years or more after the end of Ohio Hopewell. They represent at best a distorted echo of the basic mound concept. These impoverished cultures, heaping earth together in low hillocks of curious shape, have little in common with the splendor of classic Hopewell.

In the first place, Silverberg is wrong about the dating of the Effigy Mounds, failing to grasp the nearly 1000-year span of the tradition. Second, he misinterprets the "poverty" of Effigy Mound culture as a sign of *inferiority*. The ill logic of this passage leads (unconsciously, I'm sure) back to clichés about "savage red men" who came "long after" the glorious "race" of Hopewell/Temple Mound Builders, and were able to produce only a few "odd forms" compared to the incomparable "splendor of classic Hopewell." This was the official view in 1968, and it appears to remain the official view even today. The sheer *lack of taste* of orthodox archaeology (not to mention its lack of curiosity!) in relation to the Effigy Mound phenomenon constitutes one of the deepest of all the "mysteries" of Mysterious Wisconsin.

If we wish to pursue the hypothesis of the Effigy Mound culture as a "revolt" or back-to-Nature religious revival directed dialectically at the surrounding Civilization of Hopewell and Temple Mound, then obviously we need to know a great deal more about the "Empire of the Sun" throughout the entire Mississippi Valley and Eastern US—and especially the Spiro-Cahokia manifestation—and especially its colonial intrusion into the north at Aztalan…. Aztalan seems to represent a particularly ghoulish exaggeration of the Temple Mound Civilization, especially in the well-documented practice of cannibalism; see the endless dreary photos of human bones cracked for marrow and tossed into refuse heaps, in *Ancient Aztalan* by S.A. Barrett (1993). The Aztalanians apparently recruited or enslaved some local tribes, but their paranoid defense system shows that local resistance against the Sun King must have been constant and fierce. Presumably the "foreign chiefs" ate only slaves and captives—but curiously enough no cemetery has ever been found near Aztalan—maybe in the end they ate each other! It seems possible to me that the great fire which destroyed the city was set by the Effigy builders, and that the effigy mounds near Aztalan were later built by them to "hold down" the evil spirit of the place. Frank Joseph claims that when the Winnebago Elders were given an opportunity to view the enigmatic "Spirit Stone" of Aztalan (found wrapped in birch bark in a bark lined chamber beneath one of the mounds, and weighing 162.5 lbs.), the old men "recoiled in horror."[24] Of the few authenticated burials at Aztalan, one is a hunchback "princess" adorned in thousands of mother-of-pearl beads; one is a headless giant; and another consists of two little boys buried with a turtle shell.... Scherz has demonstrated that the "ceremonial poles" at Aztalan made up part of a very complex observatory (sun, moon, and stars), and that the inhabitants must have been obsessed by *Time*.

All this contrasts quite vividly with the archaeological profile of the Effigy-builders, who (as Ritzenthaler remarks somewhere) leave us an impression of ascetic nobility and a sense of powerful conviction about the right way to live—a way that included no extremes of wealth, no social hierarchy, no civilization, no cannibalism—and an emphasis on space rather than time. It would constitute the worst sort of error to believe that these "primitive" people of the Effigies (or indeed any "primitive" people) were simply too innocent or too stupid to grasp the advantages of Progress and Evolution and Development. Since the Neolithic, at least, we cannot assume that any hunter/gatherer group anywhere in the world has remained innocent (or ignorant) of the nature of the State. As Clastres shows, "primitive" tribes understand the centralization of power perfectly, but (unlike the agro-industrialists) they have actively rejected such hierarchy, and have designed their social institutions to resist it. Think of "counting coup" as a tactic of "primitive warfare" or think for that matter of the very temporary nature of "chief-ship" in most Plains and Woodlands Indian tribes. If the Effigy builders had been truly "primitive" and innocent of any threat to the harmony of Humanity and Nature, why would they bother to build the mounds at all? Why not just leave Nature untouched, as a perfectly adequate "symbol of itself"? The Effigies constitute a conscious and deliberate "sermon in earth", a minimal but potent transformation of the landscape itself into a "message" about the right way to live, about "getting back into the cycle of Nature", as Merlin Redcloud put it. The telluric geomantic ethereal energies of Earth herself are channelized in the Effigies, just as the Australians crystallized them as song-lines or the Chinese as feng-shui. The Effigies amount to a Wisdom-Teaching—about animals, birds, plants—about landscape and Earth—about *dirt*.

24. Joseph (1992). This book belongs to the "pre-Columbian contact" school of American history, of which the late Dr. Barry Fell and Cyrus H. Gordon were the doyens. Professor James Scherz and many of my other informants, including Winnebago informants, adhere to this school. Although I have great respect for their theories and especially for their field work, I decided to construct the present text without depending on any of their speculations, since my theory neither conflicts with nor supports theirs. In other words, the "reversion" I have hypothesized could have taken place *whether or not* the Cahokian Civilization was influenced by, say, ancient Libya or Ireland.

Pleasant it looked
this newly created world.
Along the entire length and breadth
of the Earth, our grandmother,
Extended the green reflection
of her covering
And the escaping odors
were pleasant to inhale.
(Winnebago song)

It is a mistake to imagine that Native Americans began to think of themselves as "guardians of the Wilderness" only after 1492, in a dialectical response to the European threat of destruction. They had already faced such a threat *from within*. They were already politically and ecologically *conscious* in 1492—they had deliberately chosen non-authoritarian *society* over the centralized *State*—and a hunting/gathering economy of leisure and excess over the *Work* of agriculture. They had deliberately overcome the "Rise of Civilization". They had in fact burned Aztalan to the ground and chased the survivors all the way to Mexico, where they seem to have become the Aztecs (of course this is a "crackpot" theory...), the most civilized and cannibalistic of all New World cultures.

The Effigy "religion" holds power for us today—whether we be Ho-Chunk or Native or Euro-american. But I believe that this power and meaning do not derive from any "philosophy of defeat" at the hands of a State or a "Race" or a Civilization. The strength of the mounds lies in the fact that they represent a *victory*, not a defeat. Civilization has not always won all the battles, and has never successfully demonstrated the "inevitability" of its "march of Progress" as anything other than a *myth of power.*

When the first Europeans arrived in the New World, the old Sun-king/Death-cult civilization had nearly vanished from North America, leaving behind it thousands of architectural and funerary mounds to baffle such later savants as Thomas Jefferson. In a sense it would seem that the entire eastern half of "Turtle Island" had already refused the kind of development (or "progress") involved in the Meso-American model, the pyramid of sacrifice. The northern tribes had, by and large, already rejected "Civilization" and *reverted* to gardening and/or hunting economies, non-authoritarian political structures, "democratic shamanism", and the general way of life called "Woodlands" by the archaeologists. The "innocent savages"—who had no concept of "Nature" because they knew nothing that was *not* "Nature"—can no longer be allowed to dominate our view of North American "pre-History". In 1492 the natives already possessed institutions that had developed dialectically out of a conflict with separation and hierarchy. They had discovered that *wild(er)ness is something that can be restored—not as "innocence" but as conscious knowledge.* The philosophy of harmony with Nature that animates Native-American religious revival today is not simply a reaction to European appropriation and immiseration. It is in fact based on a much earlier "critique" of separation, and a struggle with emergent hierarchy that had ended with victory for the "Clastrian machine". Clear records of this dialectical struggle are difficult to trace, since it involved "reversion" to forms that evade the archaeologist. But one case at least left very clear traces. The Effigy Mound builders adopted the idea of the mound from Cahokian/Mississippian Civilization, but they changed the entire *meaning* of the mounds into a symbolic language that transpires both *within* Nature and *about* Nature simultaneously. If it were not for the ravages of time and the Wisconsin dairy industry, we would possess an entire "Koran", as it were, of "waymarks on the horizons" of Nature—a "Bible" of lessons about the correct relations among humans, animals, plants, and spirits. Most of the "book" is missing and the rest in fragments—but those fragments lie before us openly on the ground. As "words" in a language of images, each Emblem seems to hold within itself the fractal image of the whole System, the entire emblematic landscape. If we offer tobacco, and receptive silence, they may still speak.

### 5. REAL DONNYBROOK

In speaking of the Land-without-Evil, and the land of Effigy Mounds, we have remained so far on the borderland between pre-history and (written) history. Our next examples will come from an area that is also ambiguous, but at least presents us with some written texts—that is, *popular* history. Logically, if we search for the continued existence of the "Clastrian machine" in history, as opposed to pre-history, we must look first where we might well expect to find such traces—at the bottom of the social pyramid, the "zone of depletion", created by hierarchy. Among the poor and marginalized we will discern areas where the rights and customs of autonomy and pleasure persist in manifestation. Luckily for us, the poor—who were voiceless in old-fashioned evolutionist "History"—have acquired some keen listeners in recent decades among the "new" historians. Bakhtin, Le Goff, Gurevich, Le Roy Ladurie, Ginzburg, C. Hill, C. P. Thompson… with guides and interpreters like these, it should be possible to apply the anthropological model derived from Clastres and Taussig to some examples culled from popular history.

We can call the *carnevalesque*, as Bakhtin conceptualized it,[25] shamanistic if not overtly shamanic; in any case, a carrier of the "shamanic trace". Carnival after all has to do with *direct experience*, and moreover with *non-ordinary consciousness*—even if the experience concerns only a simple celebratory autonomy and the pleasure of the group, and even if the consciousness "arises" only from cakes and ale. Structurally the opposition between ordinary everydayness and the carnivalesque cuts deeper than the difference between a day of work and a day of leisure. This opposition can be traced in the symbolism of Breughel's agonistic vision of "Carnival and Lent":— it is a division in *time itself* between quantitative and qualitative, between separation and presence, between exchange and gift. The "holidays" are spaces missing from the pyramid of the year, areas where the "original" abundance and excess still appear.

25. Bakhtin (1984)

Some famous carnivals such as the Saturnalia existed as literal holes in a calendrical cycle with "left-over days" at the ends of solar years. These days are exempt from the "progress" of time and still "take place" in the era of Saturnus, the golden age from whence derive all rights and customs. Saturnian time is smooth compared to the striated time of History—and it does not come to an end. The secret of carnival is that every crack in the time-structure of hierarchy will be (re)occupied by the flow of primordial time from "before" separation, before division, before "money", before work. It's often said that medieval Europe enjoyed 111 holidays a year. We can have little feeling, I believe, for the extent to which all our cognitive categories are contaminated by the deliberate erosion of carnival by mechanical/industrial time (the U.S. enjoys only twelve "legal" holidays a year). No doubt we have dismantled the pyramid of feudalism, but we have simply used the blocks in constructing a vaster edifice based on subtler forms of oppression.

The neo-conservative critique of Bakhtin is that he over-emphasized the *rebellious* nature of carnival. The fact that it occurs on a regular (calendrical) basis makes it appear that carnival is not so much opposed to measured time as complicit with it. Carnival "lets off steam" (according to the mechanistic model favored by such critics) and releases the pressure of work-disciplines, so that the people may return to their places, satisfied with their moment of "relaxation". Carnival turns the world upside down only to "right" it again the next day.

Now obviously there's some truth in this—otherwise the neo-conservatives would look pretty foolish—but it's not the only truth. Nor is it true that carnival simply equals "rebellion" (nor did Bakhtin ever suggest anything so simple-minded). Obviously, if carnival is a periodic disruption then it is also a periodic renewal—and vice versa. The critique of Bakhtin is trivial. Carnival is *both*—and we may also say that it is *neither*. We can construct a much better model for carnival by reference to the "Clastrian machine". Saturnalia is a time or space within history which has so far resisted enclosure by "History", and where the old rights and customs have been successfully defended. A portion of the year has been lost—and a portion remains "free";—the "holidays" are the parts of the year that have not been colonized by rational time. Within the "free" portion of time we can expect to find "holiday customs" based on all the original institutions of the "Clastrian machine". The economy of the Gift comes into its own again, as does the economy of Excess. Shamanic symbols and practices appear as folk dance and music (e.g., Hungarian folk-music, with clear shamanic Central Asian roots), guising and mumming (ritual lycanthropy), consumption of psychotropics, appeasement of the Dead, mock sacrifice, mock healing (e.g., the figure of the "Doctor" in the Mummer's Play), re-appearance of "pagan" figures and motifs, etc., etc. There exist entire religious systems that are both shamanistic and carnivalesque, as Jim Wafer points out in his anthropological study of Brazilian Candomblé.[26] Religion may be the opium of the people, heart of a heartless world, in some cases—but in the case of the Afro-American syncretic

---

26. Wafer (1991). Wafer's Bakhtinian reading of Candomblé is extremely entertaining and convincing.

cults religion has been a locus of resistance to power from the very beginning. Group possession in the presence of a congregation is a sort of democratized shamanism, since everyone either gets to be a spirit or to meet one. And for certain spirits, all time is festival-time.

Finally, mock warfare or ritual violence plays a major role in festival-time, and re-creates obvious patterns of "primitive" war. Authoritarian Venice, for example, was forced for centuries to put up with the "War of the Bridges", which took place on holidays, in which "armies" of faction fighters engaged in huge pushing and shoving matches on the bridges between their rival neighborhoods. Serious injury was rare. The leaders were simply bold ne'er-do-wells who could lose all their "authority" with a single dunking in the canal. The combatants were all working-class, but the aristocracy took a strong fannish interest and gambled heavily on favorites. Even for Venice the fun became too extreme, and the outraged Doges finally managed to put an end to the custom.[27] In modern America, "Halloween violence" serves very much the same function, and is viewed with very much the same cold eye by Authority. Letting off steam after all must not threaten *lèse majesté*; in the modern world, violence is the monopoly of the State—or of Capital. And the "commercialization" of holidays is nothing but an attempt to break the autonomy of the festal moment by colonizing it with money.[28]

A fine example of holiday violence is the old Irish custom of the "Pattern" or "pardon" or (most correctly) "Patron", as in "patron-saint". On certain saints' days people made local pilgrimages to Holy Wells often known for miraculous healing powers. William Carleton has left us an excellent account of the Pattern in pre-Famine (1848) days when the old customs still flourished. Vast numbers participated in services, ascetic practices like walking on knees or crawling, circumambulation of the well, and other paganish or shamanistic rites. Booths were set up, a fair was held, drinking and dancing, sparking and courting. Eventually and inevitably a faction-fight would occur:—rival gangs of men would engage in chaotic drunken brawls, using ash-sticks, black-thorns and shilaleaghs. Faction-fighting took place at fairs (e.g., Donnybrook) and other occasions as well, but the Pattern is interesting for its combination of magic spirituality and unbridled carnivalesque celebration with ritual violence.[29]

Precisely the same structures can be found in folkloristic accounts of the ancient Celtic warbands—especially that of Finn MacCumhal and the Fena (or Fianna or Fenians). As they appear in such texts as the *Dunaire Finn* or the *Colloquy of the Ancients*, the Fena appear as something more than a simple *männerbund* but differently organized than an army.[30] They are a sworn brotherhood of initiates (they must excel at druidic and bardic skills as well as war), led by a man who is both poet and battle-chief. Finn MacCumhal, a hero of semi-divine status, in turn owes fealty

27. Davis (1994)   28. Santino (1994)   29. Donnybrook Fair in Dublin gave its name to this particular type of informal/ritual violence, and was finally banned by the British in the Victorian era. See Ó Maitiú (1995). 30. On the Fenian Cycle, see MacNeill (1908), Murphy (1933) and (1953); also see bibliography in Nagy (1985).

to the High King—but very significantly this "contract" only holds good for *half the year*. From Halloween to May Day—*i.e.*, winter—the Fena must guard the throne and fight the King's wars. But from May Day to Halloween—summer—they are free men, roaming through the green wood, hunting (mostly deer), feasting, drinking, brawling amongst themselves, pursuing love affairs, and experiencing countless adventures with the *Sidh*, the "fairy-folk" or Tuatha Dé Danaan who inhabit the old megalithic mounds. Ancient Indo-European shamanistic motifs abound in the Fenian material:—humans are transformed into animals, "poetic frenzy" is acquired by entheogenic substances such as magic berries (a clear parallel to the Vedic Soma Sacrifice, as I have argued elsewhere); magical flight, healing and hexing, trance music, poets wearing cloaks of birds' feathers—the shamanic "survivals" are countless. May Day and Halloween, the "hinges" of the year, are cracks in the structure of time through which the Dead and the Spirits find direct access to the human world. But these holidays mark out a period when the Fena themselves enter the timeless world—the Forest, or "*el Monte*", as the Cuban Santeros call it: the space of wild(er)ness, shamanic space. As J. Nagy points out in his excellent study of the Fenian material, this absence from Time makes Finn and his followers *outlaws*, very much like Robin Hood and his Merry Men.[31] But for the other half of the year Finn enters Time and the World of Order, and is "loyal to the King" (although sometimes he quarrels with the King, and finally opposes him). Robin Hood too in season comes to the party of order. But it is not the party of *unjust* order (the Sheriff of Nottingham and King John), but the party of justice. The good king Richard Lionheart symbolizes this justice by donning the green garb of the Merry Men—by embracing the chaos of the forest and the outlaw code. The good king includes both chaos and order, and thereby does justice to the old rights and customs of the commons. Among the Fena, however, the transition is seasonal: half the year for chaos, half for order—or rather, half for holiday, half for work. The outlaw in-laws. Here we have a perfect image of the "Clastrian machine" as it approaches History, still intact, but already half-enclosed by the forces of separation. Finn is the "champion of the people" and of their old ways (hunting, shamanism, reciprocity), but he can preserve a space for these customs only by conceding power to the new ways of agriculture, priestcraft, and exchange. (The conflict with Christianity is boldly depicted in *The Colloquy of the Ancients*, when Finn's son Oisín—last survivor of the pagan Fena—meets St. Patrick and defends the "old ways" against the new morality.)

　　The Finn of folklore reflects patterns of Celtic social structure that can be recovered from old law tracts, annals, and from archaeological evidence.[32] The petty kings of the Tuaths or tribal confederations (there may have been more than 100 of them in Ireland) lorded over nobles, free peasants, and "client tribes" (remnants of pre-Indo-European or pre-Celtic peoples), but a great many individuals fell out of the social net in various ways. Craftsmen were free to wander, as were bards and druids. Chief Bards were considered the equals of kings, and were followed by huge retinues. Nobles were obliged to provide hospitality to such free agents (and periodi-

31. Nagy (1985)　　32. Patterson (1994)

cally also to their subjects and lords) on pain of being considered "ungenerous"—the worst sin in the Celtic book, to be sure. Each Tuath was obliged to maintain a free hostel for travelers (early Irish pilgrims to the Continent and Rome were shocked to discover hotels that charged money!), and more than one ruler was ruined by such rules. War—a seasonal affair—was largely limited to near-ritual cattle-rustling, such as the theft of a prize bull that sparks off the Irish Iliad, the *Tain bo Culaigne*. But violence was woven into the whole social fabric:—all ancient commentators emphasize the courage, amounting to blind foolhardiness, of the Celtic warrior. The orderly English (who are cruel rather than merely violent) are disgusted by this disorderly behavior. In its degenerate forms such as faction-fighting the violence comes to seem quite pointless, the turning-on-itself of a conquered and powerless people. But we should not let liberal values blind us to the fact that while we have given up our "right" of violence into the hands of the State, the Irish held on to it in the realization that violence is a means of creating freedom. The brawl at the Pattern was a device that marked it out as a "temporary autonomous zone", a crack in the space/time of Order into which flows (for a brief moment) the smooth Saturnian time of intimacy, transformation, and pleasure. The Fena enjoy the positive aspects of "outlawry" (which are nothing but the old rights and customs of "natural" freedom) because they are always prepared to defend their prerogatives by violence. In Fenian times the State has not yet grown potent enough to monopolize violence; although its power already defines the course of time, the shape of society, the State must still permit power to abandon it for "half the year". The petty kingdoms of the Celtic period remained small enough that power was forced to the level of the personal, and obligated to the function of redistribution. And they retained this intimate scale because of the fissiparous violence of Celtic politics. No one seized a monopoly of power till Brian Boru, and he only succeeded because two centuries of Viking raids had shattered the fragile pattern of Celtic society. The Celts considered themselves a free and noble people, and they would have understood quite clearly Jefferson's remark about the tree of Liberty needing a watering of blood every few years.

## 6. Unseen Tracks

In "Shamanism in Siberia: From Partnership in Supernature to Counter-power in Society", R. N. Hamayon makes three structural points that are quite relevant to our present purposes:

1. Shamanism is only present as an all-embracing system in archaic, tribal, or noncentralized, societies. Therefore shamanism is generally considered to be elementary or primitive as a symbolic system or form of religion.

2. Shamanistic phenomena are also found in centralized societies, which points to the adaptive character of shamanism. However, though shamanism is primary in archaic societies, its manifestations in centralized societies

are not only fragmentary and altered but peripheral or even opposed to the central authorities; this is a sign of the structural weakness of shamanism. Related to this simultaneously adaptive and vulnerable property of shamanism as a system is the latent availability of shamanic practices in all types of society; this availability becomes manifest especially in crisis periods, when such practices easily revive or emerge.

3. Whether in tribal or centralized societies, one encounters an absence of shamanistic clergy, doctrine, dogma, church, and so forth. Therefore shamanism is usually characterized as a politically and ideologically limited or deficient system. In other words, although shamanic phenomena are found in state societies and may even play a role in state formation, shamanism as such is not found in the position of a state religion.[33]

Except for the suggestion that shamanism is "ideologically deficient", I would agree with this.(I would prefer to say simply that shamanism is *non-ideological*.) Hamayon's thesis certainly supports out notion of shamanism as a part of the "Clastrian machine", especially in its "opposition to central authorities." Elsewhere in *Shamanism, History and the State*, however, in C. Humphrey's "Shamanic Practices and the State in Northern Asia: View from the Center and Periphery", we are told of at least one example of a "shamanic state religion"—the strange case of Imperial Manchu Court shamanism. Till the end of the dynasty in 1911, the Manchu Court at Peking continued to celebrate the ancestral rites, clear variants of well-known Siberian and circum-Arctic shamanic practices. Is Hamayon's thesis wrong then, or is Manchu shamanism the exception that proves the rule?

When the Manchus founded the Ching Dynasty they brought shamans with them—but the "great (*amba*) shamans" failed or refused to make the transition from wildness (the "raw") to civilization (the "cooked")—only the *p'ogun* or "family shamans" were to be found at Court.

The *p'ogun samans* rapidly became different from what Shirokogoroff calls "real shamans." They did not undergo the psychic sickness and spiritual rebirth of shamanic initiation but were chosen mundanely by the clanchief (*mokun-da*) at clan meetings or else proposed themselves for service. The main one, the *da saman*, was elected annually at the autumn sacrifice. Almost all of them were unable to introduce the spirits into themselves in trance or to master any spirits. In effect, Shirokogoroff maintains, they became priests. At the court in Peking, they became a largely hereditary social class, responsible for maintaining the regular sacrifices for the well-being of the government and empire. The female shamans were the wives of court officials and ministers. By the mid-eighteenth century, if we are to believe what the Qianlong emperor Hongli wrote, the court shamans, who could hardly speak Manchu, had lost touch with earlier traditions and con-

33. Hamayon, in Thomas and Humphrey (1996)

fined themselves to a ritualistic repetition of half-understood formulae. The members of the imperial family personally preferred other religions. At this point, Hongli launched his great project of "remembering," that is, the researches to revivify Manchu cultural differences from the Chinese. Histories were written, or rewritten, to establish a direct relation between the present emperor's clan, the Aisin Gioro, and the imperial clan of the Jurchen Jin, and to establish its ancestral claims over the sacred Changbaishan Mountain in northeast Manchuria. As part of this project, in 1778, the emperor issued his famous edict to renew shamanist ritual, together with some preliminary discourses about the need to transmit the correct forms to posterity.

The emperor wished to revitalize shamanism, and I suggest that a central motive for this was the renewing of the link between the imperial clan and the forces of regeneration and vitality. But we shall see that his edict in the long run probably had the opposite effect.

Shirokogoroff's picture is tendentious. It is not so clear that the court ritual was much different from what I have termed patriarchal shamanism. In this sense we can talk of a kind of shamanic state religion until the end of the dynasty.

Inspirational and performative elements were perhaps not totally absent. The shamans at the Manchu court, if they did not go into trance, certainly invoked the spirits and "invited the ancestor spirits to enter the sacred space," and they used drums and other characteristic shamanic instuments. Prayers were distinguished from other kinds of more enraptured speech. In further sequences, with the light extinguished, the shamans "murmured in the dark" (*furbure*) and then prostrated themselves and sought "to appease the spirits and to attract their favour by flattering words (*forobure*)."

But whatever was inspirational in the new register of shamanism introduced by Hongli's edict almost certainly atrophied thereafter. One of the aims of the emperor was not only to distinguish and petrify Manchu shamanism, ("If we do not take care things will gradually change," he wrote), but to give it the civilized manners of Chinese Confucian ritual. The shamanic inspirational capacities of invention and imagination must have struggled under the weight of formally prescribed written prayers, decorous gestures, and delineated movements and sounds.

Only among the "raw" Manchus left living in the forests of the north was the culture preserved. Increasingly, the emperor came to see the clans and shamanism as the central features of Manchu identity.

The bureacratization of the Manchu state in the seventeenth century, the subordination of clans to the banner system, and the decorous idiom of court ritual expelled the great "wild" shamans from metropolitan religion and tamed the patriarchal clan shamans who remained. Nevertheless, in the discourse of ethnic exclusiveness that came to be seen as necessary for preserving the legitimacy of Manchu rule over a vast and rapidly expanding empire in the eighteenth century, shamanism had a key role. It was the context in which "pure" culture from the frontier revivified the center. Incorporation of external powers to the cult of ancestors provided a centralist ideology that was at the same time an identity for the Manchus. But the means chosen by the emperor, prescribed ritual and written liturgy, served only to negate the strength of shamanic practice, its ability to deal with new forms of power.[34]

Inasmuch as the Manchu Court shamanistic revival was a failure, it clearly follows Hamayon's thesis:—that shamanism and the State are incompatible. But after all the "failure" was extremely long-lived...perhaps "failure" is not quite the *mot juste*. I suggest that we have here a "strange" case of the operation of the "Clastrian machine" from *within* the very structure of hierarchy and separation. The Court's nostalgia for the heroic and visionary life of the "periphery", carried to the extreme of re-importing it to the "center", indicates that aristocracies as well as "commons" can be touched by the movement of the "Clastrian machine". But aristocracies transform "rights and customs" into *privileges and laws*. European nobility were also descended from barbarian steppe-nomads: their heraldry was also derived from shamanic imagery, and their customs (e.g., hunting) were prolongations of the *free life* of the nomad warriors within a world of hierarchy and appropriation: a Nietzschean notion of "freedom" as will to power.

The essence of shamanism is *direct experience*. As shamanism becomes aestheticized this experience is attenuated and more thoroughly mediated—but it does not disappear. As Lin Gui-Teng says in his essay on "Musical Instruments in the Manchurian Shamanic Sacrificial Rituals",

> In sacrificial rituals, shamans experience a change of identity from man to god and from god to man, that is, in sacrificial rituals, they go through such a process as inviting gods to come down, becoming gods incarnate, giving orders and directions in the identity of gods, and then becoming man again. When it is supposed that shamans have become gods incarnate, their behaviour becomes agitated. At the same time, waistbells and magic drums give off a burst of rapid and violent sounds, form a mystical, enchanting and heavenly atmosphere, in which shamans feel themselves possessed and controlled by an ineffable yet intense passion and rise involuntarily towards the heaven. This psychological experience of shamans is not to be confined to himself, but to be imparted to others through the sound of magic drums, waistbells, songs and dances. Shamans give directions in the identity of a god, and their assistants (called *zailizi* in Chinese) explain these directions to others, and complete this process of turning an individual experience into a social one.[35]

34. Humphrey (1996): 211-216    35. Kim, Hoppál et.al. (1995):118

A similar practice of attenuation from shamanic to aesthetic expression can be traced in the famous *Nine Songs* of ancient Chinese shamanism.[36] The union between deity and shaman has become suffused with eroticism and disappoint-ment—an aesthetic of intense longing for a direct experience that is vanishing. In a sense religious Taoism "saved" Chinese shamanism by adapting as its central praxis the *direct experience* of the shamans—complete with Registers of Spirits, trance, pos-session, ecstatic flight, and probably entheogenic substances as well (especially in the Taoism of Mao Shan, and the "Seven Sages of the Bamboo Grove"). The origins of the *Chuang Tzu* in particular should be sought in such a complex; Chuang Tzu was in a sense the first "urban shaman"! Taoism was able to "save" Chinese shamanism because both were *Chinese*. But Manchu Court shamanism was the religion (or rather one of several religions) of a tiny elite of nobles and bannermen, far removed from their ethnic homeland—whereas their subjects were largely Han Chinese. Court shamanism never had a chance to transform itself or mutate into a *popular* religion like Taoism. Moreover, Taoism as a popular religion began with the peasant revolt and utopia of the Yellow Turbans of the third century AD, and Taoism remained a "repository" for many strains of resistance:—bohemian excess, egalitari-an sentiment, "heresy", deviant sexuality, and open revolution. Taoism was never popular at Court (except with a few unfortunate eccentrics), and maintained a "tra-ditional" opposition to the Confucian ideals of the Bureaucracy. Above all, in its *techniques* of mysticism Taoism offered *direct experience*—an obvious danger in an Empire based on universal Imperial mediation. In all these respects, Taoism is a reli-gion *par excellence* of the "Clastrian machine"; and this aspect of Taoism can be attributed to its "shamanic trace". Manchu Court shamanism by contrast represents an attempt by hierarchy to appropriate and ideologize or *petrify* shamanic "power". But religious Taoism also developed its Court Hierarchy of divinities and spirits (a mirror of traditional Chinese Court structures), its dogmas and "ideologies", its authoritarian and apostolic "transmissions"—and the ritual aesthetics of Taoism and Manchu Court shamanism are not that different (at least in books, that is).

The ambiguity of Manchu shamanism—its confusion of centrifugality and centripetality—is revealed in the shamanic mythology of the Daur people, Mongo-lians who joined the Manchus as bannermen. They were partly civilized, therefore, but they also retained rural roots and maintained their "great" shamans. They believed in a composite or "multiple ancestor spirit" named

> Holieli, often called *Da Barkan* (the "great deity"). People made images of this spirit, which they kept in a box in their houses. It consisted, in the best known example, of fifty-eight separate parts: bald monsters, nine-headed monsters, half-people, single legs, left-side cripples and right-side cripples, some different kinds of turtle and tortoise, a leather softener, nine fishes, a hunting gun, a dragon, and nine dancing boys and nine dancing girls.

36. Chu (1973)

There are many versions of the story of this spirit, and the components of the images also vary. In a *story* of the Nonni River Daurs, the Holieli ancestor is an antelope that emerged from a rock split asunder by lightning. It ran straight to Senyang, where it began to harass the people. The Manchu government had it seized, placed in a bag of cow leather, and thrown into the river. It drifted down the river till it met the flood dragon, where the bag burst on the dragon's horn. The antelope pushed its way out of the bag, gained the bank, and once more began to harass the people. The Manchu court again had it seized, placed in a bag, loaded on a horse, and sent off. The horse followed its nose to the Amur River, where it was captured by a tribe of strange Tungus. They thought there must be something very nice in the bag and opened it. The antelope leapt out and took to the forests. It was chased by the lightning, which struck and struck, and many creatures were killed, but the deer escaped by sheer luck. It got to the Nonni River, near the Eyiler and Bitai villages. A man was ploughing. When the antelope spirit ran beside the man, there was a great crash of thunder, and everything was smashed into ninety-nine pieces. Since then, the antelope's spirit and those of all the people and animals killed by lightning joined forces for haunting and possessing people. First, it was worshiped by the Tungus, and then it was recognized as a spirit by the Manchu court, people say.

In a shaman's *song* for Holieli, the ancestor is smashed to pieces by lightning and becomes the half-people and crippled people. It starts from the end of the earth, which is at the source of the Ergune River. It is an old man, then it becomes a fish, traveling down the Jinchili River, gathering as it goes all the people of the clans and all kinds of animals. Its aim is the southern sea, the entourage of the Dalai Lama *(dalai* means ocean in Mongol). It raids the city of Peking and occupies the seat of orthodoxy. It is a loud voice yelling in the palace. It is given a jade throne, a pearl resting-place. From there it begins its journeys again, crossing all borders, passing through all boundaries; it reaches the Daur and becomes hidden in the plowblade of the farmer. Again it is honored by the people. It is in its original place. It is given a two-dragon throne on the western wall of the house and offerings—all kinds of silks, damasks, and satins. In a robe of grass, it tramples on the clean satins. Again it seems to set out on its metamorphic journey. The song continues:

> Where the rivers flow together
> Where they flow down is a dug-out canoe,
> The Tungus who live in the dense forest
> Kill the boar and are skilfull master-hunters.
> [It is] the tracks they do not find,
> The footprints they do not see,
> The gold-colored tortoise,

> The silver-colored frog,
> A buzzing biting wasp,
> A creeping spider,
> The wriggling lizards and snakes,
> The sound of a shaken bell,
> A cuckoo calling loudly,
> The leopard growling,
> The huge and fearless wild boar...

The ancestor in a sense becomes the spirit-emperor, masterfully transcending the etiquette of the court and the boundaries of the empire. Effortlessly, it swims as a fish to the palace, where it yells; unhindered, it returns to the Daur. It cannot be pinned down: it is manifest both in the domestic sphere of the plough and the house and in the wilderness of the forests, where the best hunters cannot see it.

The ancestor Holieli has many powers because it has many transformations. It does not have all powers perhaps, because there are other spirits, with other metamorphoses. But specifically, it takes the power of the imperial ruler. Yet it seems that this is transcended by the idea of metamorphosis itself: the signs and marks of imperial rank are desecrated and abandoned as the spirit takes to the forest as a wasp, changes to a spider, and changes to the sound of a bell. In the practice of ordinary Daurs, the pacification of this spirit, which caused very great harm and mental illness, involved furnishing its representation with imperial imagery (silk, dragons, special wood for the carved models, and so on). Shamans used to order people who had costly embroidered or damask clothing, the very means of imitating the courtly Manchus in real life, to offer them to this spirit. The spirit seems both a violent rejection of and a homage to the imperial state.[37]

Shamanism does not oppose the State as an ideology because shamanism is non-ideological. Shamanism makes a big noise in Peking, but it's not clear who benefits thereby. Is "Peking" threatened or strengthened by this display? Perhaps both? In the end shamanism is not "for" or "against"—it fades into the sound of bells or the spoor of tigers. Nevertheless, in a secret temple within a secret palace within an entire "Hidden City", weighted down with gold, silk, lacquer and jewels, clouded with centuries of incense and obfuscation, something persisted—"footprints one cannot see"—organic and authentic—a homeopathic trace of chaos—a memory of the possibility of authentic vision and the "direct tasting" of non-ordinary consciousness. The dialectic between presence and representation, both their "forms" and their "spectres", is too complex to reduce to terms of simple opposition or recuperation. It might be more useful to think in terms of appearance, disappearance, and re-appearance. This process may be banal—as when a custom is simply defeated and erased—or bizarre, as when "wild" shamanism suddenly re-appears at the

37. Humphrey, *op. cit.*:220-222

center of the most centralized, hierarchic and civilized State imaginable. "Good" king Richard embraces the chaos at the heart of the greenwood in order that order may be complete; the "good" emperor Hongli's motives were no doubt similar. But perhaps chaos is that which *cannot* be "embraced". Its organicism resists all mechanization (the "Clastrian machine" is an organic and uncentered entity, quite the opposite of the *mechanical* machine based on division and centralization). In effect, the shamanic trace does not *resist*—it simply *escapes*. And, as Hamayon points out, in "crisis" situations, it "easily revives or emerges", *i.e.*, it *re-appears*. The fatality of the shamanic trace, in the view of the "State", is that it appears to be psychophysiologically inherent in the human species; it's *fated* to occur. There may even be something "cyclic" about the process; the "logic" of institutions implies a certain inevitable periodicity of commitment and crisis. From this point of view the revival of interest in shamanism in the late 20th century might be seen as (or under) the sign of such a re-appearance. The Irish used to say that "England's troubles are Ireland's opportunities"—and by extension we could say that the crisis of the "State" is the moment of opportunity for the "Clastrian machine". The crisis of the economy makes openings for violence; and the crisis in orthodoxy makes openings for shamanism—even in "Peking".

## 7. HIDDEN IMAM

However attenuated, Manchu Court shamanism is still recognizably shamanism. In order to see how shamanism re-appears as a trace within religions that have no apparent "historical links" with "primitive shamanism", we should examine a case in which purely structural parallels can be discovered. Islam supposedly offers such a test case—but it is not certain that Islam has no *historical* connections with shamanism. Many writers have commented on the shamanic motifs of the Prophet Mohammad's life story. He is prepared for his mission by spirits who split him open and wash his bones, just like a typical circum-Arctic shaman. The cave where he receives his first revelation is the haunt of the pagan Arab demon of dreams, Hiraa. He experiences "fits" similar to epileptic seizures when he recites, and is taken by some Meccans as a *sha'er* or poet, from whom such behavior was apparently expected. His *Mir'aj* or Night Ascension into a heaven of seven or nine layers certainly recalls the soul-flight of the shaman—and many more such parallels could be mentioned. There is nothing surprising or disturbing about all this from an Islamic point of view, since everyone knows there were 124,000 prophets before Mohammad, at least one for every people on Earth. In orthodox doctrine Mohammad is the "final" prophet, and this is taken to mean "last in a temporal series"; from an esoteric point of view, however, the last is also the highest or archetypal form, the "Mohammadan Light" or ray that emanates from pre-eternity and upon which all prophets and saints are situated. The historical Mohammad therefore recapitulates all possible prophetic forms and perfects them. According to sufism, this explains the esoteric parallels between Islam and other manifestations of the spirit. From this perspective one might almost say that Mohammad came not to destroy or suppress such manifestations (including Meccan paganism) but to rectify and realize them.

Be that as it may, the historian of religion must ask if Meccan paganism itself was not shamanistically structured to some degree, and therefore whether the Prophet's actions and visions cannot be seen as "historically influenced" by shamanism. Perhaps so. But then the Koran and Hadith reveal links with Christianity, Judaism, Zoroastrianism, the "Sabaeans" (possibly the Harranian "star cult") and probably other religions as well. No doubt all religions possess some "links" with shamanism, if we take "shamanism" to indicate the spirituality of the Paleolithic (and most of the Neolithic as well). Certainly when Islam came into contact with the world of the Turks and Central Asians, there were direct influences from historically attested shamanic cultures on Islamic institutions such as sufism (e.g., the Bektashi Order, or the Owaysiyya).[38] But all these links, for Islam, are unconscious links. Islam as Islam recognizes no such "historical connections". And therefore we may speak precisely of the *shamanic trace*.

If the shamanic trace re-appears most clearly in "crisis", then we might well narrow our search to an examination of Shiism, which is a religion of *permanent crisis*. According to most political analyses of Shiism it is based on the "divine right" of the Family of the Prophet to rule Islamdom.[39] But Mohammad's family (with the brief exception of his son-in-law the Caliph 'Ali) were excluded from such rule from the very beginning of the Islamic State. This is the crisis. It turned Shiism from a form of authoritarian absolutism into a "permanent revolution". Its revolutionary potential is most often veiled in quietism ("This time is not our time," as the Sixth Imam put it)—but the revolutionary implications of its origins could never be effaced. The permanent nature of the crisis is revealed by the Shiites' own belief that the first eleven of their Imams were "martyred" by Sunni Orthodoxy. But the *real crisis* occurred when the Twelfth Imam *disappeared* in the 9th century. The "Hidden Imam" is considered to be still living, but on a different plane than ours—in effect, as H. Corbin demonstrated, the *Mundis Imaginalis* or world of archetypes.[40] Although he may appear to us in dreams, or visions, or even "in person" (making use of what the Theosophists would call an "astral body"), the Imam is literally out of this world, and can never rule it—until the End of Time. The present rule of the ulemocracy in Iran is taken by some pious Shiites as a betrayal of this other-worldliness and millennial expectation, just as some pious Jews refuse to recognize Israel:—because it is not the "real Jerusalem" of perfected Time. Thus lack of power is a crisis for Shiism, but so is possession of power. And the existence of the Hidden Imam in a "heaven" that shares its position in Imaginal space with the "skies" of the ecstatic shaman, gives rise inevitably within Shiism to the re-appearance of the shamanic trace.

38. I have discussed this at some length in Wilson (1996)    39. For this discussion I have consulted Arjomand (1984), Sachedina (1981), Amir-Moezzi (1994). See also my (1988) and (1993), especially the bibliographies.    40. See especially Corbin (1978) and (1977). But Corbin developed these ideas throughout all his work.

Similarly, since Shiism is inherently "revolutionary", it has served historically as a focus for many different forms of resistance both to Orthodoxy and the State. Because Shiism is perpetually denied its "liberation", we have the paradoxical situation of an authoritarian doctrine giving rise to a libertarian practice—and even to libertarian doctrine. In other words, as a site of resistance, Shiism becomes a repository for remnants of the "Clastrian machine"—which then re-assemble themselves into a force for decentralization, egalitarianism, social/economic justice, and *direct experience* of spiritual realization.

This "direct tasting" in Shiism always takes the form of direct experience of the Imam, who is directly situated on the ray of the Mohammadan Light, and thus actually *embodies* spiritual experiences—and this is true whether the body be corporeal or astral. In practical terms, however, for the Shiite mystic this encounter does not occur merely or even necessarily on the physical plane. Inasmuch as the Imam is a spiritual reality he exists also (or even primarily) in the heart of the individual believer, as the inmost "divine" nature of the creation. Corbin discussed this concept under the rubric of "the-Imam-of-one's-own-being." On the esoteric level this doctrine "democratizes the Imamate" in that each heart contains (or, in effect, *is*) the Imam. Now, within Orthodox Twelve-Imam Shiism, this "identity" remains on the esoteric level alone; the 'ulema mediate between the people and the Hidden Imam. (Khomeini's argument that this mediation justifies the *Vilayat-i faqih* or political rule of the 'ulema was not accepted by other Ayatollahs, who argued that only the Twelfth Imam can rule—and that this rule will mark the end of profane Time.) But other more "heterodox" branches of Shiism have made much more radical applications of the doctrine of the Imam-of-one's-own-being.

In 1164 the Ismailis or "Assassins" of Alamut in northwest Persia received a message from an Imam who was then hidden and unknown to them.[41] It was relayed to them by their young leader, Hasan II (who did not claim to be the Imam himself, although that claim was made later), and it announced that profane Time had indeed come to an end. The "Resurrection" (*Qiyamah*) was declared, and "the chains of the Law were broken." That is, the Islamic Law (*Shariah*) was to be abrogated because its inner esoteric meaning was now to be openly revealed. The inside would become the outside, the world turned upside down—heaven on earth. As in heaven all actions are permitted, so now at Alamut. The revolutionary and heretical potential of Shiism was realized in an absolute opposition to orthodoxy and power, based on the universalization (through the *Da'wa*, propaganda or the "Call") of esoteric realization. The Ismaili techniques of resistance to the State had already been established by Hasan II's predecessor and namesake Hasan-i Sabbah, who first liberated the Rock at Alamut and sent out his fanatical followers to assassinate any who opposed Ismaili autonomy. Under Hasan II assassination was almost abandoned in favor of mystical enthusiasm. His open broadcasting of Ismaili "secrets" drew the shocked attention of nearby Sunni rulers. Something had to be done about Hasan II; a "conservative" party within Alamut had him assassinated, and the Qiyamat

41. See Daftary (1990)

same to a sudden end in Iran. However Hasan II had already sent his childhood friend Rashid Sinan to preach the Qiyamat in Syria. Sinan emulated Hasan-i Sabbah and liberated a network of remote castles, where he ruled as "Old Man of the Mountain." Perhaps it was here that the Assassins acquired the reputation of using hashish in certain initiatic rites mentioned by early European travelers like Marco Polo. (Northwest Iran is not known as a center of hashish production, but the Lebanese mountains of Syria have produced it since remote antiquity.) Certainly Sinan exhibited other shamanic traits that struck both the local peasants and the European Crusaders as uncanny, terrifying, and wonderful. Sinan was known for his bilocation, precognition, ecstatic flight, inspired speech, and magical invulnerability. If some of his feats strike us as stage magic, this would not make him seem any less shamanistic. In one instance he is reported to have penetrated at night into the heavily-guarded sleeping quarters of the great generalissimo Saladdin, who was then engaged in besieging Sinan's mountain fortress. Sinan left a dagger on Saladdin's pillow along with a letter—and then vanished again. Whatever Sinan's means, occult or natural, Saladdin raised the siege the next day and decamped—so much is recorded as sober fact.[42]

To the "Five Pillars" of Sunni Islam (prayer, fasting, pilgrimage, tithe, and profession of belief) Shiite Islam adds a sixth: Social Justice. As the perennial opposition, Shiism has developed an incisive critique of the State, its usurpation of right, its oppressiveness, its tendency toward corruption, its "unholy" economic practices, its intolerance, etc. In openly revolutionary Shiism the demand for social justice takes truly radical forms. Here the mysticism of the Imam-of-one's-own-being is exteriorized, so to speak, as a kind of collective messianism or eschatology of revolt. Just as the "Inner Light" Protestants of 17th century England arrived at the political position of the Levellers, the Diggers, or the Ranters, so too the revolutionary Shiites developed doctrines of mystical experience into theories of social revolution. The late Dr. Ali Shariati (probably martyred by SAVAK, the Shah's secret police) developed a system of Shiite Socialism based on the idea that the Imamate devolves upon the people as a whole. Traditional strictures on usury and unfair dealing were evolved by Shariati into a socialism of believers. His followers, the Mujahedeen, are persecuted today by the heirs of Khomeini—who believe that power rests with the 'ulema—just as Shariati was persecuted by a State that believed power belonged to the *saltanat* or rule of kings.

The existence of the "perfect state" of classical Shiism, according to the orthodox doctrine of the rule of the Mahdi or "Hidden Imam" at the end of Time, i.e., *outside* Time, also implies that it is outside Space as well—that it is literally no-where ("Nakojabad", the realm of Nowhere, or No-Place-Place, as the Illuminationist philosopher Suhravardi the "Murdered One" put it)—that it is *u-topos* and *eu-topos*, i.e., "Utopia". Here we might begin to wonder about the possibility of a coincidence involving the shamanic trace and the utopian trace. If the threads are tangled we may find a way to follow them towards an unexpected pattern. For example, we could

42. See Firas (1877)

move from the shamanic trace in the utopia of revolutionary Shiite socialism, to the shamanic trace in the "Utopian Socialism" of 19th century Europe. In following this shamano-utopian trajectory we might pause over the figure of Robert Owen, who devoted the latter part of his life to an obsession with Spiritualism (surely a kind of urban shamanism as necromancy); or St.-Simon, whose followers founded a religion and vanished into the mysterious Orient in search of the Female Messiah. But of all the Utopian Socialists we should feel most drawn to Charles Fourier.[43]

## 8. NINETEENTH CENTURY ESCAPISM

Few people actually read Fourier nowadays. He is known mostly through one or two mild rebukes by Marx and some faint praise from Engels, or in severely bowdlerized anthologies like that of Charles Gide. To read Fourier in actual whole huge pieces (one can scarcely speak of such monsters as mere "books") is to share a pleasure with A. Breton, for example, who recognized in Fourier a fellow revolutionary surrealist. Fourier's political admirers tend to censor out his obsessions with bizarre sex, gourmet food, High Magic, and the most original visionary-hermetic cosmology of the 19th century. Elsewhere in this book I've dealt at some length with precisely these aspects of Fourier's thought in an attempt to redress the balance and visualize Fourier as a whole, and not merely as a "precursor" of Scientific Socialism or the cooperative movement. His politics in fact cannot really be understood without a grasp of his cosmology, theory of Analogies, numerological mysticism, or hermetic illuminism. Here, however, I would like to concentrate not on Fourier's own self-created uniqueness, but on his relation with a whole milieu and tradition. I have already referred to this tendency or movement as the "Hermetic Left". It is here above all that we will find our "Clastrian machine" at work, combining shamanism, economic radicalism, and revolutionary strategy, into a system devoted (and devoted unstintedly!) to autonomy and pleasure.

When Fourier's first works appeared in the early 1800s, they were greeted rapturously by certain *Illuminés* of France. They perceived him as one of their own, not just for his interesting discussion of "Androgynous Freemasonry" but for his entire system, which appeared closely related to their own and yet excitingly new. But Fourier was a relatively badly-educated man and constructed his system not on references to accepted knowledge (however arcane) but on "absolute doubt" and his own wild inspiration. He never betrayed any deep knowledge of Hermeticism and it is quite possible he developed his version of it almost entirely out of his own imagination.

The key to Fourier's system is the notion that the whole universe is alive. This means that stars and planets are living sentient beings—and moreover, sexual beings. They "copulate" by means of *aromal rays* beamed through space from celestial body to celestial body. (Aromal rays are apparently polarized perfumes, as lasers are polarized light.) Since everything is alive and part of a single multiverse of life (life on

43. See Beecher (1986); also Chap. 1, "Fourier!—or, the Utopian Poetics", originally published in Waldman and Schelling (1994), and my article on Fourier in Mott (1996).

countless planets, even on stars), then everything is related to everything in a complex system of categories that Fourier called "Analogies". (One such category might contain, say, the Sun, the lion, the diamond, the color gold, frankincense, certain numbers, certain sexual acts, etc., etc.) The force that holds this complexity together is "Passion" or *desire*. Things are attracted *erotically* to things in their own "Series" of analogous forms. The primordial crisis for Fourier is that "Civilization" has literally knocked Earth "out of its orbit" in the universal complex or web of Aromal Passions. Unfructified by the exudation of the living stars, our world perishes for want of realization. Civilization can be cured only if the Passions are liberated. Desire is the only possible cohesive factor for social becoming. Without the free movement of desire, there can be no justice.

Now except for certain completely original touches (such as the "Aromal Rays") this doctrine matches point by point the cosmological teachings of Hermeticism. That the universe is a living being or Macrocosm, that Earth is alive and "holy", that the Sun is the "god of the world", that stars are alive and bathe the Earth in astral influences—all this is sound hermetic opinion. That desire or passionate love is the force that moves the universe was taught by figures as diverse as Hesiod, Avicenna, Pico della Mirandola, and Jakob Boehme. That sexuality is sacred and can be channeled for spiritual ends was taught by Renaissance hermeticists and alchemists, sufis, tantrik hindus, Dionysian pagans and neo-platonists. For "Civilization" read "false consciousness", and Fourier can be seen as an occult theorist in the grand old tradition of the Hermetic Left.

This tradition traces itself back to remotest antiquity—in fact to that Saturnian time depicted so beautifully in hermetic Emblem-books such as the *Hypnerotomachia* or the *Atalanta Fugiens*.[44] In fact on some level we are prepared to accept an "origin" for this movement in the deepest Paleolithic, since we regard the Hermetic Left as a repository of the energies of the "Clastrian machine" in history. But the Hermeticists' own explanation of the "transmission" of ancient wisdom—from mythical sages and pseudepigriphal books—interests us only as a symbol of something that persists and re-appears, no matter how "impurely", and always with the same intentions and intensity. For the purposes of the present discussion we could begin with Giordano Bruno (1548-1600), who was burned at the stake in Rome as a martyr to his cause. He believed in multiple inhabited worlds, a sun-centered planetary system, a round earth that was a living being, a system of magical correspondences or "analogies", religious tolerance, and other radical and heretical notions. Bruno, who for some time even acted as a political agent against Vatican interests in England,[45] left a legacy of occult resistance to power. The Rosicrucian Manifestoes of the early 1600s represent (as F. Yates demonstrated)[46] a *politique hermetique* of resistance to Catholic and Protestant dogmatism in the name of tolerance and a universalization of direct spiri-

44. Maier (1989). I consulted the *Hypnerotomachia* at the Biblioteca Hermetica in Amsterdam, and also the 1592 partial English translation, *The Strife of Love in a Dreame*. A modern edition and translation is much to be desired.   45. See Bossy (1991)   46. Yates (1972); see also her (1966) and ( 1964)

tual experience by occult means. The Family of Love and other radical Protestant sects before and during the English Revolution were influenced by Hermeticism, Boehme, and Bruno. John Toland (d. 1724), radical freethinker, rogue Mason, Whig spy and propagandist, and self-proclaimed Celtic Druid, modeled his life on Bruno's quite consciously.[47] Leaving aside the vast influence of Masonry on revolutionary politics in 18th century America and Europe as too dark and vexed a subject, we could, however, mention the poet and artist William Blake, revolutionary, friend of Thomas Paine, visionary, hermeticist, and also a self-proclaimed Druid. Blake's life overlapped with that of Fourier.

If we have learned to associate ceremonial magic with right-wing politics thanks to such figures as W. B. Yeats and Aleister Crowley, we should learn to be more careful in our categorical assumptions. The idea of "tradition" was only hi-jacked by the Right in very recent times (and thanks in part to such "traditionalists" as Guénon, Evola, Jung, Eliade, or T. S. Eliot). Formerly the Left had its tradition as well, the "Good Old Cause" that combined unmediated autonomy and unmediated spirituality. While the traditionalist Right veers toward a dualism of good and evil, spirit and body, hierarchy and separation, the Hermetic Left emphasizes "ancient rights and customs" of freedom, equality, justice—and bodily pleasure (e.g., Blake's *Marriage of Heaven and Hell*). The Left is "radical monist", Saturnian and Dionysian; the Right is "Gnostic", authoritarian and Apollonian. Naturally these terms and categories get mingled and confused, combined and recombined, in an excessive exfoliation of the strangest hybrids and freaks. The Right has its mystical revolutionaries, the Left has its Gnostic Dualists. But as generalizations or ideal models I believe that the rival traditions can be clearly distinguished. In this sense there exists a clear line of "transmission" between Bruno and Fourier—whether the latter had even heard of the former or not! The whole point of the history of ideas is that it is precisely not a history of detailed and documentable "influences" but of ideas that are "in the air" and "handed down" (from who-knows-where?)—a history of "diffusions", or even of disappearances and re-appearances. This is what caused the shock of recognition that greeted Fourier's work in certain (admittedly minuscule) circles of French occultists:—not his footnotes, but his "*brilliance*". The fact that some of these occultists were already socialists added to their excitement over Fourier's new synthesis.

One French occultist radical was the famous Abbé Constant, a.k.a. Eliphas Levi, who began as a defrocked priest and revolutionary agitator, moved on into journalism, and ended with the reputation of world's leading expert in ceremonial magic. I have no evidence that he took an interest in Fourier—but his secretary certainly did. This was the remarkable Flora Tristan, mystic, active Fourieriste, pioneer feminist (Fourier may have invented the word "feminism"), and champion of Labor—a hermetic heroine little-remembered outside France today.[48] Another famous radical magus was the poet Gérard de Nerval, who published some pieces in Fourierist mag-

---

47. See the Appendix on "Blake, Toland and the Druids" in my forthcoming *Ploughing the Clouds: The Soma Sacrifice in Ancient Ireland*.    48. See the introduction by Beverly Livingston to her translation of Flora Tristan's *The Worker's Union* (1983)

azines, including a long historical study of 19th-century radical French occultists, which someone ought to translate.[49] His wonderful oriental tales, based on his adventurous travels, introduced some bits of genuine Sufi and Ismaili lore to his many readers—including highly dramatized accounts of magic and hashish.

The reader may object at this point that the "Shamanic trace" has become attenuated to the point of disappearance. The Hermetic tradition held no consciousness of shamanism, and traced itself back to religious models (such as ancient Egypt) that were anything but non-authoritarian! But this is not really entirely the case. Authentic information about shamanism was widespread in 18th-century Europe, the result of centuries of research in the New World and Russia. As Gloria Flaherty demonstrates in *Shamanism in the Eighteenth Century*, this information had a profound effect on philosophy, religion, the arts, etc.[50] Early freethinkers seized on examples of "good" shamanism to emphasize that Christianity had no monopoly on truth. This positive view of shamanism influenced the occultists (who were also frequently freethinkers):—they adopted some shamanic lore into their own on-going syncretic project. Veneration was expressed for ancient Norse and Celtic shamans, who were understood to have been just like the medicine-men or wizards of 18th-century America or Siberia. By Fourier's time (thanks largely to Rousseau) the image of the "primitive" as *natural humanity* was commonplace in French culture and Europe in general. Fourier is already aware, for example, of what M. Sahlins would later call the "Aphrodisian" nature of Polynesian society (as opposed to the Dionysian/Apollonian split in Western culture);[51] Fourier had nothing but praise for the erotic freedom enjoyed by such "savages". Flaherty traces similar attitudes in Diderot's *Le neveu de Rameau*, Goethe's *Faust*, and Mozart's Masonic *Magic Flute*. Shamanism made a "hit" in the late 18th and early 19th centuries in Europe because the underground tradition of the Hermetic Left had prepared armchair travelers to understand and sympathize with *spirituality as direct experience.*

For Fourier the most direct expression of the cosmic plan for humanity was sexual pleasure. Unlike the paltry adherents of "Free Love" he did not limit sexual "health" to married heterosexuality. On the contrary, he banned marriage and permitted every sex "mania" from pederasty to flagellation (consensual, of course). Just as production could only organize itself by the complete liberation of all to choose "Attractive Labor" at will, so too society itself could not reach its true potential unless *all desire were free.* For Fourier sexuality sometimes takes on an orgiastic dimension not altogether different from de Sade's, but without the cruelty (which resulted from displaced Passion, according to Fourier). Such institutions as a utopian Church of Love (and Fourier's "Androgynous Masonry") hover on the brink of outright sex-magic. Fourier would have agreed with any pagan peasant that it was "good for the crops"—after all, it was good for the entire universe! And in the Harmonial system, as outlined in his amazing charts of universal history, an unbroken line connects the aphrodisian mysteries of Tahitian shamanism and the great feasts and Love Congresses (all the foot-fetishists in the world congregate at Constantinople!) and the

49. Nerval (1832)   50. Flaherty (1992)   51. Sahlins (1985)

spontaneous erotic rituals of the Phalansteries. Fourier proposes a kind of occidental Tantra, a sophisticated version of the "original innocence" and polymorphous perversity of primordial humanity. Fourier does not call for a *return* to Saturnian time, but rather for its re-appearance on a higher plane, a further turn of the spiral. The magic power (there's no other term for it) generated by Eros at this pitch of intensity will transform the world. The sea will turn to lemonade (just as in the American hobo-utopia song of "Big Rock Candy Mountain");[52] people will live to 144 and grow tails with an extra hand and eye at the tip. On three hours of sleep and thirty meals a day, huge erotic "armies" will transform Earth simply in an excess of creative energy, changing the climate, making contact with other planets. To believe that God wishes for anything less attractive than this future is to believe that God is unjust or ungenerous, *quod absurdum est, q.e.d.* Fourier's logic was impeccable.

Fourier's magnum opus manuscript on sexuality, *Le Nouveau monde amoreux*, remained prudishly unpublished after his death—and appeared only in 1967,[53] just in time for the events of May 1968, when rebels scrawled "All Power to the Imagination" on the walls of Paris. The Surrealists, who cherished every fragment of primitive and shamanic power—and who could understand a "Clastrian machine" if anyone can!—surely might have rejoiced at the synchronicity of these events. This is the kind of "historical link" our search affords us. The links are real, but perhaps largely in the Mundus Imaginalis—or only in the dreams of mad poets. In the end perhaps this is where the "Clastrian machine" finds its terminal incarnation, immortal because "unreal". Are we reduced to seeking it out only in old books? Or does it still operate in the world of everyday life? In Surrealist terms this amounts to asking whether everyday life can still be penetrated by the marvelous. It is a very serious question.

## 9. THE HIEROGLYPHIC MAP

The problem with Hermeticism, as Ioan Couliano pointed out,[54] is that all its best techniques have been appropriated: first by "orthodox" science in the persons of Bacon, Newton, and other Royal Society types; then by the State (modern "intelligence" and cryptography were developed by John Dee, the original "007", on behalf of Walsingham—Bruno worked for this outfit); then by Capitalism (the religious origin of money makes it a perfect subject for Gnostic speculation); and finally by the media. Couliano discusses advertising, PR, disinformation and brainwashing (by erotically-charged emblematic imagery) but he could have extended the analysis, for instance, to television and the internet as well. To understand how "Spectacle" and "simulation" work so effectively it is necessary to understand them as hermetic processes, or hermetic "perversions" in the literal sense of turning-aside-from-the-correct-path. Hermeticism was meant as an enchantment into liberation,

52. See Rammel (1990). Rammel mentions Fourier's lemonade ocean but does not speculate about whether Harry K. McClintock, the Wobbly hobo author of the song, derived his "lemonade springs" from Fourier's source.         53. DeBout-Oleskiewicz (1967)
54. Couliano (1987)

since each adept would control the hermetic powers—not be controlled by them. In effect it was also a disenchantment, a throwing-off of conditioning, received opinion, "consensus hallucination", false consciousness, and the "bad trance" of mere quotidian Civilization. Above all, it was an auto-co-divinization of humanity and nature—a process of mutual exaltation of matter and spirit. But once these techniques are appropriated by the power of separation and hierarchy, they "flip" or turn into their exact opposites. Since the individual no longer controls the powers but is controlled by them, they comprise an enchantment into alienation:—they are used to construct media that denigrate and disenchant the world of presence and difference, and exalt the world of absence and sameness. Nature and self are identified only to be denied full reality, since they are linked merely by their insignificance in the face of the monopoly of meaning epitomized by the commodity, or by money itself. Civilization is a trance-like state, and its content is bad consciousness.

Couliano's death is a case in point. Thanks to his hermetic analysis of media he was able to predict the course of events in his native Romania in 1989-1991, where television was used to simulate a revolution. Under the sign of freedom the Romanian regime was overthrown and replaced by the same regime (minus the dictator and his wife), and the world was enchanted by the televised imagery of "liberation". Reality was created through media, "action-at-a-distance"; the peoples' desires were completely recuperated by Securitate, the secret police—or, if you like, by black magic. Couliano spoke too boldly from America, not really believing he could be touched— and was martyred by a Romanian agent who shot him in the men's room of his department at the University of Chicago, an action with traces of "ritual murder" clinging to it, a mystery that remains "unsolved". Hermeticism is a double-edged sword.[55]

The question is then: what becomes of the "Clastrian machine" when its own techniques and even its goals (so to speak) are subverted, appropriated, and turned against it?

As an example we might consider television and the internet, soon to meld and merge and become one vast and "final" medium that will enclose every last open field of discourse, and become the moderator and content of every dialogue. The sense of total despair that might overcome anyone who applied a "hermetic analysis" to this situation can only be diverted by an equally immense boredom. Such ennui and anomie provide masks for an anger that can have no object (or so it appears) other than "reality" itself—since reality is now exclusively that which appears in mediation. In the past few years (mostly since around 1989-91) many people have begun to speak of a certain encroaching numbness, a feeling that "nothing is happening," or that "nothing will make any difference anyway." In America and Europe, "activism" has itself virtually retreated into mediation, to such an extent that some people equate an appearance on the World Wide Web with political action, just as the activists of the 1960s were seduced by their "fifteen seconds of fame" on television. Out of 600 channels—the bright promise of the near future—surely one or two can be devoted to "revolution", and a few more to other "alternate life-styles". The old internet of

55. Anton (1996)

techno-anarchy and "free information" will become just another channel on WWWTV, a kind of slum where the poor old original hackers can still congregate and fritter away the empty hours, while the great virtual City of Cyberspace grows up around them, dwarfing their pitiful huts and making a mockery of their "culture". The anthropologists are probably already lining up for grants to study this quaint survival; affairs move quickly when both time and space have been abolished.

The Gulf War was the first signal of the new moral sloth. A few would-be anti-war protesters watched in stunned amazement (and fear) as millions of Americans apparently went into deep hypnosis in front of CNN and the networks—literally glassy-eyed. Bush said there was no "peace movement" against this war, which would forever wipe out the shame of our (don't say the word!) defeat in Vietnam, and he was correct. Since the 60s a "peace movement" is something that appears in the media, and in 1991 no such appearance occurred. As 200,000 Iraqis died, and the USA's own troops were infected with experimental drugs and uranium-depleted weaponry, the whole thing appeared as pure simulation. Baudrillard was right to say that the Gulf War "never took place," and the proof came with the end of "Desert Storm" (the mini-series). The trance wore off, everyone snapped out of it, looked around, realized that *all was lost*—and immediately went back to sleep and voted for Clinton. The Gulf War was…meaningless. The "Hitler" Saddam Hussein is still in power and will probably end up back on the "most favored" list. The heroic Kuwaiti royal family…what happened to them anyway? Back in power, I suppose. The price of oil went up, or stabilized, or destabilized—according to plan, no doubt. A few "deranged veterans" were added to the rolls of those unfortunate and marginalized Americans whose slumber has been permanently disturbed by Late Capitalism. And that was it.

The War on Drugs is another fine example of hermeticism at work in the New World Order. Just as addiction itself is a kind of shamanism gone bad, so the sham assault on addiction is heavily compromised with the occult. The roots of this "crisis" go back to the CIA's involvement in LSD research, in which they sought the holy grail of Intelligence, a magic elixir that would allow *perfect* control. (Needless to say the Renaissance mages and their occultist heirs had already done this research long ago.) Intelligence had been involved in heroin since at least 1945 and the post-WWII alliance with organized crime. Huge profits were made in Vietnam and the "Golden Triangle", allowing for vast bureaucratic expansion. The spectacular campaign against marijuana in the 1930s was extended to other drugs because illegality made the trade more lucrative. Soon entire "dark" operations were being funded on heroin and cocaine. The pseudo-War on Drugs meanwhile created a vast boom in "security", including private police (one out of every three armed police in the US is now private), private prisons, captive slave labor (chain gangs, etc.—actually a gigantic money-spinner, monopolized by a private company called UNICORP), contracts for hundreds of new prisons, whole new police and bureaucratic structures, jobs, prosperity for all. So what if we have the largest per capita prison population in the world, with half a million inside for marijuana alone? The War on Drugs is America's *number one* business. Drugs will never be "legalized", and especially not by a liberal stooge for the multinationals like Clinton. Drugs *cannot* be legalized because, as Malcolm McLaren (I believe) once said, "Drugs are popular because only drugs can make you feel like the people in TV ads seem to feel." In other words drugs, especially addictive drugs, are the perfect commodity. With heroin cheap and legal, who would buy soap-powder and soft drinks with their spurious claims to authentic ecstasy, their meager and pitiful "utopian trace"? As for psychotropic drugs such as hemp or the hallucinogens, inasmuch as they can be experienced under the proper conditions as *"efficacious sacraments"*, means of acquiring direct experience of non-ordinary consciousness, they must always remain suspect to a psychic regime based on total mediation and alienation. The War on Drugs as a pure simulation within the media has proven to be an admirable means of controlling the drifting middle class through terror, just as the rootless underclass is controlled through violence. Drug-imagery, with its shamanic and hermetic "load" of memes, makes an ideal content for the forms of media; television itself is a kind of fifth-rate heroin—the kind that prevents junk-sickness but never gets you "off"—never "anywhere—so long as it is out of this world." When all pleasure and festivity have been *perfectly* mediated; when autonomy means the freedom to choose among 600 channels; when the Gift can no longer free itself from the market of exchange; when even violence has been taken "away into representation" and alienated from its "Clastrian" function; when nature has vanished into bioengineering, in which the human itself becomes its own commodity;—what then happens to our hermetic dialectic of re-enchantment? How does "urban shamanism" survive the compacting of all dimensions into the terminal flatness of virtuality? The *screen*, the omnipresent screen—it reminds one of nothing so much as Dr. Dee and his shady assistant Ned Kelly, peering into the sinister "obsidian mirror" wherein the angelic alphabet would appear. And it works! Cannot the media attain to the voice of angels? Why not?—since if any "real" angels exist outside that "heaven of glass", they are silent—like God, or nature. So why should we too not be silent? The screen will speak for us—and for our boredom.

The triumph of the screen is "of one nature" (to use theological language) with the triumph of Capital itself. Since 1989-91 and the collapse of Communism, the grand movement of the Social has come to an end. The "End of History" so touted by neo-liberal ideology is already a done deal. Stalinism took everything down with it in a peevish Ragnarok of Leftish impotency, and left nothing—not even "Capital*ism*"—nothing but Capital itself as power on Earth. The Global Market is not driven by ideology but by its own totalitarian logic, the bottom line of eternal growth—and that which is eternal has no history. Released from its moorings in the mire of mere production, Capital has soared aloft into a *numisphere* (a numinous and numismatic realm) of pure transcendence. Over 90% of all existing money has no relation to any other form of wealth, but only to itself (currency exchange, arbitrage, speculation in debt, etc.), and circulates in a free sphere above Earth, never manifesting as cash or even as credit. Purely spiritual, and yet all-powerful in the material realm, money has achieved what God herself could never manage. Fewer than 400 people "control" half the money in this world—how can one speak any more of a "ruling class"? The CEO is a perfectly replaceable part—a matter of mere "wetware", the human as prosthesis of the machine. Money itself makes all the decisions. There is nothing left for anyone to do. Perhaps a "bubble" stretched so thin as the numisphere will one day burst in that "final crisis" so often predicted by Marx, and so often postponed. But there will be no "working class" waiting in the wings for a smooth take-over of the means of production. Not in America or Europe anyway. The *götterdämmerung* of Capital would simply destroy the "West", because there is no viable alternative to the rule of Capital. And the "West" nowadays includes all the zones of security (e.g., the "Pacific Rim"), all zones of comfort, health, education, jobs, etc.—and excludes only the zones of depletion, where life is presumed to be a matter of mere survival, not of "expression" or realization. On the one hand you can choose capitulation to Capital (if you're lucky); on the other hand, you can choose opposition—and defeat. No wonder it feels like "nothing's happening." To allow oneself to feel what *is* happening is an impossible burden, a tragedy without katharsis, a labyrinth where every path leads to the minotaur—including the path we have marked with thread.

Now in such a situation, what could we expect of the "Clastrian machine"? For what could we *hope* (to use E. Bloch's term) from such a primitive device, and moreover a device long since looted of its valuable parts? To speak of a re-appearance *now*—wouldn't that be mere whistling in the graveyard? or a serious lapse in taste and good manners? Ethnography (which after all is what this text is supposed to concern) deals with the disappearing Other—the primitive, the "world we have lost", the verge of extinction. How can this "machine" we have concocted (and only on paper to be sure) possess any relevance to *our* condition? Knowledge (or "data" as it's usually called) may have value in and for itself—but knowledge is neither autonomy nor pleasure and as such may function only as another burden, another over-determined source of bitterness or boredom. We have been disenchanted of the "necessary illusion" (to quote Nietzsche) that some transcendent power fuels the device of our resistance. We have been "overcome"; we are the "last" humans.

This pessimism (emanating from such authors as the ex-fascist Cioran or the ex-communist Baudrillard)—this all-too-fashionable post-modern pessimism—is it a critique of the world it appears to oppose, or merely a *symptom*? In other words, are we actually to believe in the image of the world created by Capital, in which alienation and hopelessness are the just desserts of those who cannot share in the "health of the Market"? Are we to believe philosophy when it tells us it has been defeated and absorbed into the ecstasy of pure speed and the disembodiment of virtuality? Are we to accept without question the vanishment of the primitive, of nature, of the human itself? It's not a matter of "protest" nor the triviality of resentment; no one will care for our mere lamentation. Have we any *evidence* to the contrary?

In Orwell's *1984* the little rooms of the workers are overseen by panopticonographic screens which broadcast, brainwash and simultaneously snoop on every citizen of the State; only one small corner of Winston Smith's room escapes the beam/gaze of this pyramidal Eye. It is that corner we must now set out to explore.

Is the corner really so small? Metaphorically perhaps. But geographically perhaps not. In one corner of the corner, actual rebellion has broken out. If the movement of the Social is dead, the Zapatistas of Chiapas must represent either the last dying embers of the phoenix's pyre, or else the first tenuous spark of its rebirth. Owing nothing to the "historical" Revolution, which certainly imploded in 1989-91, three years before the Zapatista uprising, the philosophers of the EZLN have developed a complete critique of global neo-liberalism's meaning for the former "Third World" (how can there be a Third World when there is no *second* world?). The communiqués of Subcommandante Marcos and other EZLN writers, which have certainly influenced my thinking in this essay, were developed in conjunction with the Mayan elders of the region, many of them practicing shamans.56 In many ways the Zapatista uprising has been a model demonstration of what we've called the "Clastrian machine" functioning in the "real world" of production, geography, and war. The goals of the uprising were defined as "empirical freedoms," meaning effective autonomy, freedom from need ("In need freedom remains latent," as Col. Qadaffi puts it), freedom from disease and induced ignorance, freedom to be different (to be Mayan). Ideological or merely political freedom—which is quite capable of co-existing with Capital of course—holds much less interest for these romantic pragmatists. Hence the renewed resonance of the old anarchist slogan *Tierra y Libertad!*"—precisely at the moment when Earth and autonomy were supposed to go gently into the long good-night of the End of History. In particular, at the moment when Capital announces its unification of reality—the mall-ing and McDisneyfication of absolutely everything—the single world so long desired by Enlightenment Rationalism—just at the very triumphalist instant of Capital's psychic and aesthetic hegemony of separation and sameness—the very worst "empirical" claim made by the EZLN, the most shocking and atavistic offense against the transparent daylight of "Market values" comes to light:—the claim to the right to be different, to be Mayan. Not to be "multi-cultural". Not to be a folkloristic survival. But to be...primitive. In other words, from a certain point of view, the Zapatista uprising is a revolutionary *reversion*. Thus it meets our criteria. It is a working model of the "Clastrian machine". So far (January 1997) it even looks mildly successful.

The remnants of the Left, which believed in Enlightenment Rationalism *even more sincerely* than the Capitalists, will no doubt find this reversionism of the EZLN difficult to accept. Homosexuals, women, oppressed minorities and the like are allowed to have "identities" only on condition that consciousness itself be homogenous and transparent. Tribalism is not progressive. Over-concern with the "sacredness" of Earth is incompatible with rational goals of economic growth. Shamanism is superstitious nonsense.

All this proves is that the Left is as moribund as the Right. The fact is that in opposition to Capital, every *unassimilable difference* must be considered potentially revolutionary. Some differences may result in mere reaction and "Conservative Rev-

56. For the EZLN communiqués, see *Zapatistas! Documents of the New Mexican Revolution* (1994). For another example of shamanic warfare, see Lan (1985).

olution", while others—*non-hegemonic particularities*—will lead to the kind of revolt we can appreciate, such as *Zapatismo*! The difference between differences is not to be measured so much in ideological terms but on an empirical basis. The key to judgment is that consciousness is *not* homogenous (never was, never will be), and that the hegemonic claims of Capital in this respect are illusory—just as our "hermetic critique" would lead us to expect. In fact the very success of Capital's mediation is a function of its manipulation of consciousness, which is thereby shown to have an inner structure based on differentiation. That is: the fifth-rate trance state of commodity fetishism is no more to be identified with Enlightenment Rationality than with shamanic *enthusiasmos*. The supposed sameness of Capitalist consciousness is no more than a mask for its fragmentation and alienation. Revolutionary difference by contrast finds its own variegated cohesiveness—or "unity" if you like—on the basis of *presence*, i.e. the overcoming of separation. At such a feast, not even rationality need be turned away. (In fact, some *real* Enlightenment might be quite refreshing.)

We must doubt whether the "free peasant" aspect of *Zapatismo* can be adapted to the urban (or even post-urban) structure of America and Europe. It is true, however, that the former "developed world" has itself begun to undergo a "proletarianization of the zones" or the creation of "zones of depletion" within its own geographical and political space. The historic "deals" which bound the North's working class to Capital's interests since 1917 or 1945 have been revoked, since Capital no longer needs any allies in the battle against the Evil Empire. Labor finds itself plunged back toward the past; its vertiginous *dégringolade* has taken it down to at least 1886 or so, if not 1830. Migratory Capital can turn your neighborhood into a bit of Africa or Indonesia, just by going somewhere else—all according to "Market values". Even in the North the gap between rich and poor spreads at a dizzying rate:—your class, your profession, your "sexual preference", your *attitude* might be next in line for shoving over the edge. There may yet be some scope for "urban Zapatismo" even in the midst of our world of "plenty". There is no doubt, however, that opposition to Capital in our part of the globe is at present theoretical and nugatory at best; no one ever starts a violent revolution out of mere boredom.

But even if the thoughts of the Mayan Elders remain for us no more than distant dreams, we should still derive some inspiration from the fact that the "Clastrian machine" can function at all in this world where Capital has supposedly had the last word. In fact I would offer as evidence the entire world neo-shamanic movement, by which I mean not merely the antics of the New Agers (which range from profound to suspect to silly to sheer commodity hype) but also the definite revival of shamanism among native peoples, including their urban descendants, in the New World, Siberia, and Africa.

I will go farther and predict that the "Clastrian machine" will exercise a profound influence on the structure of the opposition to Capital that must emerge in the very near future. As the 19th century ideologies of rationalist revolution have been discredited, leading to a crisis in the movement of the Social so severe as to amount to disappearance, I suspect that the old half-forgotten radicalism of "rights and customs" may re-appear in new forms of manifestation and expression. The articulated but organically complex parts of the "machine" we have identified will be recognizable in their new guises.

On the economic level, the "Clastrian machine" always opposes exchange and supports redistribution—but reserves its unqualified approval only for reciprocity. The machine, which is always shaky in its ideology (since it essentially has none) will probably not mount a rational critique of money—and this vagueness may prove to its great disadvantage. But one thing is "perfectly clear" (as Nixon used to say)—that the "Clastrian machine" of the new millennium will attack *exchange itself*, headlong and violently, in the name of the *right* of reciprocity and the *morality* of generosity. And it will settle for *no less* than redistribution (probably in some rough and empirical form of socialism).

In the realm of polemology (=war), a crisis occurred in 1945 with the realization that one *can* possess too much fire power. Instead of dealing with this problem in a logical way, the world military plunged deeper into the mire in a huge game of bluff based on "MAD" (mutual assured destruction). It was discovered that pure war (war devoid of actual conflict) was an excellent means of staving off the perennial crisis of over-production. The final monstrosity was the "Star Wars" scenario, probably the biggest boondoggle in the entire history of war—and an ongoing scandal. But due to the largely self-inflicted collapse of Communism (almost a suicide, really) the "West" was left suddenly devoid of any enemy—just as predicted by the notorious forgery *Report from Iron Mountain* so many years ago:—the "crisis of peace". It seems that the "Clastrian machine" finds an opening here for its primitive tactic of war as the centrifugalization of power rather than its accumulation. The EZLN resorted to violence to *expel* power from its zone, not to seize it for themselves. And they did so knowing that the Mexican government would find it politically impossible to crush the revolt with superior firepower (or with US firepower), just as the US found it impossible to "nuke" Vietnam "back to the Stone Age". In North America and Europe, of course, such political conditions are absent, and all violence—whether spontaneous or deliberate—can be instantly suppressed and recuperated (as "crime" or "terrorism" for example). But this situation could change. Zones of depletion within or between the borders of "developed nations" can be controlled militarily only at great political expense to the State or regime in power. It may be that the nations will have to give up control of the zones to the privatized armies of the *zaibatzus*—but of course, Capital much prefers to leave such unpleasant tasks of discipline to the State; and besides, there are no profits to be made in the zones of depletion. In effect, vacua of power may appear in the zones. Organized crime (or even humanitarian NGOs) may attempt to replace the State—but again, not without the promise of gain or power. At this point tactics of violence might begin to make some sense.

Whatever form the "Clastrian machine" takes, display of the *shamanic trace* is always its most obvious trait. It is this sign for example that differentiates Zapatismo from all the "vulgar materialist" revolutionary forms of the 19th and 20th centuries.

(In other respects, Zapatismo owes a great deal to those systems, especially anarchism.) This visionary aspect of the machine is the most difficult part for heirs of the Enlightenment to grasp or respect. A stumbling-block…a scandal. It seems so…*anthropological*, so uncivilized. And "urban shamanism" is even worse: a hodgepodge of nostalgia, appropriation, and charlatanry. And yet somehow it seems that the "Clastrian machine" cannot operate or even survive without at least a trace of shamanism. I don't need to protest that every branch of modern thought, from quantum mechanics to existentialism, has tended to heap doubt upon the shaky edifice of rationalism—and yet we treat it like the weather, always complaining and never doing anything about it. If we once felt the courage, not to plunge into some hideous maw of occult chaos, but to allow the emergence of a *rationality of the marvelous*, then we might be able to come to terms with the shamanic trace. I don't know exactly what a rationality of the marvelous would consist of, but I suppose it to be something like the Surrealists' penetration of everyday life by the marvelous. And I would maintain, without knowing what it is, that it happens every day—especially to those who work at a certain kind of openness. And I would also claim that everyone who reads this text already knows and has always known and knows at every moment (though not necessarily "consciously") exactly and precisely what this "marvelous" is and how it enters into the rational and everyday life of body and mind. And on that wordless knowledge we must rest our case.

New York City
January 18, 1997

BIBLIOGRAPHY
Adas, Michael (1979) *Prophets of Rebellion: Millenarian Protest Movements against the European Colonial Order.* Cambridge: Cambridge University Press
Amir-Moezzi, M. A. (1994) *The Divine Guide in Early Shi'ism: The Sources of Esotericism in Islam,* trans. D. Streight. Albany, NY: SUNY Press
Angell, Norman (1929) *The Story of Money.* Garden City, NY: Garden City Publishing
Anton, Ted (1996) *Eros, Magic, and the Murder of Professor Culianu.* Evanston, IL: Northwestern University Press
Arjomand, Said Amir (1984) *The Shadow of God and the Hidden Imam: Religion, Political Order, and Societal Change in Shi'ite Iran from the Beginning to 1890.* Chicago: University of Chicago Press
Bakhtin, Mikhail (1984) *Rabelais and His World,* trans. H. Iswolsky. Bloomington: Indiana University Press
Barclay, Harold (1982/1990) *People Without Government: An Anthropology of Anarchy.* London: Kahn and Averill
Bataille, Georges (1988) *The Accursed Share: An Essay on General Economy. Vol. I: Consumption,* trans. R. Hurley. New York: Zone Books
Beecher, Jonathan (1986) *Charles Fourier: The Visionary and His World.* Berkeley: University of California Press
Bossy, John (1991) *Giordano Bruno and the Embassy Affair.* New Haven: Yale University Press

Chu, Yuan (1973) *The Nine Songs: A Study of Shamanism in Ancient China*, trans. and ed. Arthur Waley. San Francisco: City Lights Books

Clastres, Hélène (1995) *The Land-Without-Evil: Tupi-Guarani Prophetism*, trans. J. Grenez Brovender. Urbana, IL: University of Illinois Press

Clastres, Pierre (1977) *Society against the State: the Leader as Servant and the Humane Uses of Power Among the Indians of the Americas*, trans. R. Hurley with A. Stein. New York: Mole Editions, Urizen Books

— (1994) *The Archaeology of Violence*, trans. Jeanine Herman. New York: Semiotext(e)

Cohn, Norman (1970) *The Pursuit of the Millennium*. London: Maurice Temple Smith

Corbin, H. (1977) *Spiritual Body and Celestial Earth: From Mazdean to Shi'ite Iran*, trans. N. Pearson. Princeton: Princeton University Press

— (1978) *Creative Imagination in the Sufism of Ibn 'Arabi*, trans. N. Pearson. Boulder, CO: Shambhala

Couliano, Ioan (1987) *Eros and Magic in the Renaissance*, trans. M. Cook. Chicago: University of Chicago Press

Daftary, Farhad (1990) *The Isma'ilis: Their History and Doctrines*. Cambridge: Cambridge University Press

Dalton, G., ed. (1968) *Primitive, Archaic and Modern Economies: Essays of Karl Polanyi*. Boston: Beacon Press

Davis, Robert C. (1994) *The War of the Fists: Popular Culture and Public Violence in Late Renaissance Venice*. New York and Oxford: Oxford University Press

Desmonde, William (1962) *Magic, Myth, and Money: The Origin of Money in Religious Ritual*. New York: The Free Press of Glencoe

Dumézil, Géorges (1969) *Heur et malheur du guerrier*. Paris: Presses Universitaires de France

EZLN (1994) *Zapatistas! Documents of the New Mexican Revolution*. Brooklyn, NY: Autonomedia

Fadiman, Jeffrey A. (1982) *An Oral History of Tribal Warfare: The Meru of Mt. Kenya*. Athens, OH: Ohio University Press

Finlay, M. I. (1985) *The Ancient Economy*. Berkeley: University of California Press

Firas, Abu (1877) *Fasl man al-Lafz al-sharif*, in S. Guyard, "Un Grand Maitre des Assassins au temps de Saladin," *Journal Asiatique* 7/9

Flaherty, Gloria (1992) *Shamanism in the Eighteenth Century*. Princeton: Princeton University Press

Fourier, Charles (1967) *Le Nouveau monde amoreaux*, ed. Simone DeBout-Oleskiewicz. Paris: Editions Anthropos

Geddes, W. R. (1957) *Nine Dyak Nights*. Oxford: Oxford University Press

Hamayon, R. N. in Thomas and Humphrey (1996), *q.v.*

Hobsbawn, Eric (1959)*Primitive Rebels: Studies in Archaic Forms of Social Movements*. New York: W. W. Norton

Hurley, W. H. "The Late Woodland State: Effigy Mound Culture" in *The Wisconsin Archaeologist* 67:3-4

Joseph, Frank (1992) *The Lost Pyramids of Rock Lake: Wisconsin's Sunken Civilization*. St. Paul, MN: Golden Press

*The Journal of the Ancient Earthworks Society*

Kim, Tae-gon, Mihály Hoppál et. al. (1995) *Shamanism in Performing Arts*. Budapest: Akadémiai Kiadó

Kingswan, Chuck (1990) *Ho-Chunk History = A Glimpse: Notes to America = Word's Straight From the Source's Mouth = From the Ice Age to the Nuclear: Thoughts for All Ages.* Self-published: RR 2, Box 384E, Neillsville WI 54456

Krader, Lawrence (1968) *Formation of the State.* Englewood Cliffs, NJ: Prentice-Hall

Lan, David (1985) *Guns and Rain: Guerillas and Spirit Mediums in Zimbabwe.* London: James Curry

Landauer, Gustav (1919/1978) *On Socialism*, trans. D. J. Parent. St. Louis: Telos Press

Lapham, Increase A. (1855) *The Antiquities of Wisconsin as surveyed and described by I. A. Lapham on behalf of the American Antiquarian Society.* Washington DC: Smithsonian Institute

Lee, Richard B., and Irven Devore (1968) *Man the Hunter.* New York: Aldine Publishing Company

Le Goff, Jacques (1990) *Your Money or Your Life: Economy and Religion in the Middle Ages*, trans. P. Ranum. New York: Zone Books

Lewitsky, Anatole (1988) "Shamanism", in Denis Hollier, ed., *The College of Sociology, 1937-39*, trans. B. Wing. Minneapolis: University of Minnesota Press

Littleton, C. Scott (1966) *The New Comparative Mythology.* Berkeley: University of California Press

MacNeill, E., ed. and trans. (1908) *Duanaire Finn: The Book of the Lays of Fionn*, Vol. I. London: Irish Text Society Vol. VII

Maier, Michael (1989) *Atalanta Fugiens: An Edition of the Emblems, Fugues and Epigrams*, trans. and ed. by Joscelyn Godwin. Grand Rapids, MI: Phanes Press, Magnum Opus Hermetic Sourceworks #22

Mair, Lucy (1962/1964) *Primitive Government.* Baltimore: Penguin Books

Mallam, R. Clark (1976) *The Iowa effigy mound manifestation: an interpretive model.* Iowa City: Office of the State Archaeologist, University of Iowa

— (1995) "Ideology from the Earth: Effigy Mounds in the Midwest" in *Prehistoric Cultures of Iowa: A Brief Study.* Harper's Ferry, Iowa: Effigy Mounds National Monument

Martin, Joel W. (1991) *Sacred Revolt: The Muskogees' Struggle for a New World.* Boston: Beacon Press

Mauss, Marcel (1950/1980) *The Gift: The Form and Reason for Exchange in Archaic Societies*, trans. W. D. Halls. New York: W. W. Norton

Merrifield, Ralph (1987) *The Archaeology of Ritual and Magic.* New York: New Amsterdam Books

Mott, Wesley T., ed. (1996) *Biographical Dictionary of Transcendentalism.* Westport, CT: Greenwood Press

Murphy, G., ed. and trans. (1933) *Duanaire Finn*, Vol. II. London: Irish Text Society Vol. XXVI-II

— (1953) *Duanaire Finn*, Vol. III. London: Irish Text Society Vol. XXVI-II

Nagy, Joseph Falaky (1985) *The Wisdom of the Outlaw: The Boyhood Deeds of Finn in Gaelic Narrative Tradition.* Berkeley: University of California Press

de Nerval, Gérard (1832) *Les Illuminés: récits et portraits.* [Cover title: *Les Illuminés, ou, les précurseurs du socialisme*] Paris: V. Lecou

Ó Maitiú, Séamas (1995) *The Humours of Donnybrook: Dublin's Famous Fair and its Suppression.* Dublin: Irish Academic Press, Maynooth Series in Local History No. 4

Patterson, Nerys Thomas (1994) *Cattle-lords and Clansmen: The Social Structure of Early Ireland.* South Bend, IN: University of Notre Dame Press

Proudhon, P.-J. (1888) *System of Economic Contradiction, or, the Philosophy of Misery*, Vol. I, trans. Benj. R. Tucker. Boston: Benj. R. Tucker

Rammel, Hal (1990) *Nowhere in America: The Big Rock Candy Mountain and Other Comic Utopias*. Urbana: University of Illinois Press

Sachedina, A. A. (1981) *Islamic Messianism: The Idea of the Mahdi in Twelver Shi'ism*. Albany, NY: SUNY Press

Sahlins. Marshall (1972) *Stone Age Economics*. Chicago: Aldine-Atherton

— (1985) *Islands of History*. Chicago: University of Chicago Press

Santino, Jack, ed. (1994) *Halloween and other festivals of death and life*. Knoxville: University of Tennessee Press

Schmandt-Besserat, Denise (1992) *Before Writing. Vol. I: From Counting to Cuneiform*. Austin: University of Texas Press

Shell, Marc (1982) *Money, Language and Thought: Literary and Philosophic Economies from the Medieval to the Modern Era*. Berkeley: University of California Press

Silverberg, R. (1968) *Mound Builders of Ancient America:—The Archaeology of a Myth*. Greenwich, CT: New York Graphic Society

Taussig, Michael (1980) *The Devil and Commodity Fetishism in South America*. Chapel Hill: University of North Carolina Press

— (1987) *Shamanism, Colonialism, and the Wild Man: A Study in Terror and Healing*. Chicago: University of Chicago Press

— (1997) *The Magic of the State*. New York and London: Routledge

Tawney, R. H. (1952) *Religion and the Rise of Capitalism*. New York: Harcourt, Brace and Co.

Thomas, N. and C. Humphrey (1996) *Shamanism, History and the State*. Ann Arbor: University of Michigan Press

Thompson, E. P. (1993) *Customs in Common*. New York: The New Press

Thrump, Sylvia L., ed. (1970) *Millenial Dreams in Action: Studies in Revolutionary Religious Movements*. New York: Schocken Books

Tristan, Flora (1983) *The Worker's Union*, trans. Beverly Livingston. Urbana: University of Illinois Press

Wafer, Jim (1991) *The Taste of Blood: Spirit Possession in Brazilian Candomblé*. Philadelphia: University of Pennsylvania Press

Waldman, Anne and Andrew Schelling, eds. (1994) *Disembodied Poetics: Annals of the Jack Kerouac School*. Albuquerque: University of New Mexico Press

Weber, Max (1958) *The Protestant Ethic and the Spirit of Capitalism*, trans. T. Parsons. New York: Charles Scribner's Sons

Wilson (1988) *Scandal: Essays in Islamic Heresy*. Brooklyn, NY: Autonomedia

— (1993) *Sacred Drift: Essays on the Margins of Islam*. San Francisco: City Lights Books

— (1996) *"Shower of Stars": Book & Dream: Initiatic Dreaming in Sufism and Taoism*. Brooklyn, NY: Autonomedia

Worsley, Peter (1968) *The Trumpet Shall Sound: A Study of "Cargo" Cults in Melanesia*. New York: Schocken Books

Yates, Francis (1964) *Giordano Bruno and the Hermetic Tradition*. London: Routledge and Kegan Paul

— (1966) *The Art of Memory*. London: Routledge and Kegan Paul

— (1972) *The Rosicrucian Enlightenment*. London: Routledge and Kegan Paul

# A NIETZSCHEAN
# COUP D'ÉTAT

(FOR NANCY J. PETERS AND BOB SHARRARD)

"Nothing is true, all is permitted."

— *Thus Spoke Zarathustra*, 386

There is no way of telling what may yet become part of history. Perhaps the past is still essentially undiscovered! So many retroactive forces are still needed!

— *The Gay Science*, 104

## I. INTRODUCTION

Let us face ourselves. We are Hyperboreans; we know very well how far off we live. "Neither by land nor by sea will you find the way to the Hyperboreans"—Pindar already knew this about us. Beyond the north, ice, and death—*our* life, *our* happiness. We have discovered happiness, we know the way, we have found the exit out of the labyrinth of thousands of years. Who *else* has found it?

— *The Anti-Christ*, 569

The 19th century resisted coming to an end. It got off to a late start in about 1830 with the Industrial Revolution, and it held on (with increasing desperation) well beyond 1900. World War I began as the last 19th century war, an affair of monarchs and diplomats—but it degenerated into a technological hecatomb, a mass sacrifice, a potlatch of modern death—and of course, a Revolution. The 20th century really began in 1917, behind the front, in Russia. A year or so later, despite the re-appearance of the diplomats in their top hats and gleaming orders, the 20th century had reached Europe and America. And despite the declarations of eternal peace, it was to be a century of pure violence.

In 1830 the emergent world of Capital seemed fated for universal triumph. What or who could oppose such "progress"? Certainly not those backward and exhausted oriental lands that were already being added one by one as jewels to various European crowns—and most certainly not our very own pathetic "working class". These outer or inner "natives" might grow restless, but such problems could be handled by superior force. Capital was an idea whose time had come—it could be opposed only by an idea of equal power. And where could such an idea be found in 1830? In the crack-brained dreams of "Utopian Socialists"? But Capital was not a mere system, to be dismantled by reformist tinkerers. Capital was History itself—a universal fate—a natural law.

And yet by 1871 something had gone disturbingly wrong with Capital's game-plan. The revolt in Paris required more than a few police to put down—in fact, it took the massed armies of two nations, and demanded a massacre of thousands. And still the blight spread, the movement of the Social, a dialectical response to the movement of Capital—an *opposing idea*. World War I (which began in 1914 with the quintessentially 19th-century incident of a Grand Duke's-assassination) amounted to a vast tactical manoeuver for the de-railing of the Social. The workers were to be distracted by patriotism and then disciplined by war.

Instead, as the 19th century came to an end in the shambles of the trenches, something went wrong with Capital's strategy again. It lost control of Russia. Suddenly it seemed possible that the War might have been a mistake. "Soviets" of workers and soldiers were being proclaimed here and there in the oddest places, and 1918 began as the year of World Revolution—at least in the feverish imaginations of certain rebels, and certain reactionaries.

It's not easy to reconstruct this moment. Obsessive attention has been paid to the Russian revolution because it succeeded, but the other revolutions—the ones that failed—have been forgotten. One might almost say "obsessively forgotten." Capitalist historians forgot 1918-1919 because after all one need not remind one's readers that less than a lifetime ago certain incidents occurred, certain almost-meaningless incidents... and as for Communist historians, they were embarrassed by the fact that most of these incidents were not inspired by Marxism (and the ones that *were* inspired by Marxism failed like all the others). So whose responsibility was it to remember 1918-19? Obviously nobody's. And therefore it may come as a surprise to learn that in Ireland, the city of Limerick declared itself a Soviet in April 1919, and held out against the British long enough to print its own money.[1] The uprisings in Germany are perhaps better-known, although not much attention has been paid to the anarchistic *Räterepublik* in Munich that lasted tempestuously from November 1918 to May 1919, and enlisted the talents of such men as philosopher Gustav Landauer, poet Erich Mühsam, playwright Ernst Toller, and novelist B. Traven (then known as "Ret Marut").[2] In Hungary, the Marxist Bela Kun came briefly to power in 1919. In September 1919 the poet Gabriele D'Annunzio "liberated" the Yugoslavian city of Fiume and declared it independent. He promulgated an anarchistic con-

1. See Cahill (1990)    2. See my article in *Drunken Boat* (forthcoming: Autonomedia)

stitution (based on *music*) and filled his coffers with loot won by anarchist "pirates". This operatic experiment came to an end in November 1920 when the Italians bombed D'Annunzio out of his palace.3 Meanwhile in the Ukraine a revolt broke out against both the Whites and the Reds, led by the anarchist Nestor Makhno, and succeeded for a while in liberating whole areas from any government whatsoever.

The failure of the Revolution to reach world-wide proportions in 1918-1919 meant in effect that the 19th century would have to be repeated all over again. In the 19th century neither Capital nor Social had succeeded in crushing the other, and now the 20th century would have to play out all the repercussions of that failure in a world divided geographically and ideologically into two "blocs". The struggle of the Social with Capital would go on, and in that sense the 19th century would also *go on*.

In 1918 it was by no means clear that the movement of the Social would be hijacked and eventually monopolized by Marxism. The success of the Bolsheviks in Moscow was not yet seen as the signal for a *Marxist* world revolution. Other systems and ideologies competed for space within that revolution:—anarchism, for example, as well as various forms of socialism and even utopianism. Moreover, the movement of the Social had still not yet fragmented into a distinct Right and Left. Nazism and Fascism were both "Social" movements and in fact even grew out of "leftist" roots (Mussolini, D'Annunzio, and the Italian Futurists were all anarchists, and the Nazis began as a socialist workers' party). But neither of these reactionary forms had really emerged in 1918-1919,4 and strange hybrids were still possible. Fiume was a bizarre mix of anarchism, aestheticism and *fin-de-siecle* decadence, nationalism, and uniform-fetishism (black, with skull-and-crossbones insignia, later plagiarized by the SS).

One of the oddest of all the exotic revolutionary flowers of 1918-19, and one of the most thoroughly forgotten—the Autonomous Sanjak of Cumantsa, under the leadership of Georghiu Mavrocordato—demonstrates the complex fluidity of 19th century ideologies and systems in struggle against Capital *and* simultaneously against Communism. Cumantsa has never been interpreted in this light, partly because its ideological *bouillabaisse* is so strange as to be literally incomprehensible to most historians. However, there exist other good reasons for Cumantsa's obscurity. For one thing the "Provisional Government" of the Sanjak came to power not by uprising and rebellion, but by *coup d'etat*; thus it is not seen as a "revolutionary" phenomenon. Then too, Cumantsa is obscure, remote, hardly European at all—an insignificant port-town on the Black Sea in the region of Romania called the Dobruja, on one of the ancient silted-up mouths of the Danube, surrounded by hundreds of miles of desolate delta marsh-land, swamp, estuaries, creeks, lagoons and sandbars. One might almost think that Cumantsa was made to be forgotten.

The melange of intellectual and historical influences that went into the melting-pot of Cumantsa will be explored in this essay—but the main reason for our

3. See Bey (1991)    4. Although the future could certainly be read in the bloodstains on the pavement in Munich, where the Jew Gustav Landauer was stomped to death by the members of the Thule Gesellschaft.

interest in the Provisional Government of the Sanjak is not its syncretistic complexity, but rather its uniqueness. As far as I know,[5] it is the only experiment in government ever to be openly based on the philosophy of Friedrich Nietzsche. Surely *that* is worth remembrance.

## II CUMANTSA

> "Praised be this day that lured me into this swamp!"
> —*Thus Spoke Zarathustra*, 362

The ancient history of the Cumantsa region is not only interesting in itself but also provides a background without which the events of 1918-1920 will lack both depth of field and nuance. Perhaps it is merely a truism to say that geography and climate (or *landscape*), along with the memory that inheres in every building or cleared field (also *landscape*), participate in the historical events that transpire within a region—but in Cumantsa the cliché strikes us with the freshness of a new insight.

At the beginning of the Neolithic, about nine or ten thousand years ago, the entire western shore of the Black Sea belonged to that culture called Cucuteni, analyzed so brilliantly by archaeologist Marija Gimbutas and others as agricultural, "matriarchal" or goddess-worshipping, peaceful, and artistically brilliant. Gimbutas believes that sometime around the fourth millennium BC this area was "invaded" by the "Kurgan People" (named after their distinctive burial mounds) from the East, from across the great steppes beyond the Black Sea. These new peoples were pastoralist, "patriarchal" or god-worshipping, warlike, and barbaric. They were probably the Indo-Europeans. One of the chief routes from the steppes into Europe would have gone past the mouths of the Danube, and thence down into Greece or along the river into what we now call Eastern Europe. And in fact the Dobruja has been over-run countless times by an almost infinite number of barbarians. Before Classical Antiquity the sequence of invasions remains a blur in which nothing much can be distinguished, but around the 7th century BC the mists part and we find a people called Cimmerians living around the Black Sea from the Crimea down to Thrace. Semi-barbaric, perhaps Thracians or Iranians, the Cimmerii are suddenly confronted with a new set of steppe-nomads, the Scythians. According to ancient

5. Aside from a few passing references in other sources, which I shall note, all information on Cumantsa here will be derived from one book, *Hronicul Dobruja* by O. Densusianu (Bucharest, 1929), which was drawn to my attention by the dadaist poet Valery Oisteanu; I was able to acquire a summary and partial English translation of the relevant part of this text from a Romanian student in New York, Ion Barak; my thanks to both.Densusianu's sources for the period seem to have been limited to the newspaper published in Cumantsa in 1918 and 1919, *Luceafarul*, "The Evening Star". There may well exist untapped sources for further research in government archives in Bucharest or even in Cumantsa, or in private libraries in Romania, etc. These sources will have to await the researches of competent scholars, and perhaps the inadequacies of the present essay will inspire someone to dig deeper.

historians (Herodotus, Aristeas), the Scythians had been displaced by the Massage-
tae, who had been displaced by the Issedones, who had been displaced by the Ari-
maspi. This last race were cyclopeans with one eye each, who lived with griffins and
hoarded gold somewhere near the Altai Mountains and not far from Hyperborea—
such was the general opinion. The Scythians appear to have been a confederacy of
Ugrian and Irani barbarians, but Hippocrates said they were quite unlike any other
race of men. The Scyths made this impression in part because of their unusual brand
of shamanism, which involved a class of transvestite soothsayers called *Enarëes*;
Herodotus claims they were struck by the "sacred disease" of effeminacy because
they had insulted the Goddess of Ascalon. "The whole account," says one modern
scholar, "suggests a Tatar clan in the last stage of degeneracy"[6]—but in truth
transvestite shamanism is widely practised not only in Central Asia and Siberia but
also Indonesia and North America. Apparently it is "natural" in some way. The same
could be said for another Scythian custom that struck Herodotus as odd:—they
filled tents with burning hemp (*cannabis*) and breathed the smoke till they achieved
intoxication. (Archaeological evidence for Scythian hemp-use is quite plentiful.)
They worshipped the hearth, like many nomads, as well as Sky and Earth, the Sun,
and a goddess called Argimpasa (identified by the Greeks as Aphrodite Urania, the
patroness of homosexuality!)—also the Sea, and War. Their elite burials were exceedingly elaborate and involved human sacrifice. Thanks to excavations we also know
about Scythian art, one of the earliest and finest instances of High Barbarian style,
and later much imitated (for example, by the Celts who displaced the Scythians in
the interior Danubian region):—heraldic, vigorous, magical, and intricate. We also
know that the Scyths had more gold than they knew what to do with—so they
buried it. The legend of the Golden Fleece belongs to the Eastern shore of the Black
Sea (Colchis), but there can be no doubt that it represents an historical fact for the
whole region in ancient times: extreme wealth. Some of this gold came from as far
away as the Altai Mountains. For the Greeks and Romans, the Scythians were the
archetypal splendid barbarians, remote, mysterious, colorful but frightful. Neither
of the Classical "superpowers" ever managed to subdue them—but like most barbarians they were held back beyond the Danube, and their power never reached farther south than the Dobruja, which was called "Lesser Scythia" even in late Byzantine sources.

The Dobruja makes several appearances in Classical literature. In *The Voyage of
the Argo* by the Hellenistic poet Apollonius of Rhodes (third century BC), Jason and
Medea are fleeing from the "incident" in Colchis involving the Golden Fleece, pursued by the Colchian fleet. In Paphlagonia (on the southern shore of the Sea) they
stop so that Medea can offer a sacrifice to Hecate the witch-goddess—"but with
what ritual she prepared the offering, no one must hear…my lips are sealed by awe."
At this point an escape route is revealed to them by their Colchian ally Argus—on
the authority of "priests in Egyptian Thebes" who have "preserved tablets of stone
which their ancestors engraved with maps…. On these is shown a river, the farthest

6. *Encyclopedia Brittanica* (1953) XX: 235

Eastern Romania 1918

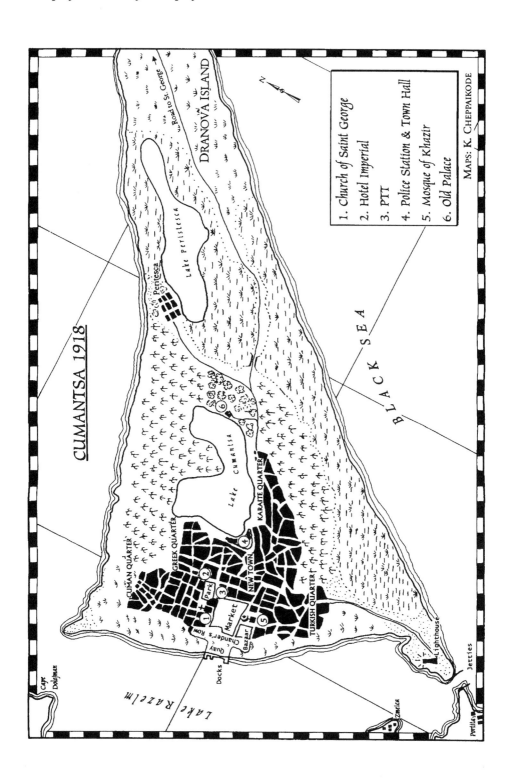

CUMANTSA 1918

1. Church of Saint George
2. Hotel Imperial
3. PTT
4. Police Station & Town Hall
5. Mosque of Khazir
6. Old Palace

MAPS: K. CHEPPAIKODE

DRANOVA ISLAND

Road to St. George

Lake Perilsessa

Pentesca

N

BLACK SEA

Lake Cumantsa

CUMAN QUARTER

GREEK QUARTER

KARAITE QUARTER

NEW TOWN

Park

Market

Bazar

Chandler's Row

Quay

Docks

TURKISH QUARTER

Lighthouse

Jetties

Portillan

Zmelca

Cape Dolojman

Lake Razelm

branch of Ocean Stream, broad and deep enough to carry merchantmen... (called the) Ister. Far away, beyond the North Wind [*i.e.*, in Hyperborea], its headwaters come rushing down from the Rhipaean Mountains. Then it flows for a time through endless plains as a single stream." It is of course the Danube. When they reach it they find the Ister "embraces an island called Peuke, shaped like a triangle, the base presenting beaches to the sea, and the apex pointing up the river, which is thus divided into two channels, one known as the Narex and the other, at the lower end of the island, as the Fair Mouth." The Colchean fleet, in hot pursuit of the *Argo*, turns up the Fair Mouth, while Jason chooses the northern mouth, the Narex. The Colchians must have used what is now called the St. George's Mouth of the Danube, just north of the present-day site of Cumantsa. The *Argo* entered the Danube at what is now the port of Sulina.

> The Colchian vessels spread panic as they went. Shepherds grazing flocks in the meadows by the river abandoned their sheep at the terrifying sight, taking the ships for live monsters that had come up from the sea, the mother of Leviathans. For none of the Istrian tribes, the Thracians and their Scythian friends, the Sigynni, the Graucenii, the Sindi, who had already occupied the great and empty plain of Laurium—none of these had ever set eyes on a sea-going vessel.[7]

The Dobruja was always half-barbarian and half-Greek. Its religion must have mirrored this synthesis—and in fact the area was always one of religious ferment. The ancient Thracian god Zalmoxis[8] had his shrines here, as did the Thracian Orpheus, and the "oriental" Dionysus. All these cults show strong evidence for shamanism or shamanic traits, which can be accounted for by "Scythian" influences. The Goddess in her orgiastic and magical forms (Aphrodite, Hecate) remained important—a link back to early Neolithic cults. This religious world lasted into the Roman Empire as the administrative unit or Province of *Dacia*.

The present town of Cumantsa dates only from the medieval period. "Ancient" Cumantsa was called Histria; its remains were discovered on Popin Island in the lagoon of Razem. Over 150 incriptions attest to the Milesian origin of the settlement, and two from the Roman period deal with Histrian fishing-rights, obviously a major source of wealth. When sand-bars formed across the estuary between the Sea and the lagoon, and the lagoon itself began to grow too shallow for shipping, Histria moved to a solid part of the sandbar and adapted an inlet as a harbor; this took place some time during the "Dark Ages", perhaps in the sixth or seventh century AD. But by this time the ethnic complexion of the region had changed, and the Greek name was abandoned.

In Classical times the area was more heavily populated and prosperous than now. Hellenic penetration was marked but never very effective and the Daco-Getic peoples of Rumania were never Hellenized as were the Balkan Thracians. But of the Greek period there are many archaeological evidences.

7. Apollonius (1959): IV, p. 155    8. Eliade (1972)

The important Milesian settlement of Histria near the Danube mouth on a lagoon island facing the modern village of Karanasuf has been well excavated.[...]

Kallatis, an old Dorian settlement on the site of the modern Mangalia in the Dobruja, was partly excavated. Inscriptions there indicate that the population was strongly Dorian and that the city, with others along that coast, was largely subject to the Thraco-Scythian kings of the interior. Kallatis was evidently one of the great grain-exporting emporiums of the Black Sea. Constanta has been identified as the ancient Tomi, the place of exile of Ovid. Remains of the city walls were discovered across the promontory upon which the residential part of the town is built. A small museum which contained all local antiquities was looted by Bulgarian soldiers during 1917 and the contents dispersed. Greek objects of commerce were found as far inland as the headwaters of the Pruth and the Argesul. Wine from Thasos and the Aegean was a much valued commodity in these regions.

The country is extremely rich in Roman remains. The great wall of Trajan can be traced without difficulty between Constanta and the Danube near Cernavoda. Extensive remains of Axiopolis at its Western end can be seen on the Danube, and excavations were carried out there. The most impressive of all the Roman monuments is the Tropaeum Trajani at Adamklissi. It stands in a wild and desolate region in the rolling steppeland between the Danube river and Constanta with much of its sculptured decoration still lying round the massive concrete core which survives. [...]

Post-Roman remains of the time before the Romanians came under the influence of Byzantium are rare, and little or nothing is known about the country at this time. The great gold treasure of Petroasa, however, which was transported to Moscow during World War I, is certainly of Hunnish or semioriental origin. It consists of two superb chalices of pure gold, inset with large garnets and with handles shaped like panthers, a large necklace of the same material, several large gold ewers elaborately chased and some superb torques.[9]

(The looted museum of Tomi and the "Hunnish gold" of Petroasa will stage a re-appearance later in our narrative.)

Ovid is still considered one of their own by the people of the Dobruja—after all, did he not actually write poems in the local Dacian tongue (and are not the Romanians actually *Romans*)? Local patriotism says yes; and the cult of Ovid was celebrated under the *coup* in Cumantsa, with translations of his *Tristia* published in *The Evening Star*. Ovid was banished by the Emperor Augustus in 8 AD; according to the poet, his crime consisted of "a poem and a mistake." The poem was the *Ars amatoria*, which was judged obscene; the "mistake" remains a secret. For eight years he languished in Pontus (*i.e.*, the Black Sea region), suffering from the climate, the

9. Xenopol (1925/1936)

threat of barbarian incursions, and intense boredom. He bombarded his friends and enemies back in Rome with bitter complaining poems (the *Tristia* or "Sadnesses" in five books) and letters (*Epistulae ex Ponto*) as well as other works. He did learn the local lingo and was adulated by the populace, but his melancholy only deepened till his death in 17 AD. Here are some of his descriptions of Pontus, selected from the poems that appeared in the *Star*, presumably the readers took a perverse pride in their dreariness:

> Beyond here lies nothing but chillness, hostility, frozen
> waves of an ice-hard sea.
> Here, on the Black Sea's bend sinister, stands Rome's bridgehead,
> facing out against Scyths and Celts,
> Her latest, shakiest bastion of law and order, only
> marginally adhesive to the empire's rim.
> [*Tristia: Book II*, 195-200]

> A region that neighbors the polar constellations
> imprisons me now, land seared by crimping frost.
> To the north lie Bosporus, Don, the Scythian marshes, a scatter
> of names in an all-but-unknown waste:
> beyond that, nothing but frozen, uninhabitable tundra—
> alas, how close I stand to the world's end!
> [*Tristia: Book III*, 4B/47-52]

> If anyone *there* still remembers exiled Ovid, if my
> name still survives in the City now I'm gone,
> let him know that beneath those stars that never dip in Ocean
> I live now in mid-barbary, hemmed about
> by wild Sarmatians, Bessi, Getae, names unworthy
> of my talent! Yet so long as the warm
> breezes still blow, the Danube between defends us:
> flowing, its waters keep off all attacks.
> But when grim winter thrusts forth its rough-set visage,
> and earth lies white under marmoreal frost,
> when gales and blizzards make the far northern regions
> unfit for habitation, then Danube's ice
> feels the weight of those creaking wagons. Snow falls: once fallen
> it lies for ever, wind-frosted. Neither sun
> nor rain can shift it. Before one fall's melted, another
> comes, and in many places lies two years,
> and so fierce the gales, they wrench off rooftops, whirl them
> headlong, skittle tall towers.
> Men keep out this aching cold with furs and stitched breeches,
> only their faces left exposed,

and often the hanging ice in their hair tinkles,
    while beards gleam white with frost.
Wine stands unbottled, retaining the shape of its vessel,
    so that what you get to drink isn't liquor, but lumps.


...as soon
as the Danube's been frozen level by [...] ice-dry wind-chill
    hordes of hostile savages ride over on swift
ponies, their pride, with bows that shoot long-range arrows
    and cut a marauding swath through the countryside.
Some neighbours flee, and with none to protect their steadings
    their property, unguarded, makes quick loot:
mean rustic household goods, flocks and creaking wagons,
    all the wealth a poor local peasant has.
Others are caught, driven off, hands tied behind them,
    gazing back in vain at fields and home;
others again die there, those sharp barbed arrows through them—
    die in agony, too, for the flying steel is smeared
with venom. What such raiders can't drag off or carry
    they destroy: unoffending hovels go up in flames,
and even while peace still prevails, men quake in terror
    at the thought of attack, the fields are left unploughed.
[*Tristia: Book III*, 10/1-24, 52-68]


You boast no fresh springs: your water's brackish, saline—
    drink it, and wonder whether thirst's been slaked
or sharpened! Your open fields have few trees, and those sterile,
    your coast's a no-man's-land, more sea than soil.
There's no birdsong, save for odd stragglers from the distant
    forest, raucously calling, throats made harsh by brine;
across the vacant plains grim wormwood bristles—a bitter crop, well-
    suited to its site.
[*Black Sea Letters: Book III*, 1/18-24]

The translator, Peter Green, adds this note:

It is hard to remember, too, when reading his descriptions of barrenness
and infertility, presenting the Dobruja as a kind of Ultima Thule on the
rim of the known world, that this area had long been famous for its wheat-
harvests, and that today Constanta raises not only wheat, but also the vines
and fruit-trees which Ovid missed so badly. If he had ever travelled in the
Dobruja, he would have known that treelessness was a merely local phenomenon: about forty miles north of Constanta huge forests began. But he
never seems to have ventured beyond Tomis itself: the terms of his *relega-*

*tio* may have forbidden local travel, and in any case conditions in the hinterland were highly dangerous. Such knowledge as he does reveal about the area he could easily have picked up from Book 7 of Strabo's *Geography*, available in Rome as early as 7 BC.

> Yet my talent fails to respond to me as it once did:
> it's an arid shore I'm ploughing, with sterile share.
> In just the way (I assure you) that silt blocks water-channels
> and the flow's cut short in the choked spring,
> so my heart's been vitiated by the silt of misfortune,
> and my verse flows in a narrower vein.
> Had Homer himself been consigned to this land, believe me,
> he too would have become a Goth.
> [*Black Sea Letters* IV: 2/15-22]

> Nor will the Cyclops out-bestialize our Scythian
> cannibals—yet they're but a tiny part
> of the terror that haunts me. Though from Scylla's misshapen
> womb monsters bark, sailors have suffered more
> from pirates. Charybdis is nothing to our Black Sea corsairs,
> though thrice she sucks down and thrice spews up the sea:
> they may prey on the eastern seaboard with greater licence,
> but still don't leave this coastline safe from raids.
> [...]
> Arrivals from home report that such things scarce find credence
> among you: pity the wretch who bears what's past belief!
> Yet believe it: nor shall I leave you ignorant of the reasons
> why rugged winter freezes the Black Sea.
> We lie veryι close here to the wain-shaped constellation
> that brings excessive cold:
> from here the North Wind rises, this coast is his homeland,
> and the place that's the source of his strength lies closer still.
> But the South Wind's breezes are languid, seldom reach here
> from that other far-distant pole. Besides,
> there's fluvial influx into the land-locked Euxine,
> river on river making the sea's strength ebb,
> all flowing in:
> [here follows a long list of rivers flowing into the Black Sea...]
> and countless others, Danube greatest among them,
> a match for even the Nile. So great a mass
> of fresh water adulterates the sea to which it's added,
> stops it keeping its own strength.
> Even its colour's diluted—azure no longer, but like some

still pond or stagnant swamp. The fresh
water's more bouyant, rides above the heavier
deep with its saline base.
[*Black Sea Letters* IV 10/23-30. 35-47, 57-64]

The translator adds this interesting note:

Reports from Rome suggest that people disbelieve his horror-stories. Very
well: he will take one of them (the freezing of the Black Sea) and offer scientific proof that he is right. A prevailing north wind combined with the
influx of numerous rivers into the sea produces the necessary conditions:
fresh water rides above salt, and is more easily frozen, while the wind aids
the process by creating a chill-factor. This not-quite-parody of didactic epic
gains considerable force from the fact that it happens to be scientifically
impeccable: cf J. Rouch, *La Méditerranée* (1946), pp. 187-93, cited by
André *Pont.*, pp. 142-3, n. 1. Dr Stefan Stoenescu informs me that 'the rich
salty waters [of the Danube delta] create a brackish region near and along
the littoral which allows an inversion of temperature to take place. The
unsalty waters of the Danube have sufficient power to maintain a thin layer
of comparatively sweet fresh water above the deeply settled salty Mediterranean current. As a result, near the Danube delta shores freezing is not an
unusual occurrence. Ovid was right.'[10]

 co    co    co

In the early Byzantine period the region was again over-run by waves of barbarians. While the Sarmatians and Gepidae and Slavs and Avars and Magyars and
Huns and Goths and Bulgars moved on to the West and into the limelight of history (or not), the Dobruja was settled by less successful tribes, content to live
obscurely in the marshes. In particular, the Cumantsa region was taken over first by
the Petchenegs (or Patzinaks, Latin *Bisseni*), and then their relatives the Cumans,
who gave Cumantsa its name. The descendants of the Petchenegs are today known
as the Sops, and live mostly in the southern or Bulgarian Dobruja, although some
remain around Cumantsa. Again the *Encyclopedia Britannica* rewards us with an
amusing example of professorial prejudice:

The Petchenegs were ruled by a Khan and organised in 8 hordes and 40
minor units, each under its khan of lower degree. They were purely
nomadic; on their raids they took their women and children with them,
forming their camps out of rings of wagons. They wore long beards and
moustachios, and were dressed in long kaftans. The food of the wealthy
was blood and mares' milk; of the poor, millet and mead. They were orig-

10. Ovid (1994)

inally "magicians," *i.e.*, fire-worshippers; but a form of Islam early became current among them and the nation was temporarily converted to Christianity in 1007-1008. They were the most dreaded and detested of the nomads; Matthew of Edessa calls them "the carrion-eaters, the godless, unclean folk, the wicked, blood-drinking beasts." Other anecdotes are current of their shamelessness, and many of their cruelty; they invariably slew all male prisoners who fell into their hands. The modern Sops are despised by the other inhabitants of Bulgaria for their bestiality and stupidity but dreaded for their savagery. They are a singularly repellent race, short-legged, yellow-skinned, with slanting eyes and projecting cheek-bones. Their villages are generally filthy, but the women's costumes show a barbaric profusion of gold lace.

As for the Cumans (a.k.a. the *Poloutsi* or *Walwen*), their moments of power came somewhat later, in the eleventh century. They are related to the Seljuk Turks but had mingled with the Kipchak Mongols as well. They defeated the Jewish Khazars and for a while held an empire centered on Kiev. For a time the Ukraine was known as Cumania.

> At this time the Cumans were partly Mohammedan, but still largely pagan. "We worship one God, who is in the sky," they told the first missionaries to them, "and beyond that we know nothing; for the rest, we have abominable habits." As to these the "Chronicle of Nestor" states: "Our Polovtsi too have their own habits; they love to shed blood, and boast that they eat carrion and the flesh of unclean beasts, such as the civet and the hamster; they marry their mothers-in-law and daughters-in-law, and imitate in all things the example of their fathers." These Cumans wore short kaftans, and shaved their heads, except for two long plaits. They seem to have been purely hunters and warriors, leaving the cultivation of the soil to their subject tribes of Slavs. Cumania, as south Russia was called, possessed thriving towns, and traded in slaves, furs and other products, but the trade was probably in the hands of Greeks and Genoese; the funeral monuments attributed to the Cumans (pyramids or pillars, each surmounted by a male figure bearing in his hand a drinking cup) were probably not their work.[11]

The Cumans were shattered by the Mongol invasions of the 13th century. Some of them ended up as far away as Egypt, where they had been sold as slaves. There they established a new dynasty, the Boharib Mamelukes, and managed even to revenge themselves on the Mongols. Some of their stay-at-home cousins in the Dobruja remained Christian, although they later supplied many Janissaries to the Sultan at Istanbul under the notorious "Ottoman boy tax". Their descendents nowadays are called *"Gagauz"*, although in the Cumantsa region (where more are

---

11. See the *Codex Cumanicus* (Kuun, 1880); partial translation in Boswell (1927)

Moslems) they call themselves Cumans. They comprise the poor peasants, hunters, and fishermen of the area.

By the early 15th century the whole of Bulgaria and Romania had been absorbed into the Ottoman empire. Cumantsa became more a Turkish town than anything else—Turkish was still spoken there in 1918—but it now began to acquire its numerous minorities as well. There were the Petchenegs and Cumans, the Greeks, Crimean Tatars, and Karaite Jews as well as Ottoman Turks and Romanians. The Karaites are an early medieval reformist sect that rejected the Talmud, and claimed to represent even earlier forms of Judaism such as the Sadducees and Essenes. At various times they were considered pro-Islamic by Moslems and pro-Christian by Christians. Although the Karaites arrived in the Black Sea region in the tenth century, their scholars (including the famous Crimean, Abraham Firkovitch, d. 1874) claimed they were already there in Classical times. Therefore the Karaites were not guilty of the Crucifixion—since they had not been in Jerusalem at the time!—and were thus exempt from the restrictions placed on Ashkenazi Jews. Similar arguments won them exemptions in Ottoman realms. In Cumantsa the little Karaite community engaged in trade but not in money-lending, and anti-Semitism never took root there.

For some time the Ottomans ruled Cumantsa directly, under a Pasha or Bey, as a separate *sanjak* of the Empire. In the late 17th century, however, the government in Eastern Europe was changed to "Phanariot Rule". In this system the Sublime Porte appointed Orthodox princes or "hospodars", chosen from among the old Byzantine royal and noble families of Istanbul, in consultation with the Patriarch of the Orthodox Church.[12] Moldavia, Wallachia, Bessarabia and other tiny principalities were passed around in these families like heirlooms. Competition was fierce and reigns tended to be brief. In 1720, due to a byzantine rivalry between two branches of the Mavrocordato family, a certain disappointed office-seeker (Constantine I) was bought off with the creation of a separate statelet in Cumantsa. At first quite bitter (he'd wanted Moldavia), Constantine soon discovered the advantages of Cumantsa:—it produced a tidy income, and...no one else wanted it. Although he never ceased to dream of bigger realms, Constantine I Mavrocordato soon settled down to one of the longest and most somnolent reigns of any Phanariot hospodar. Not only that, but he was also succeeded by a son, Constantine II, and a grandson, Georghiu I. Altogether, Phanariot rule in Cumantsa lasted from 1720 to 1811, and constituted its golden age. When its independence came to an end (it was re-absorbed into Moldavia), the Mavrocordatos remained in Cumantsa as local nobility, but their fortunes declined under the united monarchy of Romania after 1859. They were too attached to Istanbul, and their title of hospodar was not recognized by the Court in Bucharest. Cumantsa was ignored and fell into decline.

In 1888 an heir to the Mavrocordatos was born, Georghiu III. He grew up in the old family palace, which by now was crumbling away for lack of funds. He was educated at a military academy in Bucharest, and spent his vacations in Cumantsa.

12. For an excellent summary of the Phanariot period see Runciman (1968), chapter 10.

In 1905 he was sent to Germany to study philosophy at the University of Munich—where we shall join him in the next chapter.

## III The Young Hospodar

> *Happiness and culture.* We are devastated by the sight of the scenes of our childhood: the garden house, the church with its graves, the pond and the woods—we always see them again as sufferers. We are gripped by self-pity, for what have we not suffered since that time! And here, everything is still standing so quiet, so eternal: we alone are so different, so in turmoil; we even rediscover some people on whom Time has sharpened its tooth no *more* than on an oak tree: peasants, fishermen, woodsmen—they are the same.
> —*Human, All-Too-Human,* 168

Cumantsa in the last years of the 19th century must have been an interesting place to experience childhood. As a port it attracted a variety of exotic types—and it must be noted that in its decline it had turned to smuggling (grain, wine, hashish and opium, manufactured goods—and stolen antiquities) to supplement its meager income from fishing. The swamps and marshes of interior Cumantsa were the haunt of Cuman smugglers, and the little shops of the Turks, Greeks and Jews were full of surprising items. The marketplace between the Mosque of Khezr and the Church of St. George (formerly an episcopal see of the Orthodox Patriarchate) must have seemed a colorful universe to the young hospodar.

The *Hronocul Dobruja* does not mention the fact, but St. George, the Christian patron of this region, is the same person as Khezr, the Islamic patron of the region. Khezr is the Hidden Prophet or the "Green Man" of Islamic esotericism and folklore. He accompanied Alexander the Great to find the Water of Life—but he alone achieved immortality, while the Macedonian attained only the world. As a water-spirit he guards certain places by seas and rivers (including the Rock of Gibraltar)—but as a prophet he appears to spiritual seekers with no living master to initiate them or rescue them from death in the desert. Wherever he walks flowers and herbs spring up in his footsteps, and he always wears green. Why St. George (of draconian fame) should be identified with Khezr is not clear—but he is. The Dobruja is rich in folklore, but most of it has never been translated from Romanian.

The diminished estate of the Mavrocordatos was worked by Cuman peasants, who no doubt introduced young Georghiu to the mysteries of the marshes. According to a 1903 edition of a *Baedeker Guide to Eastern Europe and Turkey,* the Dobruja was a sportsman's paradise, with nine different varieties of duck, numerous other game birds, roe deer, foxes, wolves, bears, uncountable species of fish and shellfish, four varieties of crow, five of warblers, seven of woodpeckers, eight of buntings, four of falcons, five of eagles, etc. The marshes are considered desolate and uninhabitable by the inhabitants of the coasts, and of the interior, and in the entire Sanjak of Cumantsa around 1900 there were only a few thousand Cumans outside the city (which itself had a population of about 5000). In summer the marshes simmer; in winter they freeze solid. Ovid had nothing nice to say about the climate, and neither does *Baedeker*. But as every afficianado of swamps will know, such "desolation" hides a rare and elusive beauty based on sheer exuberance of life, and on a limited but subtle palette of tones and seasonal monochromatisms. The summer vacations of the young hospodar must have resembled a page out of Turgenev's wonderful *Hunter's Sketchbook*.

Based on what we know of his later life we can be certain that the Turkish culture of the town also held appeal and mystery for Georghiu. The Turks of the Dobruja were known for their old-fashioned ways, and in the late 19th century were still wearing Ottoman hats and turbans (fezzes did not come into style until later) and traditional costumes. As notorious gourmands the Turks made full use of Cumantsa's resources to create a unique cuisine, which they sold at little foodstalls in the market along with coffee and tobacco. Wherever there are Turks there are cafés, and men smoking hookahs. Greeks too are fond of good food (including wine), and also fond of the café life. A great deal of time was spent in Cumantsa arguing about politics and telling lies, fueled either with coffee or wine.

Because of Cumantsa's old connections with the Janissary corps in Istanbul— the Imperial Guard—there was also a strong connection with the Bektashi Sufi order, to which virtually all Janissaries belonged. The mosque of Khezr was used for Bektashi seances, and it is rumored that heterodoxies such as the mystical usage of wine and hashish were not unknown.[13]

Perhaps by the time he reached adolescence and had experienced Bucharest, Georghiu came to look on his childhood home as backward and boring. Many adolescents do—and with less reason. But it is certain that no sooner had he arrived in Germany in 1905 than he began to feel nostalgia and even homesickness for Cumantsa (we know because he later said so, in one of his articles for the *Evening Star*). If nothing else, this is the sign of a happy childhood.

Unfortunately we know little more about Mavrocordato's higher education than about his boyhood. Densusianu in his *Chronicle* had access only to the articles written for the *Star* and a few letters. Perhaps the archives in Munich, the records of the University, would add something to our knowledge (assuming they were not destroyed in World War II)—but for now we are reduced largely to speculation. We know that he studied law and philosophy and we know he received a degree; we do not know his teachers, his friends, his extra-curricular activities or adventures. He read Kant and Hegel. He made at least one trip to Paris, and apparently learned French. He probably traveled around Germany during his vacations, in the *Wandervogel* style then coming into fashion with German students (he mentions the pleasures of hiking and mountain-climbing). Above all—and of this there can be no doubt—he made the biggest discovery of his life. He found Nietzsche.

That is, he found Nietzsche's books. The man himself had been in a drooling stupor since 1889, and dead since 1900. But his books had finally begun to live. In

13. Birge (1937)

part this was thanks to Nietzsche's horrible sister, Elisabeth Förster, whose husband had died in South America trying to start a utopian colony for pure Aryan anti-Semites,[14] and who now ran the Nietzsche Archive in Sils Maria (where Mavrocordato probably paid pilgrimage and met her). She was then working on Nietzsche's uncollected notes for *The Will to Power*, and had already created the cult of relics, lies, and evasions that would later prove so congenial to Adolf Hitler. Despite Elisabeth's genius for bad publicity, however, Nietzsche's books spoke for themselves. (The Nazi editions, with all of Nietzsche's attacks on anti-Semitism and nice things about Jews censored out, appeared much later.) Even before he died, something very much like a Nietzschean movement had begun in Germany. Young people were particularly susceptible; and so far from being seen as a prophet of reaction, Nietzsche was considered the most radical and even revolutionary of all modern thinkers. The movement took off in the late 1890s and reached something of a fever pitch during Mavrocordato's years in Munich. One thinks of certain passages in Robert Musil's *Man Without Qualities* which describe the movement as it manifested in Vienna, with bad piano playing, *sturm und drang*, fervid sex, and monumental egotisms on display. As he himself had foreseen, Nietzsche was a kind of poison—or hallucinogen. (Nietzsche himself experimented with drugs and his works are studded with drug references.) But every fad spins off some silliness. Some fads are remembered—like Mesmerism—chiefly for their silliness. But Nietzsche was no quack. He was probably the most important thinker of the period—maybe the century (but *which century?*): a genius whose works are eternally valid, or eternally damnable, according to your taste. But…eternal. That was his wish, and it came true. And one of the peculiar qualities of his writing is that it can still ignite the same kind of uncontrollable mad enthusiasm in young readers today, even without a "movement" to encourage them. And Mavrocordato fell hard.

Nietzsche made many sneering remarks about anarchism, and therefore it may surprise the reader to learn that in turn-of-the-century Germany he was considered an anarchist thinker by many, both admirers and detractors. R. Hinton Thomas has painted an amusing picture of the situation:

In one pamphlet, the writer imagines a German, himself presumably, returning home after some years abroad to find the scene dominated by the 'cult of the self, of one's own *Persönlichkeit'*. It is plain anarchism, he thinks, and it is all Nietzsche's fault. Anarchism could easily serve as a flag of convenience for merely selfish attitudes, as in the case of the 'fanatical anarchists' who, according to Lily Braun, frequented Max von Egidy's household and 'tried to justify the freedom with which they indulged their own petty desires with the excuse that they were living out their *Persönlichkeit'*. Even simple bad manners, with no deeper purpose than to *épater le bourgeois* could count as anarchism, with the culprits instancing Nietzsche in self-justification. One writer mentions someone he knew who

14. Macintyre (1992)

thought it one of the prerogatives of the Superman to spit in public and to eat with his fingers. When those nearby objected, he 'proudly appealed to his *Individualität* and to the fact that he was a Nietzschean.' There is nothing more revolting, it was said, 'than when some vain young fathead plays the part of Superman in cafés and pubs frequented by women...or when late at night some youthful degenerate swanks around in the Friederichstraße "beyond good and evil"' and it was shocking that 'the name and the words of so pure and sublime a spirit as Nietzsche had to put up with being misused in this appalling way.' When the Crown Princess of Saxony ran off with a lover of menial standing, this was attributed to her having been reading his work. By the mid-1890s, the literary cafés in Berlin, Munich and Vienna were said to be 'so swarming with "Supermen" that you could not fail to notice it, and it left one speechless with astonishment.' When in 1897 an anarchist was sentenced for his part in a plot to kill a police officer in Berlin, he defended himself by reference to Nietzsche.[15]

Anarchist or radical admiration for Nietzsche was not limited to the rank-and-file but would even come to enflame such leftists as Emma Goldman, who said that insofar as Nietzsche's aristocracy was "neither of birth nor of wealth" but "of the spirit," he was an anarchist, and all true anarchists are aristocrats. In France the notorious anarchist bank-robbers, the Bonnot Gang, put their Nietzscheanism into action, and the philosopher was particularly admired by anarchist Individualists and readers of Max Stirner.[16] Georg Brandes coined the term "radical aristocratism" to describe Nietzsche's (non) system—but the man himself spent so much ink attacking the Church, the State, monarchism, legislative democracy, German culture and other *bêtes noires* of the radicals, that even the most egalitarian and communitarian leftists could find something to admire in his work.[17] Besides, even his criticisms of anarchism and socialism could be seen as helpful, especially on the level of psychology. Radicals were forced to examine their souls for evidence of *ressentiment*, the slave mentality of the envious *chandala*. They would have to ask themselves if their socialism were not mere camouflaged Christian sentimentality, and they would have to question the inevitability of "Progress". They would have to face the existential problem of commitment to process rather than *telos*. Nietzsche himself asked to be *overcome*—and perhaps those who wrestled with him hardest learned the most. But Mavrocordato never struggled. He was seduced.

The Munich Soviet of 1918 was packed with radicals weaned on Nietzsche. The most important were Kurt Eisner, Jewish journalist and critic, dramatist,

15. Hinton Thomas (1983): 50
16. The very obvious parallels between Nietzsche and Stirner have never really been explored. Nietzsche had read Stirner, apparently, and sometimes seems to refer to Stirnerian ideas, but never mentioned him. Many anarchists admired both, and both have been called proto-fascists. See Max Stirner, *The Ego and His Own*.
17. Nietzsche says, "We can destroy only as creators" (*The Gay Science*, 122), thus echoing Bakunin's famous line about destruction *as* creation.

philosopher and man of letters, who became the unlikely founder of free Munich, and who was assassinated by the Thule *Gesellschaft*; and Gustav Landauer, also Jewish, also philosopher, an anarchist activist, who became the Minister of Education, and was also murdered by the occult Aryan order. I feel certain that Mavrocordato read Landauer, possibly early versions of his major work *On Socialism* (published on the eve of the Munich uprising, but preceded by portions and versions in various anarchist papers), and probably his Nietzschean novel, *The Preacher of Death* (even the title was from Nietzsche). It's even possible that Mavrocordato met Landauer, although the writer was not living in Munich at the time. The key to Mavrocordato's knowledge of Landauer is contained in a reference in the *Star* to Landauer's theory of *the folk*. Landauer was the leading thinker of a school of thought that most people nowadays could never even imagine:—left-wing *volk*-ism. Like the well-known publisher Eugen Diederichs (who not only published on Nietzsche but also reprinted books that Nietzsche *liked*),[18] Landauer believed that the particularity and autonomy of any one people implied the particularity and autonomy of all peoples:—a kind of *volkisch* universal humanism. Landauer and Diederichs sponsored or encouraged left-wing *volkisch* youth groups in competition with the chauvinist (and anti-Nietzschean) *Wandervögel*. They pictured a future of agrarian and urban communes in federation, according to Proudhonian anarchist principles, all different and all free. This thinking influenced such anarcho-zionist Jews as the young Martin Buber, Gershom Scholem, and Walter Benjamin. And of course it outraged the German Nationalists, who believed in centralization and in the superiority of German culture. Left-wing *volk*-ism had a cultish aspect (like Nietzscheanism)[19] with its sun-worshipping nudists, utopian colonies, guitar-playing youth in *lederhösen*, etc. But it also had its serious side—so serious that Landauer and many others were martyred for it. Nazism erased the memory of left-wing *volk*-ism and made the whole concept of the *volk* stink of fascism and of death. But in 1900 it was still innocent and alive, and constituted a whole *milieu*. Moreover, like the Turks and Greeks back home in Cumantsa, the anarchists and poets and bohemians and madmen of Munich (like those of Vienna) liked to while away the hours in coffeeshops; Mavrocordato would have fitted in well; he probably earned points for his sheer exoticism, if nothing else. (He was said to be handsome.)

Among the Nietzschean circles in Munich at that time we might include that of the aristocratic and pederastic poet Stephan George, although there is no evidence that Mavrocordato knew him. Much more likely in this respect is the "Cosmic Circle" around the eccentric occultist Ludwig Klages, who later wrote a popular book on Nietzsche (*Die Psychologischen Errungenschaften Nietzsches*, 1926) and who preached the doctrine in the cafés and *ateliers* of Munich's bohemian quarter. Klages later veered to the Right, but culturally he was always a radical. At his salons one might meet a whole *demimonde* of faddists, cranks, health-nuts, mystics, artists, and

18. See Hinton Thomas, p. 116*ff.*    19. Nietzsche himself contradicts himself on *volk*-ism. In his earlier works he seems to share *volkisch* ideas, but in his later works he tends to make fun of the "folk-soul" and other such concepts.

dangerous women. Once again, a "Prince" from the exotic East (or nearly-East) would doubtless have been lionized in such a den.

Unfortunately, however, all is conjecture. Judging by Mavrocordato's writings the only person he "met" in Germany was Nietzsche. We also have no information on anyone he may have met in France. However, in all this dearth, one peculiar exception occurs. We know at least one person Mavrocordato met—somewhere in Europe—sometime before his return to Cumantsa in 1913. Densusianu's *Chronicle* missed it entirely. In the *Collected Correspondence* of the Romanian poet Tristan Tzara (Paris, 1967), the following telegram appears:

December 8, 1918

Zurich

To the Hospodar Georghiu III Mavrocordato Greetings old friend stop congratulations stop we have a homeland stop Tzara.

The telegraph wires into Cumantsa, which were cut during the *coup* on November 4, were restored to use only on December 1st or 2nd. Tzara's telegram must have been one of the first to reach the Provisional Government from abroad, but it was not printed in *The Star* (or else Densusianu missed it). Or perhaps Mavrocordato never actually received it. So far it remains a mystery.[20] Mavrocordato is not mentioned in any biography of Tzara known to me. The whole matter is a tantalizing dead end.

Altogether Mavrocordato spent eight years in Europe. During those years the Balkans and the Black Sea region were yanked out of their obscure backwardness and into the glare of history by a series of crises. The Bosnia crisis of 1908 drew the attention of the major European powers, and the sweet odor of decay emanating from the Ottoman Empire aroused their predatory instincts. We cannot begin here to try to unravel the intricate karmic web that sucked the world into a century of total war—a web that was spun around and from Eastern Europe. Suffice it to say that events led blindly on to the First Balkan War in 1912, in which Turkey's European colonies declared their intention to break free at last and finally from the Sublime Porte. During this war the Dobruja emerged as a bone of contention between Romania and Bulgaria. Immediately after the first round ended Bulgaria attacked its former allies (the "Second Balkan War") and attempted to occupy the Dobruja; instead a powerful Romanian army swept them all the way back to Sophia, and laid claim to the entire coastal region. Although Cumantsa was not involved in any actual battles during this Second Balkan War in 1913, the whole area was thrown into disorder, and there were reports of starvation and disease.

20. This discovery is also due to V. Oisteanu, who was led by it to uncover Densusianu's *Chronicle*. Tzara, whose real name was Samuel Rosenstock, was born in Moinesti, Romania in 1896.

As soon as peace was declared on April 10, Georghiu Mavrocordato hurried home. His mother was still alive, and living alone in the old palace. Georghiu seems to have been an only child, and no doubt he needed to return in order to assume his responsibilities as head of the family (he was then 30 years old) in such unsettled times. He arrived by boat from Istanbul, since the interior was supposedly still unsafe.

Still, peace had been declared, and Mavrocordato apparently intended to enjoy it. He arrived with two friends, a Romanian poet named Vlad Antonescu (probably an old companion from Bucharest schooldays), who had a passionate interest in Romanian folklore; and a German, a Classicist and amateur archaeologist, Wilhelm Schlamminger of Munich—no doubt a companion of university days, and an ardent Nietzschean. These two young men intended to have a long and productive holiday in Cumantsa as guests of the hospodar, collecting local myths and inscriptions, wandering about the countryside, hunting, fishing and sailing. As it turned out, they had a very long holiday indeed—seven years.

In the immediate aftermath of the Second Balkan War, the political situation in the Dobruja was precarious, and getting more so by the day. Several "peasant uprisings" had occurred both during and after the war. The Petchenegs and Cumans of Cumantsa had so far remained passive, but they were suffering the effects of absentee landlordism, tax, debt, bad harvests, and general dissatisfaction. No one had wanted Bulgarian rule, but no one was particularly happy to see the Romanians back again. In fact there were never many ethnic Romanians in the Dobruja, and the administrators sent out from Bucharest were never popular. Pro-Turkish sentiment was common, though politically unorganized. Still, there was talk (in the coffeeshops and wineshops no doubt) of an independent—or at least autonomous—Cumantsa.

The three friends decided to stay the winter. Antonescu and Schlamminger apparently found themselves in a sort of scholarly pig heaven, a virtually untouched goldmine of folk songs, superstitions, ruins, and antiques of dubious provenance; they couldn't bear to tear themselves away. As for Mavrocordato, he began to act as if he meant to stay on forever:—he started repairs on the palace, and ordered a load of books on agriculture and engineering. Perhaps he had developed Faustian impulses—a desire to donate his talents to something concrete. Action was indeed on the horizon—but not agriculture or engineering.

In June of 1914 the three friends sailed down the coast to Constanta, where they observed the state visit of the Russian Czar. They were not impressed. Neither was the rest of the world. A few days later in Sarajevo, the murder of the Austrian Archduke Ferdinand (by a Serbian terrorist) set fire instantaneously to the whole web of intrigue and hatred woven around the Balkans—and the whole world. On July 29, World War I began.

The three friends made no move to sign up in anybody's army, and apparently no one asked them. Mavrocordato's Nietzschean analysis of the war, published later (in 1918), condemns the whole affair as a conspiracy of moribund powers against

Life itself, a meaningless sacrifice, and a means of suppressing the inevitable World Revolution (which had finally broken out in Russia). In 1914 however the war probably seemed more an inconvenience to be avoided than a final cataclysm—which it certainly resembled by 1917! In brief, the friends decided to lie low in Cumantsa and *wait it out*. (At the time it was expected to last a month or so at most.)

By 1915 however it had become clear that the war had just gotten started. Still the friends demonstrated no eagerness to hurl themselves on any pyres of outraged nationalism—were they not "good Europeans?"—and as a mark of their complete rejection of everything going on in the outside world, they founded a society for the study of local languages and antiquities, and launched a periodical in its name.The organization was known as the Scythian Club, and the irregular "journal" became *The Evening Star.*

The Scythian Club was serious about its work, and the early issues of the *Star* are full of the discoveries of Antonescu and Schlamminger—and of course, of Nietzsche. But the Club, which held regular meetings at the old palace, was meant to fulfill a social role as well, with occasional gourmet dinners, high teas, and field trips. It soon acquired a surprising number of members, considering the time and place and the lofty intellectual tone of the society. Ovid would have been quite jealous, as the *Star* boasted happily. How often he had yearned to hear a word of Latin spoken in his dreary exile at Tomis—or even bad Greek! And here was a whole organization devoted to the pleasures of the mind—and the table! In Ovid's day there was no local wine, either.

Aside from a few Romanian officials and gentry, the Club enjoyed an ethnic mix worthy of the old Cumantsa tradition. First and perhaps most important was Shaykh Mehmet Effendi, the leader of the local branch of the Bektashi Sufi Order. Shaykh Mehmet owned a little antiquities shop in the bazaar, and although he was no scholar, he knew more about local history and art than the rest of the Club put together. He was a genial and liberal personality—in fact, there is some evidence that he may have belonged to the Freemasons, who were strong in Turkey and especially amongst the Bektashis. If the Shaykh also dealt in antiquities of dubious provenance—some perhaps downright "hot"—he was certainly no common smuggler, and the Club appointed him its treasurer. The Shaykh had peculiar political connections in Istanbul. It is not clear whether he was an agent of the Sublime Porte or of the Young Turks (or of both), but no one doubted he was an agent of some sort. On the subject of Turkish sufism, he was as well informed and informative as he was on Pontic relics, curiosa, and Scythian lore. Without him, as Mavrocordato wrote, the Club would have been impossible.

Another exotic member was Kuthen Corvinu, the hereditary Ilkhan of the Petchenegs and Cumans of Cumantsa. Seemingly a simple peasant, the Khan was persuaded to address the Club only with great difficulty—but then proceeded to bowl over the membership with an evening of folk songs and tales that reduced Antonescu (who wrote the report) to sheer ecstasy. The old Khan was accompanied by his daughter Anna, who helped him translate the archaic Cuman dialect into modern Romanian. Possibly it was on this occasion that Mavrocordato fell in love with her, although he may have arranged the whole affair simply to win over her father. Despite the Cuman reputation for ugliness she was said to be strikingly beautiful, and that evening she wore her nicest folkloric costume and kilos of barbaric family jewels. Everyone was charmed, and at once insisted on father and daughter joining the Club. Mavrocordato was more than charmed.

(I must admit I'm giving Mavrocordato the benefit of the doubt when I assume that he loved Anna, since, with typical self-effacement, he never says as much in print. The proof is that he later married her. As it happens, the marriage was exceedingly well-timed for political purposes, as we shall see. But my impression of Georghiu is that he would never have married simply for expediency. He was far too Romantic to be devious.)

Another indispensable Scythian was a young man from Odessa with the mellifluous name of Caleb Afendopoulo. Born a Karaite Jew, Afendopoulo had worked as a clerk in his father's shoe store in Odessa, and devoured books. He acquired a dozen languages (Russian, South Russian, Turkish, Georgian, several Caucasian dialects, Yiddish, Hebrew, Turkish, Arabic, Romanian, French, Greek and perhaps a few more)—but he lost his faith. Moreover, he was guilty of poetry, and of studying Kabbalah (strictly an Ashkenazi subject), and of despising his family trade. Adding insult to injury he became a socialist, and then—after meeting Nestor Makhno in Odessa in 1914—an anarchist. He was arrested for distributing anarchist propaganda, and after his release his father disinherited and banished him. He landed in Cumantsa, where he had distant relatives in the Karaite community, just in time to attend the first meeting of the Scythian Club and be chosen as its Secretary. His first contribution to the *Star* was a translation of some ancient riddles from the *Codex Cumanicus*—proving that he had already acquired another dialect. Presumably he also began "agitating" amongst the peasants of Cumantsa, spreading the gospel of "Land and Liberty".

Another anarchist Scythian was no savant, but a common seaman, a Levantine drifter named Enrico Elias, of uncertain nationality but lately resident of Milan, where he had joined the anarchist Mariners' Union and taken part in violent demonstrations. Elias, like many Mediterranean nomads and Italian workingclass troublemakers, was a left-wing Stirnerite Individualist Anarchist, a type that is nowadays almost forgotten. The Stirnerites—especially the Italians—made a point of joining any uprising they could reach in time, whatever ideological banner was being unfurled. Socialist, Marxist, syndicalist, anarchist—nothing mattered except that it be *revolt*.[21] The point was that the individual could realize him or herself only

21. History, materialism, monism, positivism, and all the "isms" of this world are old and rusty tools which I don't need or mind anymore. My principle is life, my end is death. I wish to live my life intensely for to embrace my life tragically.

You are waiting for the revolution? My own began a long time ago! When you will be ready (God, what an endless wait!) I won't mind going along with you for awhile. But when you'll stop, I shall continue on my insane and triumphal way toward the great and

in struggle against what was *not* self—*i.e.,* everything that denied self and suppressed the freedom to "become what you are" (as Nietzsche quoted Pindar). This existentialist insouciance obviously led some later Stirnerites into Fascismo—including young Benito Mussolini. But to true Individualists, fascism was no more acceptable than Marxism, since both were authoritarian systems. Blow it *all* up.

Elias wrote nothing for the *Star,* and held no office in the Club. But later, when the conspiracy began, he was made head of the *military committee.* Obviously Elias was the one serious and perhaps professorial revolutionary strategist in Cumantsa. Although his influence on events is difficult to trace, I believe it was crucial. I doubt there would have been a *coup d'etat* without him. And if there had been, it would not have lasted ten minutes without him. For the time being, however, there was no thought of revolt. War had thrown this motley crew together, each one perhaps in flight from something, each perhaps somehow in hiding. By sheer chance, they discovered each other and themselves together, and began somehow to enjoy life more because they were enjoying it in each other's company. Seven varieties of duck, and the amusing local vintages, probably had a lot to do with it. Coffee at Shaykh Mehmet's shop—all-night bull sessions about Nietzsche, the War, life, love, and the usual *et ceteras*—dawn strolls along the beaches—roaring fires in the huge barbaric fireplaces of the old palace, with its rotting tapestries and heavy victorian bric-a-brac—even an archaeological dig in ancient Histria across the lagoon—all this kept them occupied—all this kept them from thinking about the war—about the trouble that might be approaching…that *was* approaching. And then one day in August 1916, the trouble was almost there. The illusion of real life broke in on the reality of their Scythian dream. The Germans were coming.

sublime conquest of the nothing!

Any society that you build will have its limits. And outside the limits of my society the unruly and heroic tramps will wander, with their wild and virgin thoughts—they who cannot live without planning ever new and dreadful outbursts of rebellion!

I shall be among them!

And after me, as before me, there will be those saying to their fellows: "So turn to yourselves rather than to your Gods or to your idols. Find what hides in yourselves; bring it to light; show yourselves!"

Because every person; who, searching his own inwardness, extracts what was mysteriously hidden therein; is a shadow eclipsing any form of society which can exist under the sun!

All societies tremble when the scornful aristocracy of the tramps, the inaccessibles, the uniques, the rulers over the ideal, and the conquerors of the nothing resolutely advances.

So come on iconoclasts, forward!

"Already the foreboding sky grows dark and silent!"

—Renzo Novatore

Arcola, January 1920

## IV. THE *Coup d'Etat*

> The princes of Europe should consider carefully whether they can do with-
> out our support. We immoralists—we are today the only power that needs
> no allies in order to conquer: thus we are by far the strongest of the strong.
> We do not even need to tell lies: what other power can dispense with that?
> A powerful seduction fights on our behalf, the most powerful perhaps that
> there has ever been—the seduction of truth—"Truth"? Who has forced
> this word on me? But I repudiate it; but I disdain this proud word: no, we
> do not need even this; we shall conquer and come to power even without
> truth. The spell that fights on our behalf, the eye of Venus that charms and
> blinds even our opponents, is *the magic of the extreme,* the seduction that
> everything extreme exercises: we immoralists—we are the most extreme.
> —*Will to Power,* 396

Romania had not actually entered the war until 1916, and then on the side of
the Allies. Already Russia was beginning to lose control of its own domestic war politics, and hence of its army...the Revolution was brewing (Lenin was in Zurich—so
was Tristan Tzara, busy forming the dada movement). Romania's army had scarcely
emerged from the 19th century—it was known for its fine cavalry!—and was split
between two fronts, each waiting for a German blitzkrieg. The greater part of these
forces were positioned in Transylvania planning a pre-emptive strike across the
Carpathians; three divisions were in the Dobruja expecting Russian reinforcements
(which never arrived). In Bulgaria the dreaded German General Mackenson was
assembling a large force to invade the Dobruja—which, on September 5, he did.

Once again Cumantsa was spared any fighting (although Constanta, down the
coast, was badly shelled)—but it was not spared the German presence. A detachment of soldiers under a Colonel Randolf von Hartsheim, later memorialized in the
*Star* as a "Bismarkian Prussian of the worst sort,"[22] stormed into town and took over

---

22. In his 1918 article on the War, Mavrocordato quoted Nietzsche on Germany and the
Germans:

> *German Culture...* Political superiority without any real human superiority
> is most harmful. [PN 48]

> Against the *Germans* I here advance on all fronts: you'll have no occasion
> for complaints about "ambiguity." This utterly irresponsible race [...] has
> on its conscience all the great disasters of civilization. [BT 197 ]

> No, we do not love humanity; but on the other hand we are not nearly
> "German" enough, in the sense in which the word "German" is constantly
> being used nowadays, to advocate nationalism and race hatred and to be
> able to to take pleasure in the national scabies of the heart and blood poi-
> soning that now leads the nations of Europe to delimit and barricade them-
> selves against each other as if it were a matter of quarantine. [GS 339]

completely. The *Star*, the Club, and the good life came to an end, although it seems at least that no one was shot; I suspect that the non-Romanian contingent had meanwhile been supplied with false documents—probably by Shaykh Mehmet. But some of the Romanian members of the Club—the officials (the Postmaster and the Harbormaster, for example)—were arrested and detained, and Col. von Hartsheim rudely sequestered the old palace as his personal headquarters. The hospodar and his old mother were forced to move to a shabby hotel (the "Imperial", near the Church of St. George.)

The bulk of Mackenson's Army now (mid-November) pulled out of the Dubruja and headed for Bucharest, looking to crush Romania between the southern forces and Falkenhayn's northern forces—which were about to push their way through the Transylvanian mountain passes, already half-blocked by blizzards. Col. von Hartsheim and his contingent remained in Cumantsa. On December 6, the Central Powers occupied Bucharest, and the war in Romania came to a pause. The King, his English wife Marie, and the Romanian government fled north to the Russian border, and eventually established a regime-in-exile in Jassy. There they held out until the Russian Revolution, which caused the collapse of the Russian Army, and brought an end to the last Romanian resistance. An armistice was signed on December 6, 1917.

Germany now imposed a ruinous treaty on Romania, essentially reducing it to a slave state. A collaborationist government came to power to implement the treaty, headed by a Romanian traitor named Alexandru Marghiloman. A reign of mixed terror and confusion ensued. The Central Bank was forced to issue a run of 2,500,000,000 *lei* in paper money, which ruined the economy. Germany meanwhile began stripping the country of its resources with marked efficiency (whole factories were dismantled, entire forests cut down). Starvation afflicted everyone except Germans and collaborationists—even in well-fed Cumantsa—and the peasants and workers were on the verge of giving in to the enthusiasm they still felt for the Russian Revolution. By the spring and summer of 1918 the situation was desperate.

What had been going on in Cumantsa all this time? Our view is unclear because we no longer have the *Star* to inform us. We can imagine the usual miseries and indignities of the occupation, the growing hunger, the Germans' disdain for Cumantsa's odd racial mix (Col. von Hartsheim seems to have been an anti-Semite)[23]—and the growing sense of a will to resist. All we actually know derives

23. Nietzsche: I am…out of patience with those newest speculators in idealism called anti-Semites, who parade as Christian-Aryan worthies and endeavor to stir up all the asinine elements of the nation by that cheapest of possible tricks, a moral attitude. (The ease with which any wretched imposture succeeds in present-day Germany may be attributed to the progressive stultification of the German mind. The reason for this general spread of inanity may be found in a diet composed entirely of newspapers, politics, beer, and Wagner's music. Our national vanity and hemmed-in situation and the shaking palsy of current ideas have each done their bit to prepare us for such a diet.) [GM 294-5]

from a remark Mavrocordato later made (in the re-born *Star*): that he had been shocked to discover a German soldier reading a special "trench" edition of Nietzsche's *Thus Spoke Zarathustra*. Could it have been von Hartsheim himself? The hospodar goes so far as to repeat one of Nietzsche's famous tags: "O Nausea! Nausea! Nausea!"

Cumantsa may paradoxically have benefitted from the fact that certain areas of the Dobruja remained under direct military rule by the Central Powers during this whole period; this may have spared the populace at least from some of the sinister bumbling of the Marghiloman government. Those areas were strategically important—the ports at the various mouths of the Danube for example—and it is difficult to understand why Cumantsa should have been included in this category. In fact it had so far escaped actual violence precisely because it was *not* "strategic", never had any military presence, and produced nothing useful except fish. Why then did Col. von Hartsheim stay on and on, retaining full administrative power in Cumantsa? What value could his superiors have seen in this wastage of manpower?

The *Hronicul Dobruja*'s author believes that the explanation of this mystery lies in Cumantsa's special role as a smuggler's haven. He thinks that von Hartsheim had either managed to gain control of this illicit trade, or else at least convinced his superiors of its importance. Most interestingly, he mentions the looting of the Museum of Antiquities in Constanta, and the elusive trajectory of the famous "Hunnish" gold hoard of Petroasa. Both of these treasures may have passed through Cumantsa; in fact, the evidence suggests that both these treasures were *in* Cumantsa at some point in the summer and autumn of 1918; and this alone would explain von Hartsheim's determination to stay on and on. The really interesting question then is: *who else knew the treasure was in Cumantsa?* Was the German High Command in on the secret? Or was von Hartsheim somehow working for himself alone? As the summer wore on, the military news from Europe grew gloomier and gloomier—from the axis point of view. Germany and the Central Powers were headed for the *gotterdammerung*. The Army began to pull out of Romania. And still von Hartsheim stayed put. Was he planning to betray his superiors? his suppliers? his customers?

Now, while all this was going on, we must assume that the Scythian Club was not really ineffective and disbanded, but had become in fact a band of conspirators. At what point this transition occurred we cannot say, but by August of 1918 their plans must have been made. Col. von Hartsheim's retinue had been reduced to a mere squadron of men—albeit those men were apparently military police, and heavily armed. Everything remains quite murky up to the moment of the *coup*, but we can offer a few conjectures.

The Scythians could not have been ignorant of the looted antiquities and Hunnish gold. In fact they may have been deeply involved in the process by which these items had turned up in Cumantsa; the gaze of suspicion flickers over the personage of Shaykh Mehmet Effendi. But it seems clear that by the first of November neither the Scythians nor the Colonel actually had possession of the goods. If Von Hartsheim had the hoard, he would presumably have extricated himself from

Cumantsa post haste, especially since it was by now apparent that his masters were about to go down in flames. All over Romania Germans were being lynched and collaborationists were going into hiding. If the Scythians had the gold, they would not have needed to stage their *coup*, but could simply have waited for events to transpire—von Hartsheim's days were clearly numbered. I believe that sometime between the first and the third of November, the Colonel finally got his hands on the goods, and was preparing to decamp. Whether he intended to flit by land or by sea, his preparations would have been obvious enough to anyone who knew what to look for—and the Scythians obviously knew. *This* was the signal for their *coup*.

The *coup d'etat* as a political form would become something of a specialty of the 20th century, and eventually it would acquire certain formal characteristics, even certain "rules". If Mavrocordato and his handful of intellectual comrades could have enjoyed the advantage of reading a book like E. Luttwak's *Coup d'Etat: a practical handbook* (1968), a cynical and amusingly amoral do-it-yourself guide (by a Transylvanian author!), they would have experienced little difficulty in planning their *coup*, or even in executing it. Essentially they had no "government" to overthrow, but only a small military force with no political support. Unfortunately they *were* intellectuals, nor did they have the advantage of hindsight. They very nearly bungled it, and if it were not for two important factors, they would certainly have failed. The first of these factors was Enrico Elias, the anarchist sailor, who was made head of the military operation of the *coup*. The second was the participation of the Cumans.

If the Petchenegs and Cumans were roused from their millennial apathy to a revival of ancient warrior impulses, this was no doubt due to the fact that under the German occupation and the puppet government they had suffered beyond endurance. Moreover, there were peasant uprisings going on everywhere in Eastern Europe (wherever war or revolution left a vacuum of control), with demands for redistribution of land. The Ukraine was in turmoil, and Makhno had already declared some autonomous zones. But the Cumans had still other reasons to think well of the Scythians' *coup*. In August, Georghiu III Mavrocordato had married Anna, daughter of the Ilkhan Kuthen Corvinu of the tribes. The Khan was nominally a Moslem and Mavrocordato was nominally Romanian Orthodox, but the Cumans were never very religious and the hospodar was—of course—a convert to Dionysianism. (Moreover he was on extremely bad terms with the priests at the Church of St. George, who considered him an infidel, while he viewed them as horrid obscurantists.) As a result the marriage was held according to "ancient Cuman custom," including—despite the hard times—a wedding feast. Shaykh Mehmet officiated for the bride. The fact that Georghiu had united with the "royal clan" of the Cumans could not have gone unnoticed, and must have caused quite a stir amongst the traditionalists (and the antiquarian Scythians, of course!). When the moment of crisis came, the Ilkhan would listen to his son-in-law.

At dawn on November 4, Elias and Mavrocordato ordered the following actions:

1) A roadblock was set up to cut the "highway" to St. George's Mouth, at the point where it forks with the track through the swamp to the Petcheneg village of Peritesca. Luckily no soldiers or vehicles ever approached the roadblock—there were only about five automobiles in the entire region in any case, all of them German—because the roadblock was unarmed except for a few hunting rifles.

2) A force under Mavrocordato launched an assault on the old palace, intending to capture and arrest Col. von Hartsheim before breakfast.

3) A larger force under Elias intended to storm the police headquarters in town, near the shore of Lake Cumantsa, where the German garrison was stationed. This assault force had the best guns the Scythians could find, including one contraband (German Army issue) tripod-mounted machine-gun.

4) A boat (the hospodar's own little sloop, *The Lion and Doves*) was set to block access to the open sea; it is unclear whether the conspirators expected enemies to arrive or to depart by water—but in the event neither occured, and the sailors spent the whole day bobbing between the jetties, no doubt getting cold and wet.

5) Two men with revolvers (one of them was Schlamminger, the German philologist) were sent to take over the PTT (which also housed a small bank, stuffed with inflated *lei*) from its small staff. They expected the presence of at least two armed German guards.

6) Deep in the swamps somewhere, at dawn, a small detachment of Cumans under the leadership of the Ilkhan himself cut the telegraph wires that connected Cumantsa to the outside world, and specifically to Bucharest. This act doubtlessly saved the *coup d'etat*, which otherwise went quite badly.

7) A general strike of all merchants and workers was "declared" (but how? In any case, this proved irrelevant).

We shall now follow up the important actions one by one as they developed throughout the day.

2) Mavrocordato's assault group was detected by guards on the access road or driveway of the old palace where it meets the St. George Road. These guards opened fire on the commando, and pinned them down in the forest/marshes on the other side of the highway. Meanwhile, von Hartsheim packed all his papers into his car, loaded in the rest of his personal guard, drove to the gate, and picked up the soldiers there. (They apparently jumped onto the running-boards, and one of them was shot—by Mavrocordato—and killed as the car sped away.) Von Hartsheim turned right and headed toward the city. We surmise that the treasure was stashed at the police station, which von Hartsheim therefore considered the only objective worth defending. In any case, when the commando occupied the old palace they found nothing of value there, not even armaments. Leaving a couple of men to secure the place, Mavrocordato and his followers set off on horse or foot after the Colonel.

3) Elias failed to take the police station at the first attempt. Fighting was fierce, and it seems that several men were wounded on both sides. After about 20 minutes of intense fire, Elias fell back and occupied a building opposite the station. Here he set up the machine-gun, and when the Germans attempted a sortie he was able to

force them back into the station. A stalemate ensued. After some time, an automo-
bile careened into the street and accelerated (but remember, this was 1918) toward
the HQ. It was von Hartsheim. Riddled with machine-gun bullets, the car still managed to pull up to the door and the Germans entered the building without a single
loss. The car burst into flames. Both sides now held their fire, and began to wait—
Elias for reinforcements, and Von Hartsheim for…what? Inspiration, perhaps.

5) Schlamminger and his comrade found no German guards at the PTT; in
fact, it was not open yet. They broke in and occupied it. But there was really no
need. The telegraph wires were already cut. The pair amused themselves by forcing
open the bank vault and carting out the Romanian *lei*, which they later distributed
freely in the city. Perhaps it came in handy as fuel.

At the end of the day the *coup* was in control of the whole town—except the
one significant part of it, the part that really counted for everything. If the Colonel
held out long enough, the Germans might send him reinforcements (the telegraph-
ic silence would be taken as an alarm). True, the German Army was more concerned
with impending defeat than with any rear-guard actions. But what if someone in
Bucharest knew about the treasure, or even suspected its existence? Secrets like that
can never really be kept. One way or another, the *coup* was poised on the brink of
disaster—although by evening the city had begun to celebrate as if victory were a
foregone conclusion.

The seige of the police-station lasted all that night, and the next day, and the
next. On the seventh, the Scythians declared a Provisional Government of
Cumantsa, and announced an extremely radical land redistribution program. To
kick it off, Mavrocordato donated his entire estate (except the palace, which now
became the seat of the Provisional Government) to the peasants of Cumantsa.
Absentee landlords were declared expropriated. No holding was to exceed 50
hectares—otherwise, everyone was declared the owners of whatever land they were
occupying. The Petchenegs and Cumans went wild with joy, and immediately
flocked to sign up with the "army" of the Provisionals. About 1000 "barbarians" now
gathered before the police station and offered to storm it *en masse* and (almost)
unarmed. The Scythian leaders asked them to hold back for one more day.

On November 8 the tide turned. The Central Powers surrendered. World War
I was over. (Meanwhile in Munich the *Räterepublik* had been proclaimed by Kurt
Eisner on November 2.) By the morning of the 9th, Mavrocordato was able to send
a newspaper from Bucharest into the police station. Von Hartsheim knew he was
beaten, and sued for terms.

As a gesture of noble contempt, the Scythians decided to let their enemies go
free. The Germans were escorted by the Provisional "army" to the borders of
Cumantsa (in the Delta marshes beyond Lake Razen) where they were pointed west
and sent packing. They were arrested somewhere along the road to Bucharest by regular Romanian forces, and henceforth disappear from our story.

The *coup* had succeeded despite itself. Cumantsa was now an "independent
country". What next?

## V. BRIEF HISTORY OF AN EVANESCENT EVENT

"That something is irrational is no argument against its existence, but
rather a condition for it."
—*Human, All-Too-Human*, 238

The most obvious thing to do next would be to hand over Cumantsa to Romania, and there were advocates of that position even within the Provisional Government. (This was also the original intention of D'Annunzio when he later liberated
Fiume on September 12, 1919—but the Italian government turned him down!) But
the inner circle of the Scythians had other plans and ambitions. Apparently they had
not only succeeded in capturing the treasure, they had also kept it a secret—at least,
outside Cumantsa. They could perhaps have simply fled with the booty—but antiquities and even gold are not so easily transported or turned into hard cash. Instead
they obviously intended to sell the loot—probably to the same customer von
Hartsheim had been dealing with (the Russians?)—and use the proceeds to finance
their real intention: the creation of a revolutionary state. Obviously they succeeded,
since the autonomous Sanjak of Cumantsa never thereafter seemed to lack for funds.
Food supplies began to flow into the region almost at once, and those too poor to
buy it were fed at the expense of the Provisional Government.

Luck favored the conspirators in other ways as well. The Romanian army had
its hands full elsewhere. Bela Kun actually launched an invasion of Transylvania, and
kept Romanian forces occupied for an entire year (until November 1919). Those
troops that could be spared from the Hungarian front were too busy trying to keep
the civil war in the Ukraine from spilling over into Moldavia to worry about a few
eccentricities on the Black Sea. Moreover the winter of 1918-19 was extremely
severe. Ovid would have been perversely pleased to see the Danube and the Black
Sea freeze solid. But no barbarians approached over the ice. Cumantsa was cut off—
safe till the spring thaw.

The Provisional Government decided to remain "provisional" and not declare
itself established; moreover it proclaimed Cumantsa "autonomous" rather than
"independent", thus keeping diplomatic options with Bucharest open and fluid.
(Bessarabia had done the same thing, but later capitulated.)

In May of 1919 (as the Munich Soviet fell to reactionary forces), the Romanian government finally made an official offer of incorporation to the "caretaker"
regime in Cumantsa. Terms seemed generous enough (including "amnesty" for any
political irregularities), in keeping with Cumantsa's "heroic defeat of occupying
forces and traitorous elements" the preceding year. Mavrocordato, who was now
president of the executive committee of the Provisional Government, simply delayed
answering as long as he could. In June the pressure grew so strong that a statement
was released: Cumantsa would join Romania but only as an autonomous republic.
(The model was the Soviet Union.) This offer was indignantly refused by Bucharest.
The situation grew tense.

In July a strange telegram reached Bucharest from Istanbul. It emanated from the (almost extinguished) Sublime Porte, and in extremely torturous diplomatese it appeared to be a warning (or at least a vague exhortation) not to intervene in Cumantsa. The Romanians were outraged, and their apoplectic response was backed up by pressure from the Allies. Turkey withdrew its communiqué. The puzzle is why Turkey sent the telegram in the first place. Once again, one suspects the ubiquitous Shaykh Mehmet, "agent" of something or other, some shady faction in Istanbul. In any case, the "incident" served its purpose since it purchased time for the Provisional Government. Negotiations began concerning the possibility of a referendum. Bucharest was quite cold about it, but for some reason delayed any response. Delay seemed to suit everybody. The whole region was in turmoil, and in many ways the situation was worse now than during the War. Peasants were revolting, the Russian Whites and Reds were all over the map, the Ukraine was in open rebellion against Lenin and even against Marxism, starvation was still endemic, and Order seemed a distant dream. Who had time to deal with Cumantsa?

Amazingly enough, the Provisional Government was to survive not only another freezing winter, but also another spring and summer. The *Star*—which was now being published again—records a whole long boring series of communications and negotiations between Cumantsa and Bucharest, but in its editorial columns it makes no secret of the plans for a genuinely free Cumantsa. As we shall see, it even went so far as to publish a proposed draft of "Principles for a Constitution", which was adopted "provisionally" by the Provisionals. But still Bucharest did nothing. One suspects that the Scythians had privately communicated their intentions of creating an "incident" if any force were applied by the monarchy. At this point the Allies would not rejoice in yet another "trouble spot in Eastern Europe". And so matters went on, from November 1918, through all of 1919, and into 1920. When D'Annunzio took Fiume one of his first acts was to send a telegram of congratulations to Cumantsa. Apparently its reputation had reached him—in fact, it may even have inspired him.

Before delving into the politics, culture, social life, and achievements of the Autonomous Sanjak, let us briefly finish recounting its diplomatic history. In November 1919 the treaties of St. Germain and Trianon awarded the whole of the Dobruja to Romania. Thus Cumantsa lost a bargaining chip, and Bucharest began to step up its demands for capitulation. Only post-War chaos prevented Romania from a military solution; and so affairs dragged on till March of 1920, when—at long last—the monarchy declared itself prepared to back up its demands with force. The Provisional Government had no desire for a blood bath. On April 1, 1920, almost the entire personnel left Cumantsa as a group, including all the Executive Committee, by ship for Istanbul. There they declared themselves a provisional-government-in-exile. Cumantsa was occupied without a shot. A few arrests were made, but no one was executed. The experiment was over.

## VI Nietzschean Utopia

*Dream and responsibility.*—You are willing to assume responsibility for everything! Except, that is, for your dreams! What miserable weakness, what lack of consistent courage! Nothing is *more* your own than your dreams! Nothing *more* your own work!
—*Daybreak*, 78

"Right" and "Left", as everyone knows, derive from a seating arrangement in the old French Assembly, a circular assemblage that resulted in the two extreme wings being seated next to each other. Perhaps the sheer accident of this proximity led to a certain drift between the two factions—but the attraction of extremes would have occured at some point even without the physical proximity. Extremists, after all, are all *extreme*. And ideologies are not pure, as ideologues would have us (and themselves) believe. Every *idea*, by virtue of its organic incompleteness or irreality, can contain or reflect or absorb any *other* idea. Stalin and Hitler can make a pact and ideology can accommodate it. We see this in Russia today, with its "Red/Brown" National Bolsheviks, and we can see it in the late 19th century as well, with disciples of Proudhon and Sorel following the logic of certain "leftist" ideas toward the "Right", into monarchism or fascism. If *autonomy* and *authority* appear easily distinguishable in experience, they may perhaps become confused on paper—and when they are "rigorously" distinct on paper, they may become entangled on the level of psychology or in the confusion of "real life". For instance, one's personal desire for freedom can be projected onto the whole of society as an abstraction—one is an anarchist. But the same desire can be projected onto one particular group (nation, race, class, clique) to the exclusion of other groups—the "enemies of freedom"—without any psychological or even cognitive dissonance. Eventually one may "renounce" one's original position without qualms; one has remained "true to oneself". If this is so, even of rigorous ideologies like Marxism, it must be even more true of less systematic systems or even anti-systems such as anarchism, especially its Proudhonian or Sorelian tendencies, or its Stirnerian/Nietzschean wing. Please understand that these observations are not meant as some sort of facile "critique" of Marx, Proudhon, Sorel, Stirner, or Nietzsche. "History" can be used to make anyone look foolish, and to make all causes seem hopeless.

Walter Kaufmann to the contrary notwithstanding, there are "fascistic" elements in Nietzsche's thought:—the glorification of war, for example, or the concept of the power-elite. Nietzsche himself somewhere describes his perfect reader as one who should experience Nietzsche with equal amounts of disgust and rapture. In effect one cannot "use" him without "taking out of context"—unless one wants to share his madness. The fascists, too, found what they wanted. But Nietzsche is also an anti-nationalist (and "good European"), an anti-anti-Semite, an admirer of Jews and Moslems, a sex-radical, a pagan "free spirit", a proponent of Enlightenment rationalism, a "nihilist", an individualist, etc., etc. As Emma Goldman pointed out, his "aristocracy" was not of wealth or blood but of spirit. One might as well say there are "fascistic" elements in Marx—his glorification of the State, his bureaucratic centralism—even a touch of anti-Semitism! This rear-view mirror approach to Nietzsche is essentially *trivial*. Let the dead bury their dead. Kaufmann gets upset when people quote Nietzsche "out of context". But then—how *else* is one to quote Nietzsche? Every quotation is removed from the whole body of a writer's work only by violence; and finally one lives by the sweat of one's own brow, however deep the debt to others. In Nietzsche's case, in any case, *there is no "system"*.

Mavrocordato and the Scythians obviously intended to try to turn the Autonomous Sanjak of Cumantsa into a Nietzschean utopia; we know this because they declared it in print, in the *Evening Star*, which now resumed publication. The most important document produced during the two year lifespan of the experiment was a draft for the principles of a proposed Constitution. These principles were adopted "provisionally" by the Provisional Government, but no actual constitution was ever subsequently promulgated, since the Government remained "provisional". This may have been accidental or it may have been deliberate. I believe that the Scythians *intended* to leave everything hanging loose as long as possible. The whole point of statehood is *stasis*, the very rigidity and finality all good Nietzscheans abhor. "*Become who you are*"—Nietzsche never tires of repeating this tag from Pindar (that most Nietzschean of ancient poets)—and the process of becoming never ceases until death. On a more mundane level, the Provisionals refrained from making any irrevocable moves against Romania or the Allies; they had no desire to call down anyone's wrath simply to defend some lofty shibboleth like "independence" or "Constitution" or "rights". Mavrocordato very obviously intended that they should do whatever was best for the whole people and place of Cumantsa, not for some "philosophy" or ideology. This determination in itself was very Nietzschean.

One might, however, question the practicality of this intention. Judged by their effusions in the *Star*, and by their actions, Mavrocordato and his comrades were young romantics who saw themselves as the future. They spoke as if they expected their ideas to catch on and spread—the apocalyptic atmosphere of post-war Europe encouraged such wild speculation. The collapse of Western Civilization was expected on a day-to-day basis; the Russian Revolution was seen as the beginning of the End. We know that experiments like Cumantsa, Munich, Fiume, or the Limerick Soviet were *impractical* and doomed to failure because we know (to our sorrow) that Western Civilization was not going to collapse but to metastatize, and was about to launch a whole century of war and "cold war" that would end with the triumph of Capital in 1989-91. But it would be quite unjust of us to demand such knowledge of the revolutionaries of 1918. Gustav Landauer, as it happens, knew perfectly well that the Munich Soviet was doomed when he joined it. He even had premonitions of his own death. But as a sincere Nietzschean existentialist he did it anyway—first for *himself*, for his own becoming—and second for the *future*, for the coming-into-being of another world. But most of the rebels of the period had no such foresight. And we, who think we have such foresight, are perhaps only exhausted. "Dionysian pessimism" *knows*, but acts despite its knowledge, out of an excess of generosity—as

sheer *expression*. We know of Landauer's despair only from his letters. In his published work he never faltered, and was still issuing position papers on education
(e.g., the vital importance of teaching Walt Whitman to school children) as the Soviet began to crumble around him. Without the letters we might think him merely
absurd rather than tragic—a blind idealist, a futile intellectual. In the case of the
Scythians we have no such private correspondence to deepen our view of their motivations. We have only their public *pronunciamenti*. It is important to remember that
Cumantsa was a "failure"; thus we have already "foretold" its end in our "Brief History". But it is also important to remember that on November 9, 1918 the *coup* was
a *success*. We should be prepared to excuse some excess and jubilation. It was a kind
of "peak experience".

The Provisional Government that proclaimed itself on November 8 and assumed
power on the 9th could be called a *junta*—or it could be called simply the Scythian
Club. The President was Georghiu Mavrocordato, the portfolio of economic affairs
went to the Club treasurer Shaykh Mehmet Effendi, the Secretary (Caleb
Afendopoulo of Odessa) remained Secretary. The mariner Enrico Elias was head of the
"military committee", assisted by Mavrocordato's old friend Antonescu the folklorist.
Schlamminger the antiquarian held no office; perhaps as a German he felt awkward
about any public role, or else (very likely) he was too busy sorting out the hoard of
golden treasure which now constituted the total assets of the Provisional Government.
(Later they imposed a flat three percent harbor duty, but no customs or tax. The sheer
economic *inactivity* of the regime is the best proof of the hypothesis about the treasure.
Like Fiume, Cumantsa was literally a freebooter state or "pirate utopia"!)

On December 20, in the first issue of the new run of the *Star* (which contains
all the details of the *coup*) the junta announced the new form of government as
"Councilism"—in other words, it was to be formed out of councils or soviets, as in
Munich (or Moscow). But the Cumantsa soviets were not to be based on classes or
economic categories. A "worker's council" would have been absurd in a city where
no factories existed. The real structure of Cumantsan society was based on communities, defined for the most part by ethnic or religious identity. In other words—
*volk*. The radicalism of the proposal lay in the fact that no one community was to
be the "master" community. Each community was to choose—by whatever method
it liked—a council for itself. This council was then to send a revocable delegate to a
Council of councils, which would vote on proposals to "advise" the Junta, which
called itself the Executive Committee. This "emergency" structure was provisional,
and would eventually be replaced under a Constitution to be agreed upon *unani-
mously* in Council. Until then, the junta was obviously prepared to enforce the decisions of the Provisional Government if necessary. It is also obvious that most
Cumantsans supported the Scythian junta, since there were very few incidents of
enforcement over the next two years. The reasons for this popularity were, first, the
land redistribution scheme, which won over the peasants; second, the "free port"
arrangements which mollified the merchants; and third (I suspect) the free hand-
outs made possible by the treasure, which pleased nearly everyone else. The only

malcontents were a few Romanian gentry who lost land in the expropriation, and apparently now left Cumantsa in disgust, and—worst of all—the Orthodox priests at the church of St. George, who stayed put and caused trouble.

Two influences lie behind the "Provisional Government" arrangement, or so I believe. The first was historically appropriate:—the "*millet* system" of the old Ottoman Empire, which allowed legal and even political autonomy to ethnic and religious groups in return for taxes—and of course, the Turks were the tax-collectors and thus the rulers. In Cumantsa there were no taxes, and the Turks were on the same level as the other communities; otherwise, the Cumantsa system closely resembles the *Millet*. The other influence was clearly "left *volk*-ism" as taught by Landauer, Dieterich, and other German radicals in the Nietzschean tradition:—the freedom of one *volk* implies and necessitates the freedom of all. In this sense Cumantsa was to be a kind of Proudhonian federation, a "government" of administration rather than rule, a horizontal net of contractual solidarities. Incidentally, the announcement of this scheme in the *Star* makes it clear that *any* self-defined group could form a council and choose a delegate; it was suggested, for example, that a fishermans' council might be appropriate. In the end, however, all the "groups" turned out to be religious or ethnic—except, of course, the junta, which in any case was not a "council" at all, but a military and executive directorate.

The Petchenegs and Cumans formed one council and of course chose their Ilkhan to represent them. The Turks chose Shaykh Mehmet. The Karaite Jews chose their own traditional leader, Isaac Iskawi, who was not a junta member, but was related to Caleb Afendopoulo and apparently content to be advised by him. The Greeks were the only problem. The head of the Orthodox clergy in Cumantsa, John Capodistrias (who enjoyed the title of "Exilarch" for some reason) seems to have considered Mavrocordato the Antichrist. Fair enough, one might suppose. But Capodistrias attempted to forbid his parishioners any participation in the new government, and this the junta would not allow. First, the few Romanian Orthodox in Cumantsa were "liberals", since the "conservatives" had all been expropriated. They seceded from the Greek congregation and chose as their councillor Vlad Antonescu, the folklorist and junta-member. Second, a split—or perhaps even a schism—occurred within the Greek community. According to the *Star*, about half of Capodistrias' congregation abandoned him and declared that they had chosen as their councillor…Georghiu Mavrocordato. The hospodar now informed the Exilarch that he and his people were free to abstain from participation in the Council, but that they would also have to forego the "benefits" such as land distribution (and by implication the benefits of the treasure as well). At this point yet more Greeks (undoubtedly the poorer ones) abandoned the Church and Capodistrias was left in a powerless condition. He did not, however, cease to oppose Mavrocordato whenever possible.

The first and most important activity of the Council was land redistribution. Caleb Afendopoulo and the Ilkhan of the Cumans were appointed to oversee this process as the "Land Reform Committee". The work went rather slowly and carefully, and apparently was considered quite successful.

Otherwise, Cumantsa seemed to run itself. It had always been a peaceful back-water if left to itself—and now it was very much left to itself. "Smuggling"—now legalized as free trade—and fishing continued to support the modest needs of the people, who demanded no hydroelectric plants or higher education. The Scythians were free to meet again and to argue and discuss till dawn and draw up manifestos. The fruit of this work appeared in February 1919, in the form of an extraordinary document containing the Executive Committee's proposed platform of principles for an eventual Constitution of Cumantsa. It consists almost entirely of quotations from Nietzsche, translated into Romanian. The references to Nietzsche's works were not included, but I have been able to track down most of these quotations and find English translations for them. If ever there was a work in which Nietzsche was "taken out of context", this must be it—and yet the context is nothing but Nietzsche! Here it is, in its entirety—the finest flower of the Autonomous Sanjak of Cumantsa and its mad architects.

## Principles

*Opening Paragraphs*

It is only as an *aesthetic phenomenon* that existence and the world are eternally *justified*. [BT 52]

*Twofold kind of equality.* The craving for equality can be expressed either by the wish to draw all others down to one's level (by belittling, excluding, tripping them up) or by the wish to draw oneself up with everyone else (by appreciating, helping, taking pleasure in others' success). [HTH 177/300]

*The first thought of the day.* The best way to begin each day well is to think upon awakening whether we could not give at least one person pleasure on this day. If this practice could be accepted as a substitute for the religious habit of prayer, our fellow men would benefit by this change. [HTH 248/589]

In the main, I agree more with the artists than with any philosopher hitherto: they have not lost the scent of life, they have loved the things of "this world"—they have loved their senses. To strive for "desensualization": that seems to me a misunderstanding or an illness or a cure, where it is not merely hypocrisy or self-deception. I desire for myself and for all who live, may live, without being tormented by a puritanical conscience, an ever-greater spiritualization and multiplication of the senses; indeed, we should be grateful to the senses for their subtlety, plenitude, and power and offer them in return the best we have in the way of spirit. [WTP 424/820]

We should be *able* also to stand *above* morality—and not only to *stand* with the anxious stiffness of a man who is afraid of slipping and falling any moment, but also to *float* above it and *play*. How then could we possibly dispense with art—and with the fool?—And as long as you are in any way *ashamed* before yourselves, you do not yet belong with us. [GS, 164/107]

*Live dangerously*! Build your cities on the slopes of Vesuvius! Send your ships into uncharted seas! Live at war with your peers and yourselves! Be robbers and conquerors as long as you cannot be rulers and possessors, you seekers of knowledge! Soon the age will be past when you could be content to live hidden in forests like shy deer. At long last the search for knowledge will reach out for its due; it will want to *rule* and *possess*, and you with it! [GS 228/283]

*General Principles*

What is needful is a new *justice*! And a new watchword. And new philosophers. The moral earth, too, is round. The moral earth, too, has its antipodes. The antipodes, too, have the right to exist. There is yet another world to be discovered—and more than one. Embark, philosophers! [GS 232/289]

A concealed Yes drives us that is stronger than all our No's. Our strength itself will no longer endure us in the old decaying soil: we venture away, we venture *ourselves:* the world is still rich and undiscovered, and even to perish is better than to become halfhearted and poisonous. Our strength itself drives us to sea, where all suns have hitherto gone down: we *know* of a new world. [WTP 219/405]

*Crime* belongs to the concept "revolt against the social order." One does not "punish" a rebel; one *suppresses* him. A rebel can be a miserable and contemptible man; but there is nothing contemptible in a revolt as such—and to be a rebel in view of contemporary society does not in itself lower the value of a man. There are even cases in which one might have to honor a rebel, because he finds something in our society against which war ought to be waged—he awakens us from our slumber. [WTP 391/740]

"I say unto you: one must still have chaos in oneself to be able to give birth to a dancing star. I say unto you: you still have chaos in yourselves." [TSZ 129]

There are a thousand paths that have never yet been trodden—a thousand healths and hidden isles of life. Even now, man and man's earth are unexhausted and undiscovered.

Wake and listen, you that are lonely! From the future come winds with secret wing-beats; and good tidings are proclaimed to delicate ears. You that are lonely today, you that are withdrawing, you shall one day be the people: out of you, who have chosen yourselves, there shall grow a chosen people—and out of them, the overman. Verily, the earth shall yet become a site of recovery. And even now a new fragrance surrounds it, bringing salvation—and a new hope. [TSZ 189]

*Anti-Darwin.* As for the famous "struggle for *existence*", so far it seems to me to be asserted rather than proved. It occurs, but as an exception; the total appearance of life is not the extremity, not starvation, but rather riches, profusion, even absurd squandering—and where there is struggle, it is a struggle for *power*. One should not mistake Malthus for nature. [TI 522]

Let us not underestimate this: *we ourselves*, we free spirits, are nothing less than a "revaluation of all values," an *incarnate* declaration of war and triumph over all the ancient conceptions of "true" and "untrue." [AC 579]

It is thus irrational and trivial to impose the demands of morality upon mankind.—To *recommend* a goal to mankind is something quite different: the goal is then thought of as something which *lies in our own discretion*; supposing the recommendation appealed to mankind, it could in pursuit of it also *impose* upon itself a moral law, likewise at its own discretion. [D 63/108]

## State

Socialism can serve as a rather brutal and forceful way to teach the danger of all accumulations of state power, and to that extent instill one with distrust of the state itself. When its rough voice chimes in with the battle cry *"As much state as possible,"* it will at first make the cry noisier than ever; but soon the opposite cry will be heard with strength the greater: *"As little state as possible."* [HTH 227/474]

The price being paid for 'universal security' is much too high: and the maddest thing is that what is being effected is the very opposite of universal security, a fact our lovely century is undertaking to demonstrate: as if demonstration were needed! To make society safe against thieves and fireproof and endlessly amenable to every kind of trade and traffic, and to transform the state into a kind of providence in both the good and the bad sense—these are lower, mediocre and in no way indispensable goals which ought not to be pursued by means of the highest instruments *which in any way exist*—instruments which ought to be *saved up* for the highest and rarest objectives! [D 107-8/179]

*Apart.*—Parliamentarianism—that is, public permission to choose between five basic political opinions—flatters and wins the favor of all those who would like to *seem* independent and individual, as if they fought for their opinions. Ultimately, however, it is indifferent whether the herd is commanded to have one opinion or permitted to have five. Whoever deviates from the five public opinions and stands apart will always have the whole herd against him. [GS 202/174]

Today, in our time when the state has an absurdly fat stomach, there are in all fields and departments, in addition to the real workers, also "representatives"; e.g., besides the scholars also scribblers, besides the suffering classes also garrulous, boastful ne'er-do-wells who "represent" this suffering, not to speak of the professional politicians who are well off while "representing" distress with powerful lungs before a parliament. Our modern life is extremely expensive owing to the large number of intermediaries; in an ancient city, on the other hand, and, echoing that, also in many cities in Spain and Italy, one appeared oneself and would have given a hoot to such modern representatives and intermediaries—or a kick! [WTP 48/75]

An old Chinese said he had heard that when empires were doomed they had many laws. [WTP 394/745]

The better the state is established, the fainter is humanity. [Notes 50]

[S]tate, where the slow suicide of all is called "life." [...]

Only where the state ends, there begins the human being who is not superfluous: there begins the song of necessity, the unique and inimitable tune. [TSZ 162-163]

They have gone so far in their madness as to demand that we feel our very existence to be a punishment—it is as though the education of the human race had hitherto been directed by the fantasies of jailers and hangmen! [D 13]

The best we can do in this *interregnum* is to be as far as possible our own *reges* and found little *experimental states*. We are experiments: let us also want to be them! [D 191/453]

## Work and Capital

[Industrial culture] in its present shape is altogether the most vulgar form of existence that has yet existed. Here one is at the mercy of brute need; one wants to live and has to sell oneself, but one despises those who exploit this need and *buy* the worker. Oddly, submission to powerful, frightening, even terrible persons, like tyrants and generals, is not experienced as nearly so painful as this submission to unknown and uninteresting persons, which is what all the luminaries of industry are. What the workers see in the employer is usually only a cunning, bloodsucking dog of a man who speculates on all misery; and the employer's name, shape, manner, and reputation are a matter of complete indifference to them. [GS 107]

*Those who commend work.*—In the glorification of 'work', in the unwearied task of the 'blessing of work', I see the same covert idea as in the praise of useful impersonal actions: that of fear of everything individual. Fundamentally, one now feels at the sight of work—one always means by work that hard industriousness from early till late—that such work is the best policeman, that it keeps everyone in bounds and can mightily hinder the development of reason, covetousness, desire for independence. For it uses up an extraordinary amount of nervous energy, which is thus denied to reflection, brooding, dreaming, worrying, loving, hating; it sets a small goal always in sight and guarantees easy and regular satisfactions. Thus a society in which there is continual hard work will have more security: and security is now worshipped as the supreme divinity.—And now! Horror! Precisely the 'worker' has become *dangerous*! The place is swarming with 'dangerous' individuals! And behind them the danger of dangers—*the* individual! [D 105/173]

*Fundamental idea of a commercial culture.*—Today one can see coming into existence the culture of a society of which *commerce* is as much the soul as personal contest was with the ancient Greeks and as war, victory and justice were for the Romans. The man engaged in commerce understands how to appraise everything without having made it, and to appraise it *according to the needs of the consumer*, not according to his own needs; 'who and how many will consume this?' is his question of questions. This type of appraisal he then applies instinctively and all the time: he applies it to everything, and thus also to the productions of the arts and sciences, of thinkers, scholars, artists, statesmen, peoples and parties, of the entire age: in regard to everything that is made he inquires after supply and demand *in order to determine the value of a thing in his own eyes*. This becomes the character of an entire culture, thought through in the minutest and subtlest detail and imprinted in every will and every faculty: it is this of which you men of the coming century will be proud: if the prophets of the commercial class are right to give it into your possession! But I have little faith in these prophets. [D 106/175]]

[W]hat one formerly did 'for the sake of God' one now does for the sake of money, that is to say, for the sake of that which *now* gives the highest feeling of power and good conscience. [D123/204]

### Barbarians/Peasants

During the great prehistoric age of mankind, spirit was presumed to exist everywhere and was not held in honour as a privilege of man. Because, on the contrary, the spiritual (together with all drives, wickedness, inclinations) had been rendered common property, and thus common, one was not ashamed to have descended from animals or trees (the *noble* races thought themselves honoured by such fables), and saw in the spirit that which unites us with nature, not that which sunders us from it. [D 23/31]

[WTP 478/899]

To grant oneself the right to exceptional actions; as an experiment in self-overcoming and freedom.
    To venture into states in which it is not permitted *not* to be a barbarian. [WTP 487/921]

Best and dearest to me today is a healthy peasant, coarse, cunning, stubborn, enduring: that is the noblest species today. The peasant is the best type today, and the peasant type should be master. But it is in the realm of the mob; I should not be deceived any more.[TSZ 357]

### freedom

"That passion is better than Stoicism and hypocrisy, that being honest in evil is still better than losing oneself to the morality of tradition, that a free human being can be good as well as evil, but that the unfree human being is a blemish upon nature and has no share in any heavenly or earthly comfort; finally, that everyone who wishes to become free must become free through his own endeavor, and that freedom does not fall into any man's lap as a miraculous gift." (*Richard Wagner in Bayreuth*, p. 94) [GS 156/99]

*My conception of freedom.* The value of a thing sometimes does not lie in that which one attains by it, but in what one pays for it—what it costs us. I shall give an example. Liberal institutions cease to be liberal as soon as they are attained: later on, there are no worse and no more thorough injurers of freedom than liberal institutions. Their effects are known well enough: they undermine the will to power; they level mountain and valley, and call that morality; they make men small, cowardly, and hedonistic—every time it is the herd animal that triumphs with them. Liberalism: in other words, herd-animalization.

These same institutions produce quite different effects while they are still being fought for; then they really promote freedom in a powerful way. On closer inspection, it is war that produces these effects, the war *for* liberal institutions, which, as a war, permits illiberal instincts to continue. And war educated for freedom. For what is freedom? That one has the will to assume responsibility for oneself. That one maintains the distance which separates us. That one becomes more indifferent to difficulties, hardships, privation, even to life itself. That one is prepared to sacrifice human beings for one's cause, not excluding oneself. [PN 541-2]

*Against the tyranny of the true.*—Even if we were mad enough to consider all our opinions true, we should still not want them alone to exist:—I cannot see why it should be desirable that truth alone should rule and be omnipotent; it is enough for me that it should possess *great power*. But it must be able to *struggle* and have opponents, and one must be able to *find relief* from it from time to time in untruth—otherwise it will become boring, powerless and tasteless to us, and make us the same. [D 206]

*festival*

What good is all the art of our works of art if we lose that higher art, the art of festivals? Formerly, all works of art adorned the great festival road of humanity, to commemorate high and happy moments. [GS 144]

The states in which we infuse a transfiguration and fullness into things and poetize about them until they reflect back our fullness and joy in life: sexuality; intoxication; feasting; spring; victory over an enemy; mockery; bravado; cruelty, the ecstasy of religious feeling. *Three* elements principally: *sexuality, intoxication, cruelty*—all belonging to the oldest *festal joys* of mankind, all also preponderate in the early "artist." [WTP 421/801]

There is a need for those who will sanctify all activities, not only eating and drinking—and not merely in remembrance of them and to become one with them, but this world must be transfigured ever anew and in new ways.

[WTP 537/1044]

*Dionysus*

What hopes must revive in us when the most certain auspices guarantee the *reverse process, the gradual awakening of the Dionysian spirit* in our modern world! [BT 119]

In polytheism the free-spiriting and many-spiriting of man attained its first preliminary form—the strength to create for ourselves our own new eyes—and even again new eyes that are even more our own: hence man alone among all the animals has no eternal horizons and perspectives. [GS 192/143]

Indeed, we philosophers and "free spirits" feel, when we hear the news that "the old god is dead," as if a new dawn shone on us; our heart overflows with gratitude, amazement, premonitions, expectation. At long last the horizon appears free to us again, even if it should not be bright; at long last our ships may venture out again, venture out to face any danger; all the daring of the lover of knowledge is permitted again; the sea; *our* sea, lies open again; perhaps there has never yet been such an "open sea." [GS 280/343]

…the *Dionysian* in will, spirit, taste. [WTP 528]

*Islam*

"Paradise lies in the shadow of swords"24—also a symbol and motto by which souls of noble and warlike origin betray themselves and divine each other. [WTP 499-500/952]

Christianity has cheated us out of the harvest of ancient culture; later it cheated us again, out of the harvest of the culture of *Islam*. The wonderful world of the Moorish culture of Spain, really more closely related to *us*, more congenial to our senses and tastes than Rome and Greece, was *trampled down* (I do not say by what kind of feet). Why? Because it owed its origin to noble, to *male* instincts, because it said Yes to life even with the rare and refined luxuries of Moorish life. [...] "War to the knife against Rome! Peace and friendship with Islam"—thus felt, thus *acted*, that great free spirit, the genius among German emperors, Frederick II. [AC 652-3]

24. This is a *hadith* or traditional saying of the Prophet Muhammad, promising heaven to martyrs in holy war.

*conclusion*

*We who are homeless.*—Among Europeans today there is no lack of those who are entitled to call themselves homeless in a distinctive and honorable sense: it is to them that I especially commend my secret wisdom and *gaya scienza*. For their fate is hard, their hopes are uncertain; it is quite a feat to devise some comfort for them—but what avail? We children of the future, how *could* we be at home today? We feel disfavor for all ideals that might lead one to feel at home even in this fragile, broken time of transition; as for its "realities," we do not believe that they will *last*. The ice that still supports people today has become very thin; the wind that brings the thaw is blowing; we ourselves who are homeless constitute a force that breaks open ice and other all too thin "realities." [GS 338]

'There are so many days that have not yet broken.' Quoted from the *Rig Veda* [D xviv]

There is no indication that the Council was ever asked to approve this strange document, or even to debate it. Obviously the work of Mavrocordato, it is culled from a "complete" reading of Nietzsche, including some then-unpublished sources (the notes for *Will to Power*, which he must have seen at Sils Maria). It is difficult to see how such a "work" could be translated into a Constitution, a framework for governance. Probably this was never really intended. In some respects, it demands an impossible utopia. In other respects, however, it simply described the ad-hoc principles upon which the Junta was already acting—and undoubtedly it also represented the sincere intentions of the *coup*'s leaders.

Several months were enough to make the Autonomous Sanjak of Cumantsa more than a "temporary autonomous zone", but not very much more. For the most part, life went on as usual: fishermen fished, farmers farmed, merchants bought and sold (no attempt was made to produce a Cumantsan currency, but some attractive stamps were apparently printed, including a bust of Ovid). Unlike Fiume, which was an affair of military adventurers, Cumantsa made no great show of uniforms and parades—but Enrico Elias worked hard on building up a trained part-time "people's militia", acquiring arms and even some light artillery from the Black Sea arms smugglers market (which was enjoying a post-War boom). The "border crossing" near St. George's Mouth was kept under guard, and patrols of Petchenegs and Cumans prowled the backwaters, estuaries and lagoons of the interior. The narrow port entry was guarded night and day. The purpose of these measures was not to organize defiance against Romania or any other fully-equipped army—the junta was never mad enough to dream of such pointless bravura, whatever bluffs and boasts they may have uttered for political reasons, to frighten Bucharest with the threat of an "incident" and the annoyance of the European Powers. The real purpose of the militia was to guard against the flow of uprooted refugees, demobbed soldiers and other mobile riffraff thrown up by the end of the War and the confusion of treaties; and to regulate the black-market and smuggling trades. "Incidents" did occur in the course of the seventeen months, and some were reported in the *Star*—but none reached diplomatic status. At one point there appears to have been serious trouble with the Orthodox dissidents within Cumantsa itself—a riot? an attempted counter-*coup*? The *Star* is devoid of detail, and we do not know of any deaths or injuries. For the most part, then, the Provisionals enjoyed a reign of peace, albeit a rather nervous peace.

One important aspect of civic life—already adumbrated in the "Principles" document—was feasting. Apparently there was no shortage of food now, since the Germans were no longer stealing everything in sight. Elsewhere in the region famine was epidemic, and no doubt this explains the border patrols. But the port was busy, and it seems obvious that the proceeds of the treasure were being spent largely on food. Free food was distributed to Cumantsa's needy on a regular basis, although this program was reduced after the successful harvest of Autumn 1919. Public festivals were celebrated with tremendous spirit as part of the "Cumantsan renaissance" promoted by the Council. Christian, Jewish and Moslem holidays were all recognized, and November 7th was celebrated wildly in 1919 as the anniversary of the *coup*. Civic spirit was urged on to feats of festive creativity, with school pageants, street processions, dancing and brass band music, food-stalls in the marketplace, fairy lanterns and bunting, and free orangeade and sherbet. The *Star* never tires of recounting these happy occasions and boasting of Cumantsa's *joie de vivre*. Meanwhile the Council regaled itself from time to time with formal banquets. One of the first, held to celebrate the first seating of the Council (such sessions were known as "the *divan*") was based on Nietzsche's "Last Supper" in *Thus Spoke Zarathustra*: roast lamb "prepared tastily with sage: I love it that way. Nor is there a lack of roots and fruit, good enough even for gourmets and gourmands, nor of nuts and other riddles to be cracked"—along with wine, and water or sherbet for Moslems and nietzschean teetotalers. At other celebrations, the typical gamebirds and venison of the Dobruja, prepared in Ottoman style, Greek "bandit" style, or Franco-Romanian style, graced the junta's festive board—although they made a point of not indulging in outright gluttony on such semi-public occasions.

One important aspect of life in Cumantsa was music ("life would be a mistake without it," the sage says somewhere).[25] We have mentioned a brass band—apparently Cumantsa was able to afford at least one such, which serenaded the populace weekly and *gratis* in the small park behind the Hotel Imperial. The town also managed to put together a concert series, making use of amateur local talent (a string quartet which included the philologist H. Schlamminger on viola), and visiting professionals such as a popular violinist from Odessa named Ossip Vandenstein (who is still remembered by certain collectors of obscure 78's). Apparently there were also some Turkish musicians in town performing regularly at one of the old-fashioned cafés in the bazaar, probably in the rather louche and marvelous style known as *rembetica*, a Greco-Turkish hybrid of the levantine port cabarets, suffused with sexuality, and flavored with raki, opium, hashish and cocaine. Probably the biggest sensa-

25. "Without music, life would be in error." *Twilight of the Idols*, 471.

tion of the whole seventeen months attended the brief visit of Rosa Ashkenazi, the absolute queen of *rembetica*; the *Star* reported that every single citizen of Cumantsa, from cradle to crone, had attended at least one of her performances. (Presumably this did not include the Orthodox clergy!)

All this music reminds us of Fiume again, where D'Annunzio actually wrote his rather nietzschean theory of music directly into the Constitution. It was all part of the "Cumantsan renaissance", promoted by the junta and organized by Vlad Antonescu the folklorist. He was particularly eager to foster the folkways of the Petchenegs and Cumans, and if the results were at times a bit heavy-handed—in the style of the era, which was busily "re-discovering" the culture of the *volk*—they were nevertheless gratifying and entertaining—at least to the Petchenegs and Cumans, who attended the revivals with unwonted hilarity and enthusiasm. A "Folk Ensemble" was in the planning stages when the Provisional Government collapsed in 1920.

The Scythians may not have enjoyed anything like their former enforced leisure, but they appear to have compensated for the decline in *otium* with an excess of energy, so that affairs of state failed to keep them from their former interests. In fact one suspects that "affairs of State" took second place in their lives, and that they viewed the threat of bureaucratization with horror. Had they overthrown the Germans merely to turn themselves into…administrators? Dionysus forbid! (One is reminded of the Carlist Pretender to the throne of Spain who told a journalist that, once in power, he would spend his time "hunting and hawking". "But… what about *government?*" sputtered the reporter. "A matter for mere ministers," sniffed the King.) In short, the Scythians were far more interested in archaeology and hunting than the exchange of boring telegrams with monarchist flunkies in Bucharest. Once again, only the treasure-hypothesis can explain such insouciance. Whenever a problem arose, the junta threw money at it till it went away—or so I would conjecture. What they planned to do when the money ran out, we cannot say—since they never even admitted possession of the treasure in the first place. During the seventeen months of their run for the money, the Scythians seem to have spent the best part of their energy on an archaeological dig on Popin Island in the Lagoon, site of ancient Histri (from *Ister*, the ancient name for the Danube, which once flowed into the Lagoon at this point). Their finds—mostly inscriptions and a few gold pieces from later barbaric burials—were displayed in an exhibition held in the Old Hall of the Mosque of Khezr in November 1919, during the first anniversary celebrations. Perhaps they expected to find a great deal of gold; who knows? Perhaps they *did*.

The *Star* did not fail to publish reports on archaeology and other cultural activities. Mavrocordato handed the editorship over to Caleb Afendopoulo, but continued to contribute (mostly nietzschean ramblings) to its expanded columns. Texts were published in Turkish, Greek, and Cuman dialect, as well as Romanian. Antonescu contributed his translations from Ovid's *Tristia* and *Black Sea Letters*, as well as endless notes on folklore (sadly not included by Densusianu in the *Hronicul*). The letters column apparently contained communications from foreign scholars and notables, but the only name we know is that of D'Annunzio, who sent a booming communiqué of comradeship to the junta, offering to establish diplomatic relations between Cumantsa and Fiume! The idea was well received, but as far as we know there was no exchange of envoys.

Densusianu mentions in passing that Mavrocordato wrote a "series" of pieces on Kabbalah and sufism. Considering how little we actually know about Mavrocordato aside from his ability to paste together bits of Nietzsche, it is much to be regretted that Densusianu neglected to include any of these articles in his Chronicle. We have already noted that the "Principles" document makes clear use of Nietzsche's Islamophilic tendencies, undoubtedly in an attempt to woo the Cumantsan Moslems (Turks, a few Tatars, and some of the Cumans). Mavrocordato's quarrel with the Orthodox clergy seems to have pushed him away from Christianity toward Judaism and Islam (a fairly obvious nietzschean trajectory), and, as we shall see, there is some evidence to suggest that he actually ended his life as a sufi of some sort. It is possible that he was already secretly initiated into the Bektashiyya by Shaykh Mehmet Effendi. Its heterodoxy, wine-drinking, and political murkiness may well have appealed to his romantic nature. We shall return to these speculations.

Oddly enough, the one area upon which we can shed some light—an area scrupulously avoided by Densusianu!—is the "night-life" of Cumantsa. We owe this picture to the one non-Romanian account of the 1918-1920 period ever published (as far as I know—and I could be wrong):—a chapter in a book that appeared in Paris in 1924, *Perles d'Orient* by Adrien Villeneuve. This obscure author was somehow vaguely connected to the Surrealist movement, and was expelled from it by Breton sometime before World War II. He was also an acquaintance of André Gide, which seems quite appropriate, since Villeneuve was a leftist and a pederastic tourist, like Gide. In *Perles d'Orient* he describes his salacious and eccentric Grand Tour of the Middle East in the years 1919-1920. Most of the book deals with Egypt and Turkey, but Villeneuve also recounted his brief visit to the Autonomous Sanjak of Cumantsa in August 1919. Such characters turned up in droves in Fiume, but Cumantsa was off the beaten track.[26]

Villeneuve met Mavrocordato, whom he describes as "charming and handsome." He was invited to dine with the Scythians, and marvels at the (unexpectedly) excellent wine and venison he was served. He visited the archaeological dig at Histri, and met some Petchenegs and Cumans in the "wild". He is enthusiastic about the experiment in politics, and even mentions the land redistribution project—but having dealt thus briefly with radical ideals, he plunges headlong into the nearest "abyss of vice."

It seems that Cumantsa had a red-light district, consisting of a few dark alleyways behind the Chandlers Row section of the docks. It was here that Turkish musicians played *rembetica* in the Café Smyrna. An even lower dive, with no name, served as a rendezvous for rough sailors, smugglers, and *contrabandistas*, opium

26. See Gide's *Correspondences*, vol. II, pp. 317-19, where the *contretemps* with Breton is mentioned.

addicts, and a few hardy prostitutes. Here there was a wind-up record player, with "negro jazz". Villeneuve was pleased. But his favorite rendezvous was a café on an upper story in the "district", called The Silver Pipe, where Villeneuve was served with "a confection of haschisch and bitter coffee, by Nikos, a Greek Ganymede with violet eyes, son of the proprietor." Just how much of the sultry month of August was spent by Villeneuve in this "innocent dalliance" (he says!) is not clear, but the reader learns much more about his "long afternoons under the spell of the Green Parrot" than anything else in Cumantsa.[27] It is an amusing read, but frustrating. It tantalizes with glimpses of Cumantsa not available in the columns of the *Star*. Villeneuve's musings on the simple but elegant lines of the Mosque of Khezr, for example, or his brief description of the "Ovidian" marshes, leave us wanting more. One wonders how much of this lost world could be recaptured by visiting Cumantsa today.

## VII End and Aftermath

"All histories speak of things which have never existed except in imagination."
—*Daybreak*, 156

*Everlasting funeral rites.*—Beyond the realm of history, one could fancy one hears a continuous funeral oration: men have always buried, and are still burying, that which they love best, their thoughts and hopes, and have received, and are still receiving, in exchange pride, *gloria mundi*, that is to say the pomp of the funeral oration. This is supposed to make up for everything! And the funeral orator is still the greatest public benefactor!
—*Daybreak*, 208

In early spring of 1920, it became obvious that Bucharest's patience was wearing thin, and that its military capability was recovered, to the extent that it now contemplated a speedy resolution to the Cumantsa "crisis". If this involved an armed assault on Cumantsa, the monarchy was willing to face the flak. The junta's days were clearly numbered.

---

27. *Ensphinxed*, to crown many
Feelings into one word
(May God forgive me
This linguistic sin!)—
I sit here, sniffing the best air,
Verily, paradise air,
Bright, light air, golden-striped,
As good air as ever
Fell down from the moon—
[PN 419]

The Council decided not to contest the issue any longer. Voices were raised in favor of a last-ditch defense, but the futility of such a sacrifice was all too apparent.[28] The Council could not win such a game, and had no desire to plunge the region once again into the horrors of war. The gentlemanly thing to do was to extricate the junta from the situation in such a way that face could be saved and no one hurt. After an editorial on March 28 proclaiming its sorrow, disappointment, and intention to renew the struggle some day, the *Star* ceased publication. On April 1, 1920, the following people boarded a steamer bound for Istanbul: Mavrocordato, his wife Anna and his elderly mother, Antonescu and Schlamminger, Afendopoulo and Elias, and Shaykh Mehmet and his family. On April 2, the rump of the Provisional Government (including most importantly the Ilkhan of the Cumans) informed Bucharest that they had "expelled the foreign adventurers and anarchists" from Cumantsa, and would dissolve the Council as soon as instructions were received from the King—to whom eternal loyalty was sworn in ringing tones.

Bucharest saw through the ruse, but could do nothing about it. The ring-leaders had gotten off scot-free, and the "rump" had effectively seized power in the name of the King of Romania (who was thus bound to protect the City if he could). Romanian administrators and police who arrived in Cumantsa on April 8 were unable to arrest anyone, which must have annoyed them exceedingly. Until the Ilkhan died in 1923 he essentially functioned as political boss of Cumantsa, and was able to prevent any retaliation against citizens who had supported the junta. The fall of the Autonomous Sanjak had been handled quite cleverly.

One reason for the Scythians' decision to elude a Ragnarok situation was probably the dwindling of the treasury. No matter how much they had received for the loot from Constanta and Petroasa, they had been squandering it like there was no tomorrow—a realistic policy, actually, because in fact there was no tomorrow. I suspect that the dregs were divided between the refugees and the "rump", and that was the end of it.

Mavrocordato now settled in Istanbul. Some of the junta remained there as well, in all probability—Shaykh Mehmet for instance. Others begin to disappear.

28. But blood is the worst witness of truth; blood poisons even the purest doctrine and turns it into delusion and hatred of the heart. And if a man goes through fire for his doctrine—what does that prove? Verily, it is more if your own doctrine comes out of your own fire. [TSZ 205]

Will nothing beyond your capacity: there is a wicked falseness among those who will beyond their capacity. [TSZ 401]

Do not be virtuous beyond your strength! And do not desire anything of yourselves against probability. [TSZ 403]

The higher its type, the more rarely a thing succeeds. You higher men here, have you not all failed?

Be of good cheer, what does it matter? How much is still possible! Learn to laugh at yourselves as one must laugh! [TSZ 404]

We have no idea what became of Schlamminger, Antonescu, or Elias. It's impossible to believe that such unusual and energetic men simply did nothing for the rest of their lives, and some research might prove rewarding. At present, however, we remain in the dark.

Meanwhile, the civil war in the Ukraine continued unabated, with Makhno now in control of quite a lot of liberated territory. In Romania the peasants were dissatisfied with the government's lukewarm land reform[29] and the workers were dissatisfied, period. Makhnovist ideas were popular. In October of 1920 a general strike broke out. Many of the strikers were anarchists, but they were less well-organized than the socialists and the Communists. What began as a spontaneous and non-violent uprising degenerated into factional squabbles—and violence—among the strikers. At this point, Mavrocordato issued a *pronunciamento* from Istanbul, dated October 20, 1919. In it he declared that the Provisional Government in Exile of the Autonomous Sanjak of Cumantsa supported the Strike, and recognized the "liberated communes of the Ukraine under Makhno" as the legitimate regime in South Russia. I suspect that Mavrocordato may then have returned to the Dobruja clandestinely, and attempted to organize the strike in Cumantsa. Rioting against government land policies broke out there in late October. But it was soon repressed. The General Strike failed before the end of the month, and the Communists took over the labor unions. Not long thereafter, Makhno fled the Ukraine and ended up in Paris, where he proceeded to drink himself to death and write his memoirs.

Mavrocordato did neither.

The last news we have of Mavrocordato, thanks to Densusianu, is the text of the final (?) communiqué of the Government in Exile, dated November 7, 1924, from Istanbul. In it the Council is said to have proclaimed Georghiu III Mavrocordato the hereditary hospodar and prince of the Autonomous Sanjak of Cumantsa.

Had Nietzsche finally driven Mavrocordato mad? Was this mere "prankishness" (a sure sign of the "free spirit"), or did it have some deeper significance? I believe that it was a gesture of defiance—and I also suspect it means that Anna had given birth to an heir. Who knows what history would cook up in the future? It was best to stake a claim, just in case. Perhaps the "Phanariot" atmosphere of old Constantinople had gone to the hospodar's head.

A postscript to this telegram reveals, I believe, Mavrocordato's growing interest and involvement in sufism. Typically enough, it consists of a quotation from Nietzsche:

> There has never been a saint who reserves sins to himself and virtues to others: he is as rare as the man who [...] hides his goodness from people and lets them see of himself only what is bad. [HTH 253/607]

---

29. In fact, several landowners in Cumantsa were given back their expropriated estates by Bucharest, which must have caused much ill-feeling among the Cumans.

After this is added, *"Al mulk li'llah"*, which means, "The Kingdom belongs to Allah." The evocation of the hero who allows only his faults to be seen, while attributing all his virtues to others, reminds one irresistably of the Turkish sufi order of the *Malamatiyya* or "Blameworthy Ones". This order, which included the infamous Shams-al-din Tabrizi, the companion of the great poet Jalal al-din Rumi, developed a means of spiritual concentration that involved outrageous behavior such as public wine-bibbing and hashish-smoking, in order to ruin their reputations as saints. In the 20th century the Order has read deeply in Western philosophy—including Nietzsche. It seems clear enough to me that Mavrocordato was now an adept of the *Malamatiyya*. Perhaps, in the end, this was *his* escape from the 19th century.[30]

If there remains nothing more to say, this is because Densusianu's *Hronicul* now comes to an end.

We might, however, append a brief note on the role of Cumantsa in the events that shook Romania in 1989, with the death of the dictator Ceaucescu. The television station in Bucharest, which constituted the actual focus of the "Revolution", reported that 200 people had been massacred in Cumantsa by Securitate (Intelligence) forces loyal to the Stalinoid regime.

Later reports "admitted" that in fact only six people had been killed—but film footage was shown of many corpses.

30. Nietzsche himself sometimes implied that only religion can overcome religion; one of his last "insane" letters was signed "Dionysus *and* the Crucified One". He also said:

It is in this *state of consecration* that one should live! It is a state one can live in! [D223]

And is *this* human beauty and refinement which is the outcome of a harmony between figure, spirit and task also to go to the grave when the religions come to an end? And can nothing higher be attained, or even imagined? [D37]

"What is this I hear?" said the old pope at this point, pricking up his ears. "O Zarathustra, with such disbelief you are more pious than you believe. Some god in you must have converted you to your godlessness. Is it not your piety itself that no longer lets you believe in a god? And your overgreat honesty will yet lead you beyond good and evil too. Behold, what remains to you? You have eyes and hands and mouth, predestined for blessing from all eternity. One does not bless with the hand alone. Near you, although you want to be the most godless, I scent a secret, pleasant scent of long blessings: it gives me gladness and grief." [TSZ 374]

"It is immoral to believe in God"—but precisely this seems to us the best justification of such faith. [WTP 524]

—And how many new gods are still possible! As for myself, in whom the religious, that is to say god-forming, instinct occasionally becomes active at impossible times—how differently, how variously the divine has revealed itself to me each time!

So many strange things have passed before me in those timeless moments that fall into one's life as if from the moon, when one no longer has any idea how old one is or how young one will yet be—I should not doubt that there are many kinds of gods— [WTP 534]

Still later it was "admitted" that *no one* had been shot in Cumantsa. The corpses were fake (dug up from new graves and shot in obvious places, like the forehead, so the wounds could be seen on television).

The truth of the matter—in which Cumantsa was no more than a microcosm reflecting similar events all over the country—is that there had in fact been no "Revolution". The television had *simulated* a revolution (in which to be sure several hundred people died bravely and needlessly) in order to cover up what was *really* happening.[31] In truth, Ceaucescu had been deposed by a faction of Securitate, which now called itself the "Front for National Salvation", and had taken over the television station. While Romanians thought they were dying for "freedom", they were simply watching the *same people* take power, hidden behind a few brave and deluded rebels, and a barrage of highly sophisticated media manipulation (including *recordings* of machine-gun fire, used to terrorize crowds of demonstrators). There was no "Revolution". There was no "betrayal" of the Revolution because there was no revolution to betray—except in the media-entranced consciousness of a whole world glued to the tube and willing to believe *anything they see on video*. Compared to this Ionescu-like "absurdity", the Autonomous Sanjak of Cumantsa seems like a solid piece of history.

Once again the world failed to put an end to the 19th century. The rebels of 1918 dreamed of a new era. The rebels of 1989 dreamed of a new era.

But all they got was Capitalism.

NYC
February 7, 1997

32. See Codrescu (1991)

BIBLIOGRAPHY
(Note: Sources of Nietzsche quotations are identified by the abbreviations used in the text.)
Apollonius of Rhodes (1959) *The Voyage of the Argo*, trans. E. V. Rieu. London: Penguin
Bey, Hakim (1991) "The Temporary Autonomous Zone" in *T.A.Z.* Brooklyn, NY: Autonomedia
Birge, John Kingsley (1937) *The Bektashi Order of Dervishes.* London: Luzac Oriental
Cahill, Liam (1990) *Forgotten Revolution: Limerick Soviet 1919, a Threat to British Power in Ireland.* Dublin: O'Brien Press
Codrescu, Andrei (1991) *The Hole in the Flag: A Romanian Exile's Story of Return and Revolution.* New York: William Morrow
Densusianu, O. (1927) *Hronicul Dobruja.* Bucharest
Eliade, Mircea (1972) *Zalmoxis, the Vanishing God: Comparative studies in the religions and folklore of Dacia and Eastern Europe*, trans. Willard R. Trask. Chicago: University of Chicago Press
*Encyclopedia Brittanica* (1953), vol. XX
Gide, André (1953) *Correspondances*, vol. II
Hinton Thomas, R. (1983) *Nietzsche in German Politics and Society, 1890-1918.* La Salle, IL: Open Court
Kuun, Count Gezu (1880) *Codex Cumanicus.* Budapest; partial translation in A. B. Boswell, "The Kipchak Turks." *Slavonic Review*, June 1927
Luttwak, Edward (1968) *Coup d'Etat: A Practical Handbook.* London: Penguin
Macintyre, Ben (1992) *Forgotten Fatherland: the Search for Elisabeth Nietzsche.* New York: HarperCollins
Nietzsche, Friedrich (1954) *The Portable Nietzsche*, ed. and trans. Walter Kaufmann. New York: The Viking Press. Pieces used from this volume include AC: *The Antichrist; Notes*; TSZ: *Thus Spoke Zarathustra*; and TI: *Twilight of the Idols.*
—(1956) BT and GM: *The Birth of Tragedy: and, the Geneology of Morals.* Trans. Francis Golffing. Garden City, NY: Doubleday
—(1974) GS: *The Gay Science*, trans. Walter Kaufmann. New York: Vintage
—(1982) D: *Daybreak*, trans. R. J. Hollingdale. Cambridge: Cambridge University Press
—(1986) HTH: *Human, All Too Human*, trans. Marion Faber. Lincoln: University of Nebraska Press
—(1968) WTP: *The Will to Power*, trans. and ed. Walter Kaufmann. New York: Vintage
Ovid (1994) *The Poems of Exile*, trans. with introduction and notes by Peter Green. New York: Penguin
Runciman, Steven (1968) *The Great Church in Captivity: A Study of Constantinople from the Eve of the Turkish Conquest to the Greek War of Independence.* London: Cambridge University Press
Stirner, Max (1907) *The Ego and His Own.* New York: Benj. R. Tucker
Wilson, Peter Lamborn (1988) *Scandal: Essays in Islamic Heresy.* Brooklyn, NY: Autonomedia
— (forthcoming) *Drunken Boat*, vol. 3. Brooklyn, NY: Autonomedia
Xenopol, A. D. (1925/1936) *Istoria Românilor din Dacia Traina.* Bucharest; abridged French translation, *Histoires des Roumains*, 1936

opium, 158, 192-93
orgies, 12, 13-14, 20, 31, 33
*Origins of the German Tragic Drama* (Benjamin), 35
Orwell, George, 135
Ottoman Empire, 156-57, 163, 179
Ovid, 151-53, 155, 159, 165, 174, 188
Owaysiyya, 124
Owen, Robert, 31, 35, 43, 127

paganism, 11, 113, 123, 124, 128
Paine, Thomas, 129
Paleolithic age, 73, 76, 77, 81, 85, 124, 128
pantheism, 11
Paracelsus, 7, 35
paranoia, 12-13, 28
Paris Commune (1871), 62, 144
parliamentarianism, 183
parties, 26
Passion, Fourier's concept of, 22, 28, 33, 128
Passional Attraction, 5, 7, 34, 36
*Passions of the Human Soul, The* (Fourier), 29, 33
pataphysics, 7
"patriarchal" societies, 146
patron-saints, 114
Patterson, Ian, 36
pederasty, 13, 19, 130, 191
perfecti, 5
Perfectionists, 29
Perles d'Orient (Villeneuve), 191
perspectivalism, 10
Petchenegs, 137, 155, 157, 164, 165, 171, 179, 188, 190, 191
phalansteries, 8, 11-12, 29, 43, 131
*Philosophy of Poverty, The*

(Proudhon), 57-61
*Physiognomy of Taste, The* (Brillat-Savarin), 9
Pidgeon, William, 102-4, 108
Pindar, 143, 167, 177
"pirate utopias," 178
planets, 7, 15, 16, 20, 29, 127-28
pleasure, 6, 15, 21-22, 31, 85, 180
of banquets, 9-10
in hunter/gatherer societies, 73, 76, 77
messianism and, 34
spirituality of, 35
Polanyi, Karl, 80
polytheism, 187
Pontus, 151-52
Postmodernism, 30, 69
potlatch, 78-79, 97, 143
*Poverty of Philosophy, The* (Marx), 59-60
*Preacher of Death, The* (Landauer), 162
priests, 81, 84, 85
"primitive" societies, 73, 77, 89
*Principle of Federation, The* (Proudhon), 67
progress, concept of, 96, 110, 111, 144, 161
proletariat, 46-47, 49
property, 44-48, 49, 50, 55, 60, 63, 76, 78, 80
Protestantism, 87, 126, 128-29
Proudhon, Pierre Joseph, 11, 43-52, 68, 70, 176
on authority and organization, 63-64
correspondence with Marx, 54-56
early Marx and, 44-52
on federalism, 66-67, 69
on God and religion, 58-59
on money, 82

personality of, 51
political legacy of, 63-64
quarrel with Marx, 52-60, 62
Proudhonian federalism, 67, 179
psychedelics, 13
Putnam, F.W., 108

Qadaffi, Col. Muammar, 136
*Qiyamah/Qiyamat*, 125-26
*Quest for the Origins of the First Americans, The* (Dixon), 108

racism, 31, 87, 96, 102, 108
rationalism, 34, 40, 67-68, 136, 139, 176
"red/brown" alliance, 176
Redcloud, Merlin, 99, 100-101, 103, 110
Reich, Wilhelm, 19
reincarnation, 16-17
religion, 16-17, 21, 88, 118, 127. *See also* shamanism; specific religions
anarchism and marxism likened to, 46, 54, 59
Capital and, 42
in Dobruja, 150
Fourier's view of, 11, 23-24, 32-34, 35
links between religions, 124
money and, 81, 82
Nietzsche's view of, 195n
"Religion of Effigies," 98, 101, 106
resistance and, 113-14
rembetica, 189-90, 191
revolution, 65, 78, 136-37, 138. *See also* anarchism; communism; socialism
end of the Social and, 41-43
following World War I,